Analyzing the Different Voice

New Feminist Perspectives Series
General Editor: Rosemarie Tong, Davidson College

Analyzing the Different Voice

Feminist Psychological Theory and Literary Texts

Jerilyn Fisher and Ellen S. Silber

ROWMAN & LITTLEFIELD PUBLISHERS, INC.
Lanham • Boulder • New York • Oxford

ROWMAN & LITTLEFIELD PUBLISHERS, INC.

Published in the United States of America
by Rowman & Littlefield Publishers, Inc.
4720 Boston Way, Lanham, Maryland 20706

12 Hid's Copse Road
Cumnor Hill, Oxford OX2 9JJ, England

British Library Cataloguing in Publication Information Available

Library of Congress Cataloging-in-Publication Data

Analyzing the different voice : feminist psychological theory and
   literary texts / [edited by] Jerilyn Fisher and Ellen S. Silber.
      p.   cm. — (New feminist perspectives)
   Includes bibliographical references and index.
   ISBN 0-8476-8640-X (hardcover : alk. paper). — ISBN 0-8476-
8641-8 (pbk. : alk. paper)
   1. Feminist psychology.   I. Fisher, Jerilyn.   II. Silber, Ellen S.
III. Series.
BF201.4.A53   1998
150'.82—dc21   98-30697
                                                              CIP

ISBN 0-8476-8640-X (cloth : alk. paper)
ISBN 0-8476-8641-8 (pbk. : alk. paper)

Printed in the United States of America

♾ ™ The paper used in this publication meets the minimum requirements of
American National Standard for Information Sciences—Permanence of Paper for
Printed Library Materials, ANSI Z39.48-1984.

Lovingly dedicated . . .

*to Jules, Arielle, and Devan
and to my parents, Arlene and Arthur Fisher*
J.F.

*to Al and Kenny
and to Mother, Pearl, March, Grace and Lynn*
E.S.S.

Contents

Contents

Foreword

Wild Voices: Fiction, Feminism, and the Perennial Flowering of Truth

Carol Gilligan

You who do not remember
passage from the other world
I tell you I could speak again: whatever
returns from oblivion returns
to find a voice:

from the center of my life came
a great fountain, deep blue
shadows on azure seawater.
from Louise Glück, "The Wild Iris."

Voices wild, breaking free, telling the truth—"Then it was over: that which you fear, being / a soul and unable / to speak, ending abruptly, the stiff earth / bending a little" (Glück 1993). This age-old signal of psychological liberation, the wellspring of art and political resistance, has become the centerpoint of feminist psychological theory, joining the awareness that "It is terrible to survive / as consciousness / buried in the dark earth" with the realization that freeing the human voice unsettles the foundations of patriarchy. Reading "The Wild Iris," I remember the passage from the other world, being able to speak again—oddly simple, "like birds darting in low shrubs," the earth bending a little under the weight of truths that once spoken seemed so obvious as to raise the question: What stopped the great fountain coming from the center of my life: my voice, suddenly sounding like me?

When Cynthia Ozick, in her essay "Notes toward Finding the Right Question," asks us to consider how we will respond to the awareness that women have been omitted "by purposeful excision" from traditions commonly represented as the collective endeavor of an entire people, she is asking us to see the "plain whopping lie" contained in such representation, and also to consider the immensity of the loss which this lie covers (Ozick 136). Making a move which perhaps only she could risk, Ozick connects the legacy and the lesson of the Holocaust—learning how to mourn the loss of so much life and so many talented and creative people—with the need to grieve having lost women's talents, knowledge, creativity, and judgments century after century. Yet speaking of this loss of the available minds of half the population, Ozick notices "a curious absence of grief" (Ozick 138). As if nothing was lost, or nothing of value. Finding the right question, then, begins with sadness. Feeling the absence of women as a loss, not simply an injustice suffered by women, leads eventually to the realization that the avoidance of grief signifies an avoidance of love. We cannot grieve what we cannot love. To love women, however, means to harbor the suspicion that women's minds would change the tradition, reopening the most basic human questions including how we experience ourselves, how we know what we know, how we love, and what we value.

The luminous essays that compose this book join the feminist project at this level. More specifically, they mark the completion of a cycle. Literary voices that over the centuries have provided resonances for people that could not be found in other places are now themselves brilliantly illuminated by the psychology which they helped to create. Voice is the tie between psychology and fiction, and as the dialogue between feminist psychology and literary texts continues in these pages, new voices and new linkages enter the conversation. The vibrancy of the essays comes from the fact that they draw constantly on people's voices—literary characters as well as the writers themselves—and from the rush of discovery in bringing new evidence, new cultural resonances, and new psychological insights. Women's voices, the range of women's voices, have changed the voice of human psychology. And girls, a vital part of women's history, contribute centrally to feminist psychological theory because they articulate with such clarity the shock of coming of age in the landscape of patriarchy.

I have long written in dialogue with the voices of writers and literary characters, finding validation in novels, plays and poems for what I was hearing from real people. That others had heard what I was hearing testifies to the material nature of voice, its sound. Voice is part of the physical world, and its psychological power comes in part from this fact: that it transposes what has no physical manifestation—the psyche, the soul, ourselves—into sound, carried on breath, creating vibrations in the world. As voice is physical, part of nature, it is also cultural, shaped by language, so that a voice-centered psychology resists the dichotomizing of nature and nurture, bridging the either–or with the realization that as human beings we are always in nature and in culture, and also ourselves. Voice is the footprint of the psyche.

The theme of finding a voice comes up over and over again in these essays: finding a voice that has been lost, meaning swallowed, buried deep within oneself, held in silence; finding a way to say what could never be said because there were no words or no possibility of being heard or because speaking was too risky, too dangerous; finding a way to be present in places of absence—the experience of returning from oblivion and suddenly hearing oneself. Both literally and metaphorically, finding a voice means bringing oneself into relationship.

My work began with the realization that women's voices were being distorted by the sound-system of the world, so that a woman, speaking in public, often found it extremely difficult, sometimes impossible to hear herself. What she said seemed to make no sense. By disentangling the voice from distorting resonances and bringing a different acoustic—different resonances and a different interpretive voice—I found that suddenly women's voices made all kinds of sense. They changed the conception of the world in fundamental ways. Basic psychological and philosophical concepts like identity or the sense of self, and morality, and processes such as knowing and loving and development take on new meanings when reframed in light of women's experiences and also in light of the realization that psychologies and philosophies that have not seriously attended to women are out of touch with the human world.

This is a crucial point. To release women from a patriarchal ghetto means to see women as human, just as human as men. Difference becomes interesting rather than a measure of greater or lesser. Then comes a new and revolutionary question: Can there be an order of living that is nonhierarchical and loving? This question lies at the center of the feminist project, which in deconstructing the hierarchy of patriarchy exposes its racism and homophobia, as well as the class structure and sexism that hold in place what is an essentially gendered social order: a pyramid of power and privilege with fathers, or a father, at the top. A feminist psychology brings home the reality that psychoanalysts and psychologists have read patriarchy as nature, falling into the naturalistic fallacy by moving from *is* to *ought*. Gender, along with race, class, and culture, has guided the selection of whom to study and whom to consider exemplary of human development and health.

In reading these essays, it is critical to distinguish between a view of women that emphasizes that women are simply different and a feminist psychology that brings a different voice to the interpretation of human—not just women's—experience. I titled my book *In a Different Voice,* not *In a Woman's Voice,* to make this point. I found that listening to women led me to speak differently about self, relationship, morality, adolescence and other landmarks of human life. When Belenky, Clinchy, Goldberger and Tarule (1986) studied women's ways of knowing, they addressed the conception both of women and of knowing, given that historically women were not taken seriously as knowers. Knowledge, like women, was considered to be a man's possession. Jean Baker Miller's (1976) insight that women provide "a crucial key to understanding the psychological order" led to a new psychology of women and also to a new psychology (Miller 1).

Yet women's voices, however distorted by interpretation or driven into silence, have been present throughout human history, and listening to women's voices and silences—even when barred from official knowledge—has always been a source of psychological insight, in daily life and in the work of artists. Long before the dawn of modern feminist consciousness and consciousness-raising, from the very beginnings of patriarchy, the germs of the contemporary critique have been present in art—in the voices of Iphigenia and Lysistrata, in the biblical Eve, and in folktales. This perennial flowering of truth attests to the creativity of the human spirit—wild voices resisting the colonization of patriarchy, undoing dissociation, people saying what they know.

Finding a voice is a human quest that has been profoundly illuminated in recent years by research on women's psychology and girls' development and also by the study of trauma (Brown and Gilligan 1992; Gilligan 1997; Gilligan, Rogers and Noel 1992; Herman 1992; Rogers 1994; van der Kolk 1996). To feel voiceless, without the ability to speak or represent oneself, is to feel helpless and powerless, small and ultimately vulnerable to all forms of humiliation and degradation. The experience of being voiceless lies at the heart of psychological trauma, creating the sense of utter terror and leading to dissociation. Loss of voice was noted by Freud (1895) as the most common symptom of hysteria, and this observation, made at the end of the nineteenth century, returns in light of feminist research on psychological development to raise a radical question: Is the internalization of patriarchy inherently traumatic, setting off a struggle for voice and a process of resistance and leading to a series of splits that have been interpreted as part of human nature when in fact they are symptomatic of an enforced adaptation to a particular political and social arrangement?

"You can't say anything," girls will say to one another at adolescence, signaling their descent into the underground. I have studied this passage and listened to girls doubling their voices, telling different stories, concealing parts of themselves, playing with disparate realities, using humor but also showing signs of dissociative processes—splits in consciousness that leave girls not knowing or not feeling what they want and feel and know (Gilligan 1990a and b, 1992). Girls may discover at this time that it is dangerous for them to speak the obvious and also confusing when what they see happening is said not to be happening. Women develop life-long strategies for holding disparate realities, intricate forms of narrative that are culturally scripted as well as private speech and body language. But girls often feel helpless and powerless in the face of a social construction of reality that eclipses their experience, so that speaking seems hopeless or terrifying, and their voices sound too loud or too small. I have suggested that girls' sense of being overwhelmed in the struggle to find a voice and to be present in their relationships, which is readily interpreted as part of normal development or even neurotic, may be more akin to trauma—more confusing precisely because the traumatic nature of this struggle is not named. "You can't say that," people tell girls repeatedly; "You listen to me, young lady," conveying a fear that girls will listen to themselves and say what they know.

This underground surfaces in fiction. Women and men writers have seeded truths in the voices of literary characters, so that the line between autobiography and fiction is deliberately unclear and the relationship between fiction and life becomes of great interest. Charlotte Perkins Gilman in *The Yellow Wallpaper* writes a story about a woman who is unable to leave her husband, and after writing the story Gilman leaves her husband; Nathaniel Hawthorne marries Sophia Peabody, one of the early feminists, and in *The Scarlet Letter* analyzes why the feminist project stalls.

In voicing the human world, novelists create narrative strategies that can hold the distinctness of voice and the layered nature of psychological realities. As the essays in this book elucidate these strategies, they also reveal the act of love that is at the heart of this intimate knowing. Reading these essays, I am deeply moved when love of women becomes palpable in the writing. The brilliance of joining feminist psychological theory and literary texts lies in matching the novelist's ear with a theoretical ear that is also attuned to women's voices, bringing out inner voices in the novels with stunning clarity. In "With Whom Do You Believe Your Lot is Cast?" Shoshanna Felman (1993) records her personal and intellectual struggle to cast her lot with women. Bringing herself into the presence of another woman to witness her creativity, she discovers that the act of bearing witness is, "crucially, a noncoercive act." It means opening oneself to being surprised by the other, and Felman, reading women's autobiography, finds herself experiencing the "unexpected revelation," a resistance in the text unexpectedly, unwittingly stirring "some forces, some desires, some events in our own life" (133).

Writing against a legacy of loss, the writers of the essays in this book demonstrate the power of building on women's work. Their analyses of novels, stories and fairy tales have the quality of revelation—new ways of speaking and seeing, at once familiar and surprising. The difference in voice comes from placing connection with women at the center of their own analytic endeavor, stressing the primacy of voice in the development of relationship, holding differences by resisting a series of polarizations that serve to undermine the feminist project, and seeing the seeds of truth buried in women's consciousness as groundbreaking.

Note

My thanks to Bill Cutter for steering me to Cynthia Ozick's essay, to Marsha Levy-Warren and Lisby Mayer for inspiring conversations, and to Normi Noel, my guide always into voice and silence. I thank the Spencer Foundation for so generously and freely supporting my research and also for providing a research endowment for the Chair in Gender Studies at Harvard.

Works Cited

Belenky, Mary, Blythe Clinchy, Nancy Golberger, and Jill Tarule. *Women's Ways of Knowing*. New York: Basic Books, 1986.

Brown, Lyn Mikel, and Carol Gilligan. *Meeting at the Crossroads: Women's Psychology and Girls' Development*. New York: Ballantine Books, 1992.

Felman, Shoshanna. "With Whom Do You Believe Your Lot is Cast? Woolf, de Beauvoir, Rich, and the Struggle for Autobiography." *What Does a Woman Want?* Baltimore: Johns Hopkins University Press, 1993. 121–151.

Freud, Sigmund. "The Case of Elisabeth von R." *Studies on Hysteria. Standard Edition, Vol. II*. Ed. J. Breuer and S. Freud. London: The Hogarth Press, 1895.

Gilligan, Carol. "Teaching Shakespeare's Sister: Notes from the Undergroud of Female Adolescence." *Making Connections*. Ed. C. Gilligan, N. P. Lyons, and T. Hanmer. Cambridge: Harvard UP, 1990a.

Gilligan, Carol. "Joining the Resistance: Psychology, Politics, Girls and Women." *Michigan Quarterly Review*. XXIX. 4 (1990b): 501–537.

Gilligan, Carol (1992) "Response to Melanie: Reflections on Case No. 1 ("Courting Danger")." *Adolescent Portraits: Identity, Relationships, and Challenges*. Ed. A. Garrod, L. Smulyan, S. Powers and R. Kilkenny. Boston: Allyn and Bacon, 1992. 41–47.

Gilligan, Carol. "Remembering Iphigenia: Voice, Resonance, and the Talking Cure." *The Inner World in the Outer World: Psychoanalytic Perspectives*. Ed. E. Shapiro. New Haven: Yale UP, 1997.

Gilligan, Carol, Annie G. Rogers, and Normi Noel. "Cartography of a Lost Time: Women, Girls and Relationship." Paper presented at the Learning from Women conference, Harvard University, 1992.

Glück, Louise. "The Wild Iris." *The Wild Iris*. New York: The Ecco Press, 1993. 1.

Herman, Judith. *Trauma and Recovery*. New York: Basic Books, 1992.

Miller, Jean Baker. *Toward a New Psychology of Women*. Boston: Beacon Press, 1976.

Ozick, Cynthia. "Notes toward Finding the Right Question." *On Being a Jewish Feminist*. Ed. S. Heschel. New York: Schocken Books, 1983. 120–151.

Rogers, Annie G. "Voice, Play, and a Practice of Ordinary Courage in Girls' and Women's Lives." *Harvard Educational Review*. 63.3 (1993): 265–295.

van der Kolk, Bessel. *Traumatic Stress: The Effects of Overwhelming Experience on Mind, Body and Society*. New York: Guilford Press, 1996.

Acknowledgments

Many people have helped us in the making of this book. We are indebted to Jules Trammel for his invaluable technical assistance and to Jay Vande Koppel for the help he gave us early on in the project.

At a crucial time, Cynthia G. Jones gave us her expert, sensitive reading of an essay-in-progress and important resource materials. For her contributions to our work, we express sincere appreciation. We are also grateful to Lyn Mikel Brown, Nellie Teresa Justicia and Pat Sharpe for connecting us with three of our many talented contributors.

We are indebted to Sr. Ellen Marie Keane for the numerous references she suggested in women's epistemology and moral development; she was also generous enough to share her personal library with us. Thanks go to Wendy Goulston and Kathleen Gregory Klein, perceptive readers of our essay on fairy tales: we feel fortunate to have had their refreshing comments.

This volume found its source of inspiration in our having participated in annual meetings of interdisciplinary feminist educators committed to studying applications of psychological theory to our various fields of specialization. It was at a meeting of this group, known as Education for Women's Development, that we first experienced the excitement of analyzing literary texts through the lens of feminist psychological theory, beginning with a study of Zora Neale Hurston's *Their Eyes Were Watching God*. In particular, we would like to acknowledge several members of that group, Blythe Clinchy, Nancy Goldberger, and Janet Kalinowski, each of whom offered both encouragement and intellectual support for this project.

Rosemarie Tong, the editor of the New Feminist Perspectives series in which this volume appears, showed confidence in both our idea and our ability to produce. We thank her for her commitment to interdisciplinary feminist scholarship.

At Rowman & Littlefield, we were assisted ably by several editors. We thank Jennifer Ruark for her work with us early in the process; we thank Robin Adler for her consistently good advice and both Robin Adler and Christa Acampora for their patience and willingness to think through practical concerns. Lynn Weber, production editor, helped us with important details toward the end of the process, and was extraordinarily patient when the unexpected occurred.

Also, for technical assistance, we thank Frannie Lindsay and Ken Silber.

It is true, however, that this volume would not "be" without the creative analysis and eloquence of each of our contributors. Every one of them has been wonderful to work with; indeed, we wish we could say thanks in person. Unable to fulfill a fantasy we've had of giving a fabulous party for all of them, we wish, more simply, to express our appreciation here.

Jerilyn Fisher: My debt for support from my husband, Jules Trammel, and my children, Arielle and Devan Trammel-Fisher, can never be repaid fully. They gave me unqualified encouragement even as they sacrificed plans or put aside their needs so that I could continue attending to this work. I owe them each innumerable nights and weekends.

Ellen Silber: The support of my husband, Al, and the special inspiration of my son, Kenny, have been vital to my sustaining the effort required.

Last of all, and not least of all, we are thankful for each other. Ours is a partnership that has survived and even flourished as we worked through the multi-faceted travails of creating a book: building on our respect and love for one another; working out our differences, with tolerance and a tacit commitment to meeting half way almost all of the time. We come out of this experience not only with a book we cherish, but also with a friendship and colleagueship that has been strengthened by withstanding the test of true, intensive collaboration.

The editors gratefully acknowledge permission to use the following material:

Lyn Mikel Brown, "The Dangers of Time Travel: Revisioning the Landscape of Girls' Relationships in Margaret Atwood's *Cat's Eye*," LIT, Vol. 6, 1995: 1–14.

Gail L. Mortimer, portions of "Initiation Stories and Gender" were originally published in *Approaches to Teaching Faulkner's The Sound and the Fury*. Eds. Stephen Hahn and Arthur F. Kinney. New York: Modern Language Association, 1996: 128–133.

Barbara Schapiro, "The Bonds of Love and the Boundaries of Self in Toni Morrison's *Beloved*," *Literature and the Relational Self*, Barbara Schapiro, New York: New York UP, 1994: 127–143.

Mirella Servodidio, "A Case of Pre-Oedipal and Narrative Fixation: *The Same Sea as Every Summer*": An earlier version of this essay was published as "A Taste of Pre-Oedipal and Narrative Fixation: *El mismo mar todos los veranos*," in a special issue of *Anales de la literatura española contemporánea* entitled *Reading for Difference: Feminist Perspectives on Women Novelists of Contemporary Spain*," Vol. 12, 1987: 157–173.

Susan Rubin Suleiman, "Maternal Splitting: 'Good' and 'Bad' Mothers and Reality," *Risking Who One Is*, Susan Rubin Suleiman, Cambridge, MA: Harvard UP, Copyright 1994 by the President and Fellows of Harvard College.

Of the articles reprinted, Lyn Mikel Brown's essay and Gail L. Mortimer's essay were originally prepared for inclusion in this volume.

I

Psychological Development during Adolescence: Girls' Voices of Surrender and Resistance

In their studies of identity and constructions of the self, psychologists frequently examine the values people hold and the choices they make at different points in the life cycle. During puberty, we undergo dramatic physical and emotional changes that deeply affect how each of us envisions ourselves, the world, and our possibilities. Generally considered a phase of intensive identity formation, the adolescent years have been seen by feminist psychologists as a crucial period in which to understand the dynamics of girls' lives and the women they soon become.

Freud and Erikson have influenced conceptions of adolescence by defining it as that time during which the youngster strives to moderate childhood dependencies, such as those on parent figures, in order to foster adult development. Freud insists that during puberty, "detachment from parental authority" is a process "through which all human beings ought by rights to pass," noting that girls much more often than boys fall short developmentally in their apparent inability to distance themselves from the influence of their parents' affection (227). Erik Erikson repeats Freud's privileging of masculine development patterns: in *Identity: Youth and Crisis,* he characterizes adolescence as a life stage in which the central task is to forge an autonomous identity, leaving girls—whose emerging sense of self primarily takes shape through their relationships with others—to appear developmentally deficient. Likewise, Daniel Levinson, in *The Seasons of a Man's Life* (1978), values individuation over relational capacities as a maturational marker. A man devotes his life to realizing "the Dream," and Levinson describes this quest as a lifelong process in which a young adult begins to build a "life structure," requiring that relationships be modified or terminated if they do not support his goal of autonomous achievement.

1

As early as 1976, Jean Baker Miller recognized from clinical practice that throughout her life span a woman's sense of self is constructed within the context of building and maintaining relationships. Contrasting this model of development with the accepted male model, Miller proposes that if, in Western culture, "affiliation were valued as highly as self-enhancement," men and women alike would understand that "individual development proceeds *only* by means of affiliation" (83). Two years later, Nancy Chodorow published *The Reproduction of Mothering*. She responds to masculine dominance in psychoanalytic writings by reinterpreting girls' continuous connection to their mothers as empowering and progressive. Her theory that "women, as mothers, produce daughters with mothering capacities and the desire to mother" (7) leads Chodorow to conclude that, through maternal gender role identification, girls acquire "a basis for 'empathy' built into their primary definition of self in a way that boys do not" (167). Thus, when she examines the onset of adolescence and the resolution of the Oedipal complex, Chodorow observes the contrasting orientations from which boys and girls arrive at puberty and resulting distinctions in masculine and feminine personality development. Specifically, she clarifies why and how "relational capacities and senses of the self" (173) differ in the experiences of girls and women, boys and men.

Subsequent feminist psychological theory about girls' and women's lives builds upon Chodorow's work. Documenting benefits teenage girls derive uniquely from continued attachment, Terri Apter argues that extended intimacy with mothers in particular promotes, not retards, girls' growth. Apter's work on adolescence—and, correspondingly, that of Carol Gilligan, Judith Jordan, Nona Lyons, Lori Stern, Irene Stiver, and Janie Victoria Ward—reveals an urgent need for more flexible, more inclusive models of burgeoning adulthood to widen constricted definitions of growth that render girls developmentally deficient.

Deploring gender inequity in developmental studies, feminists in this field first employed the powerful metaphor of "voice" to capture neglected female points of view and a woman's sense of self (Gilligan, *Different Voice* 1; Belenky et al. 18). Lyn Mikel Brown and Carol Gilligan, in conjunction with their associates, expand the original metaphorical concept of "voice" to represent girls' and women's frequently difficult "struggle to authorize or take seriously their own experience" (*Crossroads* 6). According to recent research, girls of seven to ten or eleven speak freely without masking their disagreements or angry feelings; they remain confident that relationships they hold dear will survive the expression of opposing opinions or values (Gilligan, "Women's Psychological Development" 13; Rogers, "Voice, Play," 270). But lengthy interviews with preadolescent and adolescent girls reveal that by the age of eleven or twelve, girls' voices often change: they no longer "know what they know" (Gilligan, Rogers, Tolman 1). Observing repeated instructions to hold back or disguise bad feelings that may hurt others, unwilling to speak their privately held truths, girls routinely begin to "lose voice." This split in their sense of what they see and know and what they can let others know results in a swirling confusion of honesty and masquerade.

Thus, what poses itself as a serious crisis for an adolescent is the unbridgeable rupture between her authentic inner voice—recording, for example, disagreements, hurt, or envy—and the disingenuous behavior required among girls to sustain an illusion of their unfailing sweetness and good will. As Gilligan describes it, adolescence for girls hastens a crisis of identity, with girls frequently "us[ing] the phrase 'I don't know' to cover knowledge which they believe may be dangerous . . ." ("Women's Psychological Development" 11); for Brown and Gilligan, adolescence is the time when girls must disconnect parts of themselves in order to "enter, without disrupting, the world they are to live in as young women" (3).

In longitudinal studies, girls negotiating these turbulent developmental waters speak in voices of "surrender" and "resistance," alternately registering conformity with and defiance of gender expectations about allowable female self-expression.[1] Carol Gilligan, Annie Rogers, and Deborah Tolman shift the clinical meaning of "resistance" from negative associations with avoidance to positive associations with girls' strategies for challenging falseness in relationships (1). They find that girls' voices are strengthened by adult women's openness about their experiences in private and public spheres dominated by men. Brown and Gilligan reach the same conclusion (220–32). For example, one of the young girls that Brown and Gilligan interview is Janice, who reports finding strength in her relationship with her mother. Bonding easily with her mother, Janice listens to female elders in her community, who teach her to question or "resist" what isn't being taught about African American history in her textbooks (227).

Each of the four essays found in this section throws light on girls' development, focusing particularly on adolescents' struggle between surrendering to or resisting the demands of conventional femininity. In "Initiation Stories and Gender," Gail L. Mortimer analyzes the onset of adulthood in characterizations by three southern writers—Faulkner, Porter, and Welty. Using Nancy Chodorow's work to suggest "how such stories by male and female authors differ, and why they do," Mortimer reads "Barn Burning" as a quintessentially male quest in which Faulkner leaves no doubt that young Sarty's complete break from his family is a morally right, courageous, and admirable decision.

Yet Mortimer finds "a very different picture" in several stories by Katherine Anne Porter and Eudora Welty. Both writers repeatedly portray an adolescent girl desiring relational distance from kin—Miranda in Porter's "Old Mortality," the protagonist in Porter's "Theft," and Laura in "Flowering Judas;" Dicey in Welty's "Kin"—but in each case the main character discovers that she cannot disconnect fully from family attachments and strike out on her own. Caught in the mesh of responsibility for others, female protagonists in these works never achieve complete autonomy, since for them, the choice to detach is "pervaded by complexity and pain." Thus, Mortimer argues, the male initiation plot which presumes the necessity of separation from childhood attachments "cannot easily serve as the climax or epiphany of a young girl's story."

In "The Dangers of Time Travel: Revisioning the Landscape of Girls' Relationships in Margaret Atwood's *Cat's Eye*," Lyn Mikel Brown describes the protagonist's memories of her painful and confusing surrender to expectations that she speak and act falsely if she wants acceptance by the neighborhood girls. In Elaine's re-created scenes of capitulation to cruelties enacted by childhood friends, we see the "terror of uncertainty, the panic of shifting reality" that many girls suffer when they can no longer "stay with" their knowledge to resist the disconnection between false versions of reality and what they honestly see around them.

Probing this story of a woman's dangerous journey back through time, Brown correlates the novelist's revelation—and, indeed, Atwood's implicit warning—with her own research. In Elaine's story, as in her own longitudinal interviews with girls, Brown notices how quickly an adolescent's voice is forced underground when her expression of rage or frustration is not sanctioned—particularly by adult women—as a legitimate response to "the daily barrage of subtle and not-so-subtle messages . . . that first turn girls against each other, and then eventually against themselves." In her studies with adolescent girls, Brown has witnessed the dynamics of this conflict captured in *Cat's Eye*. Her analysis of the novel leads her to conclude that when women ignore girls' confusion and refuse to validate girls' resistance to the "narrowing effects of conventional femininity," we act out of "the legacy of our own trauma and loss."

Writing "In the 'I' of Madness: Shifting Subjectivities in Girls' and Women's Psychological Development in *The Yellow Wallpaper*," Annie Rogers also argues that adult women's freedom in self-expression may be key to girls' resistance against cultural imperatives that bind them. This essay focuses attention on the psychological significance of the narrator's shifting voices in Gilman's short story. Describing the narrator's fragmenting of her self into the writer of truths and the dutiful patient who lies to please her physician-husband, Rogers draws parallels between this woman's strategy of resistance and how adolescents cope when adult rules of gender interrupt "what they once knew from experience." The result for girls, says Rogers, is that they experience their own knowledge and "what is said to be reality" as representing two different, conflicting perspectives. Rogers finds this same "double-subjectivity" at the heart of Gilman's nineteenth-century characterization.

Rogers listens to Gilman's mad narrator alongside the voices of girls she has interviewed before and during their adolescence. Juxtaposing the young and adult voices, Rogers explores *The Yellow Wallpaper* as a story about what a woman will do to keep sane when she can no longer sustain self-knowledge in the face of imposed, patriarchal constructions of her identity. Gilman's story of her narrator's entrapment and demise leads Rogers to discuss psychological processes that women can learn from pre-adolescent girls to struggle against self-dismissal. However, it is women's double subjectivity—the "capacity to hold two contradictory voices or perspectives"—that proves "crucial in [women's] helping one another and girls to sustain resistance and avert the edge of madness."

Fisher and Silber find feminist psychological theory particularly useful in revealing the extent to which fairy tales imprint conservative cultural values on young girls and women alike. In "Fairy Tales, Feminist Theory, and the Lives of Women and Girls," the authors analyze both well-known and lesser-known stories that contain themes related to mothers and daughters, deception, desire, and "happy endings" in the patriarchal kingdom.

Along with the other contributors to this section, Fisher and Silber consider the damaging effect of repeated characterizations in which girls and older women remain relationally disconnected. Noting that in Grimm's stories the "bad mother . . . dominat[es] not just the princess, but the plot," while the good mother appears "for a sentence or two before dying," the authors recognize the impossibility of a girl reader identifying with any adult woman in the tales. Feminist psychological theory "gives the lie to pervasive 'happy endings'" that consistently exclude older female characters from final scenes in which "perfect happiness" is restored. Offering adolescents no effective models of female resistance, the tales imagine instead "a young woman in the prime of her life who has lost not only a healthy relationship with her mother and all other women, but also her own identity and voice." Losing voice, she learns to resist cultural mandates through lies, betrayals, and silence.

Like the other literary selections analyzed in this section, Grimm's fairy tales illustrate real-life limitations girls face today as they take those defining steps toward adulthood. The works of fiction explored in this essay have not always been seen in their capacity to illuminate girls' psychological struggles of surrender and resistance. Read in this way, these stories surely suggest the far-reaching significance of women's and girls' mutual influence on each other's development. Moreover, an analysis of literature using feminist developmental theory shows how profoundly ideas about gender, connection, and separation affect not only characterizations rendered vividly in art, but also the world in which we live.

Notes

1. For examples of longitudinal, feminist research on adolescent girls, see, for example: Gilligan, Rogers and Tolman, *Women, Girls & Psychotherapy: Reframing Resistance*, Binghamton: The Haworth Press, 1991, 1–3; Brown and Gilligan, *Meeting at the Crossroads*, Cambridge: Harvard UP, 1992; Apter, *Altered Loves*, New York: St. Martin's Press, 1990.

Works Cited

Apter, Terri. *Altered Loves: Mothers and Daughters During Adolescence*. New York: St. Martin's Press, 1990.

Belenky, Mary Field, Blythe Clinchy McVicker, Nancy Rule Goldberger, and Jill Mattuck Tarule. *Women's Ways of Knowing: The Development of Self, Voice and Mind*. New York: Basic Books, 1986.

Brown, Lyn Mikel and Carol Gilligan. "The Psychology of Women and the Development of Girls." Manuscript, Harvard University, Graduate School of Education, 1990, p. 3; as quoted in *Silencing the Self: Women and Depression*. Dana Crowley Jack. New York: HarperCollins, 1991.

Brown, Lyn Mikel and Carol Gilligan. *Meeting at the Crossroads: Women's Psychology and Girls' Development*. Cambridge: Harvard UP, 1992.

Chodorow, Nancy. *The Reproduction of Mothering: Psychoanalysis and the Sociology of Gender*. Berkeley: U of California P, 1978.

Erikson, Erik. *Identity: Youth and Crisis*. New York: W.W. Norton, 1968.

Freud, Sigmund. "Three Essays on the Theory of Sexuality." *The Standard Edition of the Complete Psychological Works of Sigmund Freud*. Ed. James Strachey. Vol. 7. London: Hogarth Press, 1961. 125–78.

Gilligan, Carol. *In a Different Voice: Psychological Theory and Women's Development*. Cambridge: Harvard UP, 1982.

Gilligan, Carol. "Women's Psychological Development: Implications for Psychotherapy." *Women, Girls and Psychotherapy: Reframing Resistance*. Ed. Carol Gilligan, Annie G. Rogers and Deborah L. Tolman. New York: Haworth Press, 1991. 5–31.

Gilligan, Carol, Nona Lyons and Trudy Hanmer, eds. *Making Connections: The Relational Worlds of Adolescent Girls at Emma Willard School*. Cambridge: Harvard UP, 1990.

Gilligan, Carol, Annie G. Rogers, and Deborah Tolman, eds. *Women, Girls & Psychotherapy: Reframing Resistance*. Binghamton: Haworth Press, 1991.

Jordan, Judith V., Alexandra G. Kaplan, Jean Baker Miller, Irene P. Stiver, and Janet L. Surrey. *Women's Growth in Connection: Writings from the Stone Center.* New York: Guilford Press, 1991.

Levinson, Daniel. *The Seasons of a Man's Life.* New York: Alfred A. Knopf, 1978.

Miller, Jean Baker. *Toward a New Psychology of Women.* Boston: Beacon Press, 1976.

Rogers, Annie G. "Voice, Play, and a Practice of Ordinary Courage in Girls' and Women's Lives." *Harvard Educational Review* 63 (1993): 265–95.

1

Initiation Stories and Gender

Gail L. Mortimer

Among the most provocative concepts influencing feminist thought in recent years has been the notion that young children's recognition of their separateness from other human beings, so central to the development of their identities, is crucially affected by the fact that primary caretakers in our culture have been almost exclusively women. Theorists Nancy Chodorow, Carol Gilligan, and Dorothy Dinnerstein, among others, have explored various implications of this phenomenon for both male and female children. Chodorow, for example, has shown how the child's tasks of learning about and adjusting to its separateness from this woman figure (most often, its mother) and establishing a sense of its own identity necessarily differ because of the need, psychologically, to understand one's identity in the context of the mother's identity as a woman.[1]

Little girls, according to Chodorow, establish their identity directly with the mother; a decisive separation from this crucial figure is not necessary to the process. Little boys, however, form their identities through relationship with a father figure who has often been of secondary importance in the child's experience, in the sense that he arrives on the scene after the powerfully experienced mother. The male child's identity must be formed in many ways in opposition to the feminine identity he originally found to be virtually omnipotent. Decisive separation from the mother is essential to the development of a boy's sense of identity precisely because of his mother's emotional importance in his life. As a consequence of the young male's emergence from such a context, masculinity comes to be defined as a configuration of characteristics that are decidedly *not* "feminine" ones, and the need to maintain separation from the

9

feminine remains (*Feminism* 109). Chodorow argues that masculinity in our culture is associated with a high valuation of autonomy and a tendency to see other individuals as decidedly separate from the self.[2] Femininity, in contrast, has been associated with greater conscious concern with the "retention and continuity of external relationships" and a vulnerability to relationships that Chodorow sees as the consequence of "more permeable ego boundaries" (*Reproduction* 169 and 93).

This model can serve as a valuable heuristic device for illuminating differences in the styles of men and women as they make choices, determine the values that matter to them, and interpret their experiences. In exploring human development through their fiction, some of our most insightful authors have intuitively understood the nature of the issues to be resolved by children moving toward adulthood. The symbolic moment at which adulthood is achieved—or signaled—in a child's life is a favorite subject for writers because it provides an occasion for showing a pivotal point in a life from which all else appears to follow. The initiation story is especially important in American literary history, because our stories have so often taken place in the context of myths—the frontier, the American Dream—implying that all things are possible. Authors who write such stories seem especially fascinated with the turning points in our lives when some possibilities are chosen, while others are relinquished. Nancy Chodorow's work is invaluable, because she suggests new questions to ask about how such stories by male and female authors differ, and why they do.[3]

By "initiation story," I do not necessarily mean stories reflecting systematic rituals like those enacted in various societies to formalize a young person's entrance into the world of adult responsibility—such as we see, for example, in William Faulkner's hunting stories, "The Old People" and "The Bear." The stories I have in mind do, however, share one important feature with explicitly ritualistic stories: they record the point in a youngster's development when he or she embraces particular adult standards and leaves behind the (ostensibly) more comforting world of children. Rituals of various societies enact this assumption of new values by symbolically separating the initiate temporarily from the world he or she has known. Only after internalizing newer, "adult" values and perhaps proving that they are now part of one's behavior is the young person free to return home, but he or she has changed. Childish dependence has been left behind. In American literature, the child usually does not experience specific rituals, but initiation stories *do* characteristically explore the mind of the child as he or she encounters previously unknown forms of knowledge (whether kept from the child or simply not yet recognized) at precisely the point in the child's life when he or she must choose whether to be part of the group/context/world signified by those values.

Adolescence intrinsically involves—at a somewhat greater level of sophistication—an explicit and necessary reenactment of the earliest separation experience.

I want to focus, then, on the initiation motif as the chronicle of this emotional or moral event in a young person's life. Characteristically, such stories about children and adolescents emphasize occasions of disillusionment that precipitate one's movement into adulthood. These texts are permeated often with a moral questioning of adult values and reach their crisis with the protagonist's decision either to adopt or abandon them. The ethical consequences of these choices are paramount, for the child may embrace or disavow values such as honesty, loyalty, or a belief in justice, depending upon his or her assessment of the adults who have embodied (or claimed to embody) them and, in doing so, become a particular kind of adult.

Carol Gilligan's research proves especially beneficial at this point, for she has cogently argued that ethical decision-making is deeply influenced by gender and by the sorts of values males and females in our culture have been taught to embrace. Attempting to understand varieties of "relational potential" long associated in our culture with males and females,[4] Gilligan explores how males and females perceive specific ethical dilemmas and decide what is to be done. When Gilligan asked her subjects to react to pictures of human beings in different situations, she found striking confirmation of Chodorow's observations about the high valuation males in our culture place on separateness and autonomy. Gilligan's male subjects more often found danger in pictures reflecting (even potential) relationships and created stories expressing fantasies of violence. Conversely, women subjects more often perceived violent outcomes in scenes implying individual achievement, suggesting that negative consequences were, for them, associated with independent, successful behavior. Gilligan concludes that men "projected more violence into situations of personal affiliation than they did into impersonal situations of achievement," whereas women "saw more violence in impersonal situations of achievement than in situations of affiliation" (41). In other words, her subjects appeared to project fears of dependence on others, on the one hand, and of abandonment, on the other, in patterns at least to some degree associated with gender identity.

The interplay of separateness and connection in all of our lives and their specific significance in the perceptions of (at least some) men and women in our culture have potentially widespread implications for understanding social assumptions and behaviors—and, consequently, for understanding such issues when they surface in particular fictional plots. The initiation story, echoing our earlier, crucial separation experience, seems a natural place to begin asking to what degree narrative decisions, plot, and theme may be affected by a writer's gender.[5]

Let us begin by considering a characteristic initiation story: William Faulkner's "Barn Burning." In the course of this story, the protagonist, a young boy named Colonel Sartoris Snopes, comes to terms with the meanings of his father's life and has to decide whether his loyalties lie in "blood ties" or in the moral values he begins to perceive in the wider society. He finds these latter values explicit in the behavior, demeanor, and very environment of Major de Spain, a character whose dignity and apparent desire to be fair seem at odds with and even to belie the instinctive hatred and contempt Sarty recognizes in his father. The significance of Sarty's name (composed, in part, of the aristocratic name "Sartoris") is, of course, that Faulkner has embodied in it Sarty's capacity to make a choice between the values of his grudge-ridden, vindictive father ("Snopes") and a value system characterized by notions of honor, compassion, honesty, and personal courage that Faulkner often associates with aristocratic names.[6] If we think in terms of the psychoanalytic paradigm, Sarty must choose between two "fathers," must find the figure with whom he will identify himself and so determine the sort of adult he will be.

The turning point in the story—the moment at which Sarty chooses how he will live his life—is foreshadowed throughout the text by Faulkner's depiction of Sarty's "readiness" to recognize the disjunction between what his father tells him is true and apparently contradictory realities that exist in the larger world. At the outset, Sarty is shown to be totally immersed in the world view held by his father; he simply does not know that other, less bitter ways of seeing things exist. Faulkner emphasizes his limited perceptions from the beginning by establishing differences between what Sarty can see and what he can smell and hear. The latter senses somehow offer him truer information. He smells the otherness of others (whom his father has defined, uniformly, as enemies), the cheese in the store where the Justice of the Peace is holding court, the "hermetic meat" in tin cans. The phrase "he could not see" is repeated several times to show us that both Sarty's limited experience and his very height distort his perspective on what is happening. When the Justice of the Peace tries to show him compassion by not putting him in a position where he will be forced to lie out of loyalty to his father, we are told that Sarty "could not see that the Justice's face was kindly nor discern that his voice was troubled when he spoke . . ." (Faulkner 4). Instead, this threatening world is a "fluid world," rushing beneath Sarty, and he hears only "voices coming to him again through the smell of cheese and sealed meat" (Faulkner 5). Immediately upon leaving the makeshift courtroom,

Sarty jumps on someone who has hissed "Barn burner!" at them: "Again he could not see, whirling . . ." (Faulkner 5).

Later in the day, Sarty's father strikes him, accusing him of being on the verge of betraying his family:

> You're getting to be a man. You got to learn. You got to learn to stick to your own blood or you ain't going to have any blood to stick to you. Do you think either of them, any man there this morning, would? Don't you know all they wanted was a chance to get at me because they knew I had them beat? Eh? (Faulkner 8)

The narrator explains that "never before had he paused afterward to explain why; it was as if the blow and the following calm, outrageous voice still rang, repercussed . . ." (Faulkner 9). The juxtaposition of punishment and of an explanation that Sarty recognizes as flawed and distorted begins to awaken his capacity to see a difference between his father and other people.

The next day, the lesson is completed when Sarty first views the home of Major de Spain. He and his father have gone there to set the terms for their tenancy on one of de Spain's farms, and at first sight Sarty is awestricken.

> he saw the house for the first time and at that instant he forgot his father and the terror and despair both, and even when he remembered his father again (who had not stopped) the terror and despair did not return. . . . *Hit's big as a courthouse,* he thought quietly, with a surge of peace and joy whose reason he could not have thought into words, being too young for that: *They are safe from him. People whose lives are a part of this peace and dignity are beyond his touch, he no more to them than a buzzing wasp: capable of stinging for a moment but that's all.* (Faulkner 10)

The child's hopes are raised: "*Maybe he will feel it too. Maybe it will even change him now from what maybe he couldn't help but be*" (Faulkner 11).

The convergence of these two events—the explanation for his punishment and his powerful admiration for the de Spain mansion—becomes important when Sarty sees his father deliberately defile the de Spain home by dragging and smearing horse droppings into the front hall onto a pale French rug after the well-dressed black servant who has answered the door tells them to wipe their feet. His father's self-justificatory and bitter pronouncements about de Spain's insulting intentions toward him so clearly do not fit anything that has happened that Sarty is shaken. The events surrounding the spoiled rug (which Abner causes to be destroyed by being scrubbed with a rock and lye) make Sarty realize that his father's motive is vengeance, that de Spain's barn is the next likely target, and (for the first time) that this retaliation is not at all justified by what has transpired. Readers recognize it too, for after the trial in which Ab Snopes is told he will have to pay ten bushels of corn over his contract to compensate de Spain for the rug, the father keeps his sons in town for a leisurely afternoon, making clear that he feels no urgency to begin planting: they will not be staying.

When Abner gathers kerosine and leaves, Sarty escapes from his mother and aunt, who try forcibly to hold him back, runs to de Spain's house, shouts a warning about the barn, and then leaves, not returning to his home. He hears shots. It is never clear whether his father is killed, wounded or missed by the bullets. But from Sarty's perspective, it does not matter. He cannot return home. If his father is alive, he will know Sarty betrayed him, and Sarty will face the consequences. If he is dead, then Sarty has no reason to go home, because the family is impoverished and ineffectual; there is nothing there for him. He does not consciously think of the alternatives, perhaps, but he instinctively knows he cannot return.

What is crucial for our concerns is not the fact that Sarty leaves but the manner in which Faulkner narrates the departure. He has already set the stage for us to understand this final separation in purely positive terms by having the narrator refer, during the story itself, to Sarty's later adult understanding of these earlier experiences. As Sarty's father beats him and expresses his paranoid view of the urgency of family solidarity, for example, we are told: "Later, twenty years later, he was to tell himself, 'If I had said they wanted only truth, justice, he would have hit me again.' But now he said nothing" (Faulkner 8). In the same vein, Faulkner devotes a paragraph to the smallness of the campfire Abner customarily builds. "Older," he writes,

> the boy might have remarked this and wondered why not a big one . . .
> Then he might have gone a step farther and thought that that was the reason
> . . . And older still, he might have divined the true reason . . . But he did not
> think this now. . . . (Faulkner 7–8)

What these passages show us is that Sarty will go beyond this crisis with his family to become morally admirable, an adult who values truth and justice.

The language of the final paragraph itself is also telling, for it frames Sarty's final walk down the dark road precisely in terms of the *moral correctness* of his decision by repeatedly reassuring us that everything is going to turn out well. Faulkner suggests several of the difficulties Sarty will face, young and alone as he is, but immediately ameliorates their seriousness:

> It would be dawn and then sun-up after a while and he would be hungry. But that would be to-morrow and now he was only cold, and walking would cure that. . . . He got up. He was a little stiff, but walking would cure that too as it would the cold, and soon there would be the sun. (Faulkner 25)

As Sarty walks away, moreover, he is accompanied by the "silver voices" of birds that make up "the urgent and quiring heart of the late spring night" (Faulkner 25). He is made part of a larger, harmonious universe ("The slow constellations wheeled on."), and his recognition of the time of night it is ("He could tell that from the whippoorwills.") shows that Sarty is a part of this world. The moral positiveness of this last scene, the apparent peace of mind seen in Sarty's assimilation by nature, is in sharp contrast to the fear and despair his life in his family had caused him. Faulkner, moreover, makes Sarty's leaving of his family emotionally appropriate by depicting the only caring members of that family—the women—as completely ineffectual in dealing with Abner or in protecting Sarty from his father. They are seen as comic, bovine creatures, not to be taken seriously as beings who might have legitimate emotional claims to make on him. As a result, we as readers are discouraged from empathizing with their loss when he leaves them.[7] Thus, Faulkner handles Sarty's departure in ways that lead us to believe his courage in striking out on his own *is* the act of leaving Snopesian values behind him and a sign of the morality he is beginning to embody. We are led to believe that his final act is positive, laudable: "He did not look back" (Faulkner 25).

In contrast to the moral approval with which Faulkner sanctions Sarty's abandonment of his family, we find a very different picture when we turn to the work of two Southern women writers depicting similar crises in children's lives. Near contemporaries of Faulkner, Katherine Anne Porter, and Eudora Welty devote a larger proportion of their writing to children and their perceptions than he does. Yet we find in their stories nothing precisely analogous to the initiation story per se. Perhaps this is because our very definition of what an initiation story is—the decisive movement of a young person toward adulthood and a deliberately chosen value system—does not often correspond with feminine experience. Females don't (according to Chodorow and Gilligan) tend to experience a break with their families as decisive, and so it seems plausible to argue that such an act cannot easily serve as the climax or epiphany of a young woman's story. Breaks from one's family are prolonged, painful, and incomplete, and in women's stories about such events, there is rarely, if ever, the sanction of moral approval and implicit joy we have found in Faulkner's tale.

Those familiar with the details of Faulkner's life may well point out that he did not himself achieve the freedom from family ties exemplified by Sarty Snopes. On the contrary, throughout his life Faulkner felt deeply responsible to his family. Whenever he was in Mississippi, for example, he visited his mother virtually every day. Joseph Blotner reports that Faulkner's friend, Phil Stone, had said "that all the Faulkner boys were tied to their mother and resented it" and that this was "probably partly responsible . . . for an animosity toward women that he saw in Bill" (Blotner 1: 631). These apparent facts about Faulkner's life do not, however, invalidate the argument I am making. Rather, in their light, Sarty's story comes to seem a kind of compensatory fantasy. It is almost as if Faulkner were saying by means of this tale of how Sarty achieves moral stature, how much easier it would be to live one's life honorably if one were not entangled in family responsibilities. It was Faulkner, after all, who said that he knew why there would always be war: "it's the only condition under which a man who is not a scoundrel can escape for a while from his female kin" (Blotner 2: 1106). Virtually all of Faulkner's stories about aristocratic protagonists confirm their inability ever to escape what families signify. For the purposes of my argument here, what is important is that such compensatory fantasies as the one he creates for Sarty Snopes *work* as fiction about male protagonists. Such pure fantasies of successful separation are rarely attempted by women writers—at least when they choose female protagonists—probably because they would be implausible. *Even as fantasy*, such a plot about a female character would not ring true.

Dealing with similar contexts—especially in a series of stories centered on the figure of Miranda—Katherine Anne Porter, too, emphasizes the evolving process of her protagonist's discovery of adult myth-making, of the stories that families create to explain their lives to themselves. Or, alternatively, she focuses on the aftermath of leaving one's family, on the many ways in which the "break" from them has been incomplete or ambiguous. What Porter tends *not* to address directly is the act of separation itself, because, as we shall see, for her characters this event is pervaded by complexity and pain. Porter's characters powerfully exemplify the difficulty in separation that Chodorow and Gilligan see as so typical of female experience.

The central theme of Porter's "Old Mortality" is Miranda's emerging awareness of how false the stories are that her family tells about its past. Seeing artifacts from that past in the faded flowers and other mementos of her long-deceased Aunt Amy and meeting at last Amy's former husband, Uncle Gabriel, now bloated with self-pity, an alcoholic, Miranda cannot reconcile the tangible evidence of the past with the romantic aura in which Aunt Amy's story has always been told. Miranda is chagrined, moreover, as adults in her world repeatedly ruin the pleasure of current moments by dismissing them as hopelessly inferior to occasions that happened before Miranda and her sister Maria were born. The impossibility of arguing or competing with these long-dead, "perfect" moments from the past, the consequent destruction of present joys, and the recognition of the shabbiness that remains of that ostensibly glorious past cause Miranda to begin to turn away from her family and its stories in disappointment and near despair. She marries very early just to escape them.

Some years later, her hasty marriage now failing, Miranda encounters an older relative, her bitter Cousin Eva, on a train. Eva's spiteful version of Amy's story sickens Miranda further, so that she turns even more decisively away:

> her blood rebelled against the ties of blood. She was sick to death of cousins. She did not want any more ties with this house, she was going to leave it, and she was not going back to her husband's family either. She would have no more bonds that smothered her in love and hatred. She knew now why she had run away to marriage, and she knew that she was going to run away from marriage, and she was not going to stay in any place, with anyone, that threatened to forbid her making her own discoveries. . . . (Porter 220)

Believing that she *can* leave the ugliness of family entanglements behind, Miranda determines not to participate any further in the stories—the lies—her family builds around itself. Porter records her thoughts: "At least I can know the truth about what happens to me, she assured herself silently, making a promise to herself, in her hopefulness, *her ignorance*" (Porter 221, emphasis mine). These are the last words of the story; Porter's narrator ends with words reminding us that Miranda, too, is deluded in her belief that she can free herself from her family through any simple choice.

In stories like "Theft" and "Flowering Judas" featuring young women protagonists in many ways indistinguishable from Miranda, Porter chronicles the aftermath of the break from one's family: the sense of loss and of self-betrayal in the decision to avoid entangling relationships. In these two stories, the pull back toward relationship and responsibility for others is experienced as so strong that only an abrupt and deliberate rejection of relationship per se seems to promise release. Yet that decision, in these stories, has led each protagonist into a sense that life itself has been rejected or missed, and both characters reveal a numbness that seems self-inflicted. In both stories, the protagonists have moved to different environments (a large city and Mexico, respectively) and adopted radically independent lifestyles (as a journalist and a revolutionary sympathizer), yet, despite their physical distance from their families, both women feel that their current, ostensibly more superficial relationships threaten to pull them back into responsibility for others, powerfully resurrecting that dimension of relatedness that for Porter is most compelling and disturbing. The geographical distance these characters insist upon and the fierceness of their denial of these human claims are signs of the desperate need they feel for separation and the impossibility of their achieving it. The very titles of the stories ("Theft" and "Flowering Judas") emphasize the feelings of betrayal—of self and of others—that are the price of separation. Laura, in the latter story, struggles with despair brought on by her very indifference to people, for she has failed to intervene to save the life of a young man in prison. Her final dream discloses her feelings of complicity and guilt. She tries to deny everything (Porter 97) and ends waking from a nightmare of reproaches, trembling. Similarly, in "Theft," the unnamed protagonist, having turned away a lover by her ultimate refusal to make a commitment to him, recognizes at the last that *her* "principle of rejection" (Porter 64), so like Laura's, has created her own overwhelming sense of loss: "I was right not to be afraid of any thief but myself, who will end by leaving me nothing" (Porter 65). Physical distance, each of these characters learns, has little to do with feelings of freedom; Porter's characters carry with them their entangling emotions.

The efforts of Porter's protagonists to escape connection with others are consistently exposed as self-deceptive. The very feeling tone of many of her stories, that of disappointment and sorrow, seems to follow from her theme, as if she sees her protagonists' efforts to live self-sufficient lives as inherently doomed. The sense of personal failure permeates her stories both of these failed attempts at freedom from entanglement and of other, very different characters who allow themselves to become emotionally involved with others. Examples of the latter are found in "Pale Horse, Pale Rider" and "The Jilting of Granny Weatherall"; for them, connection leads directly to abandonment, loss, or betrayal. There seems in Porter's world to be a permanent frustration and unhappiness about the impossibility of freedom, on the one hand, and of viable connectedness, on the other. Katherine Anne Porter records what Faulkner had described as a decided move away from one's past as an *illusory* separation, necessary perhaps to a sense of adulthood, but ephemeral as well. In Porter's fictive world there is no permanent release from the webs of meaning and relationship into which families (and others) weave us.

Eudora Welty, too, seems to write about the long preliminary disenchantment of children as they come to understand adult truths and their discrepancy from reality as the child perceives it, but her stories differ markedly from Porter's. In her stories about young protagonists, while the narrator makes clear to the reader that some new knowledge has taken place, Welty's child characters remain only dimly aware of these discrepancies and of the possibility of choosing one's own values. Never do they attempt to break away from the parents as a direct result of these revelations—at least at this young age—and Welty typically stays *outside the mind of her character* rather than revealing the evolving consciousness as it explores, compares, and understands what is happening. A characteristic example of Welty's style of presenting such material is offered by "A Visit of Charity," in which the young protagonist, a fourteen-year-old named Miriam, goes to visit two old ladies in a nursing home in order to earn points as a Campfire Girl. Welty playfully echoes "Little Red Riding Hood" throughout this story, as she does other intertextual sources, to show us that this is indeed a type of initiation story. Miriam is faced for the first time with the facts of elderly pain and the bitterness that can come at the end of a long life in the persons of two elderly ladies who live together in the same room, bleat like sheep, and hate each other. Welty, in a characteristic move, enacts a cliche in her story, that of the wolf in sheep's clothing, both to show the discrepancy between what lies beneath and what is on the surface of adult behavior and to suggest that Miriam is indeed encountering evil (the women's malice and bitterness), as Little Red Riding Hood had done. But instead of having this revelation make an immediate impact on Miriam's consciousness so that she is moved to make some decision vis-à-vis the adult world, Welty simply signals the event by having Miriam take a bite out of an apple, after which she catches a bus home (*Collected* 113–18). We are not to know in this or in Welty's other stories about children how or how soon the new knowledge glimpsed in the events of the story will make itself felt in the child's development. Oddly enough, then, despite several wonderful stories of childhood experience, Welty has written no stories that record a child's explicit rejection of particular adult values, no initiation involving an attempt to separate oneself from those values. Instead of depicting understanding of these matters as something that occurs at a single moment in time, Welty tends to show her child characters as being fully immersed in the world as relevant adults have defined it. Only the reader understands the implications of the fictive events.

Epiphanies for Welty's characters occur somewhat later, retrospectively, when as adults they find themselves capable of recognizing the differences in the world as they now know it from the world they knew so well as children. Knowledge for her characters consists of a recognition of the limitations of one's own prior thinking. It is *as an adult* that the protagonist becomes aware of the perpetual pull back toward the powerful myths of childhood. Another of Welty's stories, "Kin," offers a good example. Its protagonist has assumed the possibility of breaking from her childhood and its entangling connections, only to discover how powerfully adults would like to restrain her. Dicey Hastings, raised in Mississippi, has lived in the North long enough at the time the story begins that she feels her identity is no longer in the South, until, that is, she returns to visit her Aunt Ethel and cousin Kate. Like many of Welty's protagonists, Dicey is an outsider who was once an insider in a particular family, and her story consists of her partly dismayed, partly amused recognition that the family has not in the least released its emotional hold upon her. Filled with an exuberant happiness in the news of her engagement to a young man up North, she is amazed to discover that her aunt and cousin treat her as if she has barely left and that, in fact, she must postpone her desire to share her confidences with them. They still live "as if they had never heard of anywhere else, even Jackson" (*Collected* 539), and in their preoccupation with their own extended family's life, they assume that she should "keep up in spite of being gone almost [her] whole life, except for visits"(*Collected* 538).

To a large degree, the point of this story is that Dicey's status as an outsider has enabled her to see things about this family that its insiders, engrossed in its myths, fail to grasp. Her ability to imagine, because she has lived it, a life not rooted in this particular family, gives her a breadth of sympathy that makes her alone recognize—late in the story—the dimensions of her elderly, ill Uncle Felix's life and what it may have consisted of before the family took it over in his feeble old age. The stable, absorbing reality at the center of this, as so many of Welty's stories, is the family that (however benignly) swallows up individual priorities and desires in its larger purposes, defines individual experiences in terms of its own needs, and, inevitably, to some degree, chokes off an individual's freedom. Welty records and hints at the suppression of individual desire brought about by family claims.

The difference in understanding between Dicey and her cousin Kate, who is about her age (in her twenties), but has never left the family home in Mississippi, is humorously suggested early in the story by Dicey's recognition that they tend to use different adverbs: "I was thinking, if I always say 'still,' Kate still says 'always,' and laughed, but would not tell her" (*Collected* 546). In phrasing her questions to the family in terms of whether or not something is still the same ("'Uncle Felix! Is *he* still living?'"), Dicey proclaims how much has happened in her life beyond this family and her bemusement that things have remained unchanged. Using "always" to refer to the way things are, Kate unwittingly expresses the stability, the sameness through the years, of *her* world. Dicey notes this difference—just as she notices them throughout the story—but she does not tell Kate, who she feels would not understand. This distinction between them sets the stage for Dicey's and Kate's very different abilities to comprehend what has been happening in Uncle Felix's life when they finally visit him later in the story.

Before this later scene, however, Welty sets the stage for Dicey's moment of understanding through episodes revealing how tenaciously people, including her family, cling to romanticized versions of their own lives. Arriving at Uncle Felix's home, where he is now being cared for by one of their mutual kin, Sister Anne (whose exact relationship to them all seems indeterminable), Dicey and Kate discover the house taken over by a photographer who has rented their parlor for the day to take pictures of people in the neighborhood. Everyone is dressed up in the least normal way possible, "'like Sunday and Election Day put together'"(*Collected* 550), to have pictures taken against a totally fake and improbable photographer's backdrop. As payment for letting the photographer use the parlor, Sister Anne receives her own photograph, in which she chooses to hold an archaic fan covered with forget-me-nots "languidly across her bosom," as the picture is taken against the "absurd backdrop" (*Collected* 562). She is, it seems, quite willing to be remembered as she never was.

On the wall behind the photographer's backdrop is the only painted portrait in this home, that of Dicey's ancestor: "the romantic figure of a young lady seated on a fallen tree under brooding skies: my great-grandmother Jerrold, who had been Eveline Mackaill" (*Collected* 561). Dicey remembers the picture now, even more vividly than if she could see it:

> And I remembered—rather, more warmly, *knew*, like a secret of the family—that the head of this black-haired, black-eyed lady who always looked the right, mysterious age to be my sister, had been fitted to the ready-made portrait by the painter who had called at the door . . . (*Collected* 561)

The utter unreality of this portrait, with its "forest scene so unlike the Mississippi wilderness" (*Collected* 561), and Evelina's submission to the painting of her portrait in so false a way (with a large, beaded necklace painted in to disguise where her head has been added on) persuade Dicey that she and her ancestor both have been seduced into accepting false versions of reality for the sake of their family. The old stereopticon that Uncle Felix had used to share with Dicey on Sunday afternoons after the huge family meal (when everyone else was napping) set the stage for the version of reality she now understands, but the then-young man allowed Dicey to see only some of the slides, including the "'Ladies' View, Lakes of Killarney,'" just as the family still only admits to particular versions of its own history. The family is protective, creating and sustaining a special view of reality for its women. Much of this story, then, emphasizes the gap between appearances and underlying truth, between what her family insists upon remembering and what Dicey now knows.

The young women visit Uncle Felix in a room in the back of the house, where Sister Anne has placed him to keep him unaware of the invasion of his home by the entire neighborhood. Unable to talk, he nevertheless seems to recognize Dicey, and he writes a brief, cryptic message on the torn-out page of a hymn book, slipping it into her hand: "'River—Daisy—Midnight—Please'" (*Collected* 561). Dicey seems ready to understand what Kate cannot, that Daisy is a woman's name and what the message might mean about him. Because his wife's name had been Beck, Kate is simply bewildered. When she declares, " 'I expect by now Uncle Felix has got his names mixed up, and Daisy was a mistake,' " Dicey cannot so easily dismiss the truth she has now glimpsed: "It was the 'please' that had hurt me . . . some things are too important for a mistake even to be considered. I was sorry I had showed Kate the message . . ." (*Collected* 564). Uncle Felix may have lost track of things in some sense, but what is beyond doubt is that he has turned to Dicey to share something precious, something his family cannot understand, and Dicey feels by the end of the story how irrevocable is the difference in understanding between herself, Kate, and the rest of her Mississippi family. Separation here is not willed; it is the result of Dicey's final, adult recognition of the vast difference in her capacity to see clearly, or at least more clearly than those immersed in her family's myths.

What these stories by Katherine Anne Porter and Eudora Welty suggest is that, for women, the moment of separation leading to an adult sense of autonomy or self-sufficiency is so far from being a single moment, a simple event, that it does not serve as a natural sort of dramatic center around which a story can be built. The dramatic disillusionment we find in such stories as "Barn Burning" or, to cite another example, in Sherwood Anderson's "I Want to Know Why," does not normally correspond to the experience of women. This is true, as well, of other famous stories in our culture of men who separate decisively from their families, such as Washington Irving's "Rip Van Winkle" and Nathaniel Hawthorne's "Wakefield," both centering on men who leave their families behind for twenty years. Rip Van Winkle is celebrated on his return from hills where he has slept; his "demanding" wife has, conveniently, died in the interim, so his fantasy of blissful irresponsibility is fulfilled as he lives out his life being taken care of by others. Wakefield simply walks back into his house as if nothing has happened after his twenty-year absence, with apparently no consequence other than his peaceful resumption of his former life. We should also recall James Thurber's "The Secret Life of Walter Mitty," in which Mitty's *emotional* separation from his wife is as complete as if he were thousands of miles away; he, too, is sympathized with in his desire to escape, for his wife is depicted as pure harridan. If we even try to imagine such plots as lived by female protagonists, we quickly see the impossibility of depicting women characters happily and fully separated from their families. What evokes sympathy for "oppressed" males would be very differently viewed if the characters were women.

In the stories of women writers, rather, characters' attempts to secure a relatively autonomous sense of self are part of a prolonged disengagement that is never fully achieved, is characteristically wrenching, and leaves a residue of guilt, a sense of failed responsibility, and even (in Porter) a sense of self-betrayal that cannot be finally overcome.[8] Welty expresses the feminine experience of even temporary separation succinctly in her autobiographical *One Writer's Beginnings*, when she describes how she and her family felt when one of them would take a train ride (as, for example, to New York, to see her publishers). She says that she would lie back in the seat of the train with "an iron cage around my chest of guilt"; taking trips was to her sheltering family "something that had better be momentous to justify such a leap into the dark" (93). Adulthood for Welty's and Porter's young women characters becomes a delicate and disturbing *balancing* of claims, not the clean sense of a fresh beginning that we found in Sarty—or that we find throughout American fiction, for that matter, in those joyous young male adventurers who have followed Huck Finn in lighting out for the frontier.

Notes

1. Chodorow, *Reproduction* and *Feminism*, especially chapter 5: "Gender, Relation, and Difference in Psychoanalytic Perspective," 99–113; Gilligan; and Dinnerstein. For a consideration of the implications of this theory for a variety of disciplines, see the essays in *The Future of Difference*.

2. Chodorow, *Feminism* 110, and *Reproduction* 174. An interesting variation on this idea as applied to how people sort through data looking for truths is found in Peter Elbow's "The Doubting Game and the Believing Game—An Analysis of the Intellectual Enterprise," an Appendix Essay in *Writing Without Teachers*, 147–91.

3. Literary applications of this paradigm have for the most part consisted of attempts to understand more fully the narrative content of texts by male and female writers, as in recognizing the importance of female networks and friendships in novels by women. See, for example, Abel.

4. The term "relational potential" is cited by Chodorow as coming from Henry Dicks' *Marital Tensions*. See *Reproduction* 166.

5. It is the *writer's* gender that is crucial for how such stories tend to evolve. It is significant, perhaps, that initiation stories nearly always involve protagonists of the same gender as the writer, so that no distinction need be made, but in other

sorts of fiction—where the protagonist may be, for a variety of reasons, of the opposite gender from the author—the character's sensibilities will often echo those of the author's gender, rather than the character's. This is a complex phenomenon, and it is beyond the scope of this Chapter to substantiate this idea fully, but consider as examples Virginia Woolf's characterization of Septimus Warren Smith in *Mrs. Dalloway* or William Faulkner's depiction of Addie Bundren in *As I Lay Dying*.

6. While Faulkner challenges this association of aristocracy and positive values by suggesting their potentially self-aggrandizing and self-deluding nature in such texts as *Flags in the Dust*, in "Barn Burning" he never questions that noble values are embodied in such figures. The fact constitutes an unqualifiedly positive goal toward which Sarty moves. "Barn Burning" 3–25.

7. Sarty cries out for his father as he runs away and tries, one final time, to justify him by saying, "He was brave! . . . He was in the war! He was in Colonel Sartoris' cav'ry!" but Faulkner's narrator reminds us that Sarty did not know his father had been a mercenary, loyal to neither side if he could profit by stealing from them (Faulkner 24–25). This final correction of a final misconception emphasizes once again the changes of understanding Sarty must undergo to reach fuller, adult comprehension.

8. In analyzing a different sort of initiation story—Sarah Orne Jewett's "A White Heron"—Carol Singley sees the protagonist's choice as being between the values of "the external male world" and the protagonist Sylvia's own value system, based in a reverence for nature. Singley argues that the cost of Sylvia's integrity in choosing to save the white heron is "social isolation," that the very fact of choosing entails alienation. Jewett is like both Porter and Welty in depicting the female's choice between following others' values or following one's own as invariably alienating: if you choose your own values (that is, some degree of spiritual separation), you "pay" through social ostracism—whether self-imposed or imposed by others—and if you choose the values of the culture, which entail for women capitulation to the social expectations of others, you become entangled in those values to the point of losing part of your "self." Sylvia's turning toward nature in Jewett's story is both a sign of her integrity and compensation for the loss of human relationship (with the young hunter) that her integrity has cost her. Jewett's story differs from those I am considering because she depicts separation as an unanticipated consequence of a moral decision, rather than as the nature of the decision itself. See Singley 76.

Works Cited

Abel, Elizabeth. "(E)Merging Identities: The Dynamics of Female Friendship in Contemporary Fiction by Women." *Signs* 6.3 (Spring 1981): 413–35.

Blotner, Joseph. *Faulkner: A Biography.* 2 vols. New York: Random House, 1974.

Chodorow, Nancy. *Feminism and Psychoanalytic Theory.* New Haven: Yale UP, 1989.

————. *The Reproduction of Mothering: Psychoanalysis and the Sociology of Gender*. Berkeley: U of California P, 1978.

Dicks, Henry V. *Marital Tensions*. New York: Basic Books, 1967.

Dinnerstein, Dorothy. *The Mermaid and the Minotaur: Sexual Arrangements and Human Malaise*. New York: Harper & Row, Harper Colophon, 1977.

Eisenstein, Hester, and Alice Jardine, eds. *The Future of Difference*. New Brunswick, NJ: Rutgers UP, 1985.

Elbow, Peter. *Writing Without Teachers*. New York: Oxford UP, 1973.

Faulkner, William. "Barn Burning." *Collected Stories of William Faulkner*. New York: Random House, Vintage, 1977. 3–25.

Gilligan, Carol. *In A Different Voice: Psychological Theory and Women's Development*. Cambridge: Harvard UP, 1982.

Porter, Katherine Anne. *Collected Stories of Katherine Anne Porter*. New York: Harcourt Brace Jovanovich, Harvest, 1979.

Singley, Carol J. "Reaching Lonely Heights: Sarah Orne Jewett, Emily Dickinson, and Female Initiation." *Colby Library Quarterly* 22.1 (March 1986): 75–82.

Welty, Eudora. *Collected Stories of Eudora Welty*. New York: Harcourt Brace Jovanovich, Harvest, 1980.

————. *One Writer's Beginnings*. Cambridge: Harvard UP, 1984.

2

The Dangers of Time Travel:
Revisioning the Landscape of Girls' Relationships in Margaret Atwood's *Cat's Eye*

Lyn Mikel Brown

You don't look back along time but down through it, like water. Sometimes this comes to the surface, sometimes that, sometimes nothing. Nothing goes away.

Atwood, *Cat's Eye*

In the parallel universe, the laws of physics are suspended. What goes up does not necessarily come down; a body at rest does not tend to stay at rest; and not every action can be counted on to provoke an equal and opposite reaction. Time, too, is different. It may run in circles, flow backward, skip about from now to then. The very arrangement of molecules is fluid: Tables can be clocks, faces, flowers.

Susanna Kaysen, *Girl, Interrupted*

Nothing will come of nothing. Speak again.

Shakespeare, *King Lear*

Perhaps there is a point in each one of our lives when we are moved by some force or event, conscious or unconscious, to reflect on those relationships that have in some fundamental way shaped us, fully captured our will and attention, held us in place for a time. It is testament to the power and force of those relationships that, once triggered, we are so easily pulled back to know suddenly and without warning what we have struggled for years not to know, to feel again what we have, we thought, so successfully buried. In Margaret Atwood's *Cat's Eye,* this event for Elaine Risley, a successful artist living in Vancouver, is her arrival in Toronto, her childhood home, for a retrospective of her work. At this time in her life, a time she thinks of "as a place, like the middle of a river, the middle of a bridge, halfway across, halfway over" (13), Elaine's psychic life is brought to a halt as she relives in a flood of memories and feelings her girlhood relationships, particularly with her friend and nemesis, Cordelia.

In this chapter, I journey back with Elaine to the psychological roots of her present day feelings about herself and her life. In doing so, I attempt to show the relationship between Elaine's experiences as a girl and her particular struggles as a woman. I highlight, through Elaine, the trauma of a girl's life in patriarchal culture; not trauma as we usually think of it—acute emotional crisis or the psychological residues of physical or sexual assault—but the daily barrage of subtle and not-so-subtle messages about being female in a male-defined culture that seep into girls' ears, into their speech, their feelings and thoughts: messages that first turn girls against each other and then, eventually, against themselves.

Elaine's childhood illustrates with stunning clarity a transformation that I, and other feminist psychologists of late, have witnessed and documented in girls' interviews over time—a shift from a lively embodied young girl, outspoken, direct, in touch with her senses, her feelings and thoughts, to a girl at the inside edge of adolescence struggling to speak, to stay with her feelings, to know what she knows (Brown and Gilligan 1992; Gilligan 1990; Gilligan, Rogers, and Tolman 1991; Rogers 1993). Elaine's journey through girlhood reveals the depth and complexity of this conversion, the almost imperceptible ways eight-, nine-, and ten-year-old girls take in the world around them, translate the voices and imitate the actions of adults in their lives, dramatize the relationships between men and women, and become themselves, over time, interpreters and carriers of a male-defined culture. What begins for Elaine, as with so many girls, as a desire for connection and inclusion becomes the pull of expectation, the demands of conventional femininity, of white middle-class female perfection. Elaine's struggle to stay with herself reveals girls' initial resistance to these pressures and her eventual capitulation, the psychological suffering many experience as a healthy resistance fades into the underground and, voice faltering, vision blurring, girls feel themselves disappearing.

Elaine's journey back through time is, for her, a matter of survival. "Vancouver is the suicide capital of the country," she says. "You keep going west and you run out. You come to the edge. Then you fall off" (45). Standing precariously at the edge of this psychic precipice, Elaine can only turn inward to follow the labyrinthine associative pathways that will bring her back to herself. For years her feelings and memories, not fully known to her, have filtered out through her art, like light through the crack of a door—incongruent images of beauty and anger, hate and pleasure seep into her paintings, underscoring both the depths of her feeling and the degree of her amnesia.

A reluctant time traveler, Elaine moves slowly at first. But memories are summoned by the simplest act; the vaguely familiar smell of a place or the look of a person conjure up vivid scenes long forgotten. She begins her journey boldly enough it seems—with a memory of herself and Cordelia at the edge of womanhood:

> Cordelia and I are riding on the streetcar, going downtown, as we do on winter Saturdays. . . . Cordelia sits with nonchalance, nudging me with her elbow now and then, staring blankly at the other people with her gray-green eyes, opaque and glinting as metal. She can outstare anyone, and I am almost as good. We're impervious, we scintillate, we are thirteen. . . . Our mouths are tough, crayon-red, shiny as nails. We think we are friends. (4)

This memory comes readily to Elaine, itself tough and shiny like protective veneer. It's the feeling beneath it, the time before it, a "black square of time" that Elaine has lost and that she will be moved to retrieve, to remember, in Toronto.

Elaine is unwilling but unable to stop this transmigration to a past life because she is not firmly anchored in the present. She is, as she says, "transitional," still unconvinced she "could ever get away with, or deserve" the life she now lives, certain that "everyone else my age is an adult, whereas I am merely in disguise" (15). In the midst of her public success as an artist, Elaine struggles privately against the voices and images she has taken in and taken on over the years, but which she cannot fully know or claim as her own. Secretly, she longs to give up, to give in to a seductive inertia, to give herself over to persistent, insistent feelings of depression and worthlessness. Like invisible threads, these feelings tie Elaine to the past; the daily rhythms of her life—the struggle to see herself clearly, to move forward, to do the simplest things—reverberate their message. She cannot elude them until she revisits them.

Soon Elaine is transported to another time and dimension: to childhood, to girlhood. It is not a girlhood very often spoken out loud or permitted by girls to be seen, and yet it is startlingly and disturbingly familiar. It is relationship in bold relief: wants and needs and feelings before layers upon layers of not knowing, "like a series of liquid transparencies," cloud the vision.

A Story of Loss and Resistance

When time stops still, Elaine is a girl, herself stopped in time by a Brownie box camera she received for her eighth birthday; its color and shape—"black and oblong" (28)—portending certain death, even as it now preserves the happiest moments of her life. This fleeting moment of stillness—posing for the camera, dressed in her brother's clothes, in front of a door that could be any motel door—belies a childhood filled with the pleasure of movement. Elaine remembers this day vividly:

> Right after the picture it begins to snow. . . . We're running around outside the motel, wearing nothing but our worn-out summer shoes, with our bare hands outstretched to falling snowflakes, our heads thrown back, our mouths open, eating snow. If it were thick on the ground we would roll in it, like dogs in dirt. It fills us with the same kind of rapture. (32)

The children of an insect field researcher father and a loving, unconventional mother, Elaine and her brother follow the migrant rhythms of the natural world. Against the dark backdrop of the Second World War, theirs is an "irregular, and slightly festive" life. Elaine's memories of this time fill her senses: She tastes once again the "Habitat pea soup, heated up on the two burner stove in a dented pot," feels "the saggy pull-out bed," sees with her mind's eye the car headlights through the motel window (30).

And yet, in the midst of this irregular, sensuous life-on-the-move, eight-year-old Elaine longs for something else: "Friends, friends who will be girls. Girl friends. I know that these exist, having read about them in books, but I've never had any girl friends because I've never been in one place long enough" (29).

The objects of Elaine's desire take physical shape as she reads her school primers; and yet the life there—the "two children who live in a white house with ruffled curtains, a front lawn and a picket fence" (30)—is unrecognizable to her: "Nothing in these stories is anything like my life. There are no tents, no highways, no peeing in the bushes, no lakes, no motels (30). But to Elaine, "these books have an exotic appeal"; the images tug at her senses, draw her away from herself, away from her experiences and the reality of her family. An "elegant, delicate picture" forms in her mind of other little girls, "always clean," living life differently, dressed in "pretty dresses and patent-leather shoes with strap" (30).

As providence would have it, Elaine receives what she most longs for when her father takes a new job. Now the daughter of a university professor, Elaine finds her small body situated: in a house that is "really ours," in a regular school, and with the possibility of friends who are girls. No longer acceptable to her older brother, with whom she has spent her nomadic childhood playing war and gathering insects, "I am left to the girls, real girls at last, in the flesh" (50). But these strange beings and the world they inhabit present Elaine with an entirely new set of problems.

As Mrs. Lumley, her new teacher at Queen Mary Public School, propagates the virtues of the British Empire and its many gifts to the "heathens" in Africa and India and Canada, Elaine undergoes the narrowing effects of another sort of colonization. Here she begins her lessons in a different kind of girlhood than she has known. She cannot, she discovers, "wear pants to school." She must, against her impulses, "sit still at a desk." And when the bell rings, under the threat of punishment, the children line up in twos, "girls in one line, boys in another," and file in their separate doors, above which elaborately ornate insets announce in "curvey, solemn lettering: GIRLS and BOYS." "Very curious" at such an odd state of affairs, Elaine asks herself the disruptively logical questions of an eight-year-old: "How is going through a door different if you're a boy? What's in there that merits the strap, just for seeing it?" (49).

Clearly, the door Elaine the girl is required to pass through will take her further away from the familiar world she has known. Crossing this threshold, Elaine enters a culture as yet unfamiliar and unreadable, but where the rules are rigid and precise.

An eager student, Elaine begins to suspect that the something that she is, is nothing of importance or value in the world of girls. Her first guides through this new landscape, Carol Campbell and Grace Smeath, introduce Elaine to the requirements she must meet to fit in. Carol teaches her what she must know to survive: what to wear, how to act to be desired by boys and how to avoid the shadowy world of bad men who wander the ravine beneath the wooden bridge the girls cross to school. From Grace, who "never raises her voice, gets angry, or cries" and who "is quietly reproachful" (55), Elaine learns about God the Father and also how to get what she wants without actually saying what she means. And with her new friends come new models of home life—fathers who cast shadows everywhere and nowhere in particular, who appear like ghosts in the evenings "with their real, unspeakable power" (175). Mothers rule the daylight here; mothers like Mrs. Campbell, wry-mouthed, in her beige twin set, cleaning her perfectly symmetrical house, or Mrs. Smeath, plain and heavy with religious principles, with her potato face and spectacles, napping on the couch in her one-breast bibbed apron. Against these models of girl and womanhood, Elaine and her mother are sorely lacking. The inadequacy of Elaine's life is laid before her, her marginality visible to all, especially herself.

Although at first Elaine secretly suspects her new friends are "sissies," she longs to be part of the world they inhabit. In order to at least pretend to take seriously their ever pressing questions and expectations, Elaine learns to keep her feelings and thoughts to herself. In touch with what she knows, she must remain silent or at least appear unsure if she is not to betray herself—which she is not, as of yet, prepared to do—or disrupt this new reality of her friends. "Playing with girls is different," Elaine thinks, "and at first I feel strange as I do it, self-conscious, as if I'm only doing an imitation of a girl. But I soon get more used to it" (55).

As time passes, Elaine spends less and less energy arguing with her brother or playing with the microscopes in her father's lab and more time with Carol and Grace practicing how to be the right kind of girl: giving life to Grace's movie star coloring books, playing school, cutting models of women, cookware and furniture out of *Eaton's Catalogues* and pasting them into scrapbooks.

But cutting and pasting is only part of the game; Elaine learns that such activities demand a sufficiently humble demeanor and an appropriate tone of voice: "Oh yours is so good. Mine's no good. Mine's *awful*" (57). Although Elaine hears the fraudulence in her friends' voices, "can tell" the duplicity, her desire to be connected and included, to enjoy the pleasures of friendship, to feel worthy of these relationships, draw her into these false scenes. And even though she finds the games her friends play "tiring," she practices daily and soon, appropriately, begins "to want things I've never wanted before: braids, a dressing gown, a purse of my own" (57).

In spite of the daily lessons in humility, the voice-training, the hours upon hours of diligent practice in what to want and feel, what to say and do, Elaine's pleasure in movement and fearless nature are difficult to contain. Occasionally, at her own peril, physically and socially, Elaine bursts out, tempted by the sight and smell of the forbidden. She relishes the evenings clambering about the unfinished houses in the neighborhood, smelling "the fresh wood smell of shavings, walking through walls that don't yet exist, climbing ladders where there will soon be stairs" (66). While Carol and Grace, in fear and propriety, stand on the ground floor in their pretty dresses, Elaine climbs upward, "basking in the red-gold sunset. . . . not yet afraid of heights" (66).

And at school, Elaine plays marbles at recess with the boys, "drawn in by the rules of the game and the excitement, the avarice," the "pleasurable terror" of winning or losing her favorites, the cat's eyes. To Elaine, the cat's eyes "really are like eyes" (67). Translucent, but "with a bloom of colored petals in the center" (66), the cat's eyes, like her own thoughts and feelings, are to be guarded, protected from loss. Elaine keeps her precious blue one close, hidden, does not risk it to be shot at.

It is in this liminal state between her self-possessed desire for full plea-sure of expression and movement and the wish for inclusion and accep-tance by her girlfriends that Elaine meets Cordelia. So different from Grace and Carol, Cordelia is "thin without being fragile." Dressed in "corduroys and a pullover," smart and sassy, Cordelia is, on the surface at least, more like Elaine. And yet, Elaine observes in her fascination, something is strange, off; "she has a smile like a grown-up's, as if she's learned it and is doing it out of politeness" (74).

At ten, Cordelia—a year older, taller, more experienced—is herself a naturalist, watching and listening closely to the way the *social* world is named and described, especially the world of women. Even as she re-sounds the shape and content of her older sisters' "extravagant, mocking way of talking," which seems to Elaine inauthentic, "like an imitation of something" (76), she critically scrutinizes women—their bodies, their relationships, their sexuality. Like other womanly things, "breasts fasci-nate Cordelia and fill her with scorn" (97). With disdain, she bypasses the cookware and appliances in *Eaton's Catalogue* for the "foundation garments"—the brassieres, "the elaborately laced and gusseted corsets."

> [She] draws mustaches on the models . . . pencils hair in, under their arms, and on their chests between their breasts. She reads out the descriptions, snorting with stifled laughter: "Delightfully trimmed in dainty lace, with extra support for the mature figure. That means big bazooms. Look at this—cup sizes! Like teacups!" (97–98)

In Cordelia's impertinence and sarcasm, Elaine finds a dangerous edge, a fascinating invitation to know the unknowable, to speak the unspeak-able. Given Elaine's ambivalence about Carol and Grace, Cordelia's cut-ting wit must seem refreshing and exciting. Through her older sisters, Cordelia passes on the mysterious future, reveals women's bodies "in their true, upsetting light: alien and bizarre, hairy, squashy, monstrous." Led by Cordelia, the girls peek through the keyhole of her sisters' room, where they "are peeling the wax off their legs while they utter yelps of pain" (97).

> This frightens us. What has happened to them, bulging them, softening them, causing them to walk rather than run, as if there's some invisible leash around their necks holding them in check—whatever it is, it may happen to us too. (97)

But it is Cordelia, her family well-off and proper, who most feels the tug of this leash, feels the pressure to fold in on herself, to narrow the full range of her feeling and movement into the bottleneck of womanhood. Under the authoritarian rule of a father-king and a compliant mother, the youngest of three sisters, Cordelia, like her Shakespearean namesake, suffers greatly for her knowledge and her stubborn resistance. Punished for speaking directly the extent and depth of her sadness and rage, Cordelia's scorn and sarcasm reveal the outer edges of deep frustration and fear; they are the bitter remnants of feelings she cannot otherwise express, pressures she cannot control.

And so, perhaps it is not surprising that Elaine, the least adept at being what Cordelia is so pressed to become, soon finds herself the target of Cordelia's resentment. Through her friendship with Elaine—whose mere difference and unintentional lack of conformity threaten to disrupt the idealized scene Cordelia has not yet resigned herself to play, and yet whose innocent wish to please, to comply must enrage her—Cordelia acts out the dimensions of her father's anger and her mother's quiet disappointment. And nine-year-old Elaine, who wishes more than anything to fit in, to belong, to be loved, opens herself fully to her new friend.

In her vulnerability and desire to please, Elaine is unaware that the large square hole Cordelia digs obsessively day after day in her backyard has meaning beyond play. For Cordelia, the hole is a desperate attempt to find sanctuary—a place to escape the relentless judgments and expectations she endures from her father, a safehouse from her feelings of rejection and invisibility in her family.

Cordelia, Grace, and Carol take Elaine, clothed in a black dress and cloak, playing "Mary, Queen of Scots, headless already," to the deep hole. Holding feet and underarms, the three girls lower Elaine into the hole and arrange the boards over the top. "The daylight air disappears, and there's the sound of dirt hitting the boards, shovelful after shovelful" (112).

> Up above, outside, I can hear their voices, and then I can't hear them. I lie there wondering when it will be time to come out. Nothing happens. When I was put into the hole I knew it was a game; now I know it is not one. I feel sadness, a sense of betrayal. Then I feel the darkness pressing down on me; then terror. (112)

For Elaine, this single event becomes "a time marker that separates the time before from the time after. The point at which I lost power" (113). As Mary the Queen is headless, so is Elaine separated from what was once so clear and certain, no longer able to know for sure what, up to this point, she has known. What she realizes suddenly, lying in the hole, is the awful truth of these relationships—they were not what they seemed, she is not who she thought she was to her friends. Separated from her knowledge, no longer able to trust the evidence of her own senses, Elaine faces the terror of uncertainty, the panic of shifting reality. Grief and loneliness are buried alive with her in the suffocating darkness. "It's as if I've vanished at that moment and reappear later but different, not knowing why I have been changed" (113).

Like the red berries and dark purple blossoms of poisonous nightshade Elaine associates with this time of loss and deep sadness, what seems on the surface lovely and innocent can be deadly when taken in. From a distance, the four girls look like children playing; to the untrained eye, they are simply girlfriends, harmonious. Her father thinks Cordelia has beautiful manners.

Over time, Elaine suffers all variations of Cordelia's wrath—she must pay penance for her inadequacies, her unpracticed voice, her lack of knowledge—exclusions, derision, public humiliations. "What do you have to say for yourself?" Cordelia asks. "And I have nothing to say." Against her friend's admonishments and others' perceptions, Elaine feels helpless. If Cordelia so perfectly resembles the model image of what adults want and value, then perhaps what she says about Elaine is true: she is not matching up. She is not normal, not polite enough, happy enough, pleasing enough. She does not know the right things to say and do, and Cordelia does. Cordelia, Elaine begins to tell herself, can teach her. "She is my friend. She likes me, she wants to help me, they all do. They are my friends, my girlfriends, my best friends. I have never had any before and I'm terrified of losing them. I want to please" (126).

Cordelia's power over Elaine sustains itself in the secrecy that blankets the girls' actions and protects them from the watchful gaze of adults. Above all else, Elaine takes in the importance of this secrecy: "to violate it would be the greatest, the irreparable sin. If I tell, I will be cast out forever" (126). Even if she could speak her feelings, Elaine thinks, who would listen to her? She could tell her brother, perhaps. "But tell him what exactly? I have no black eyes, no bloody noses to report: Cordelia does nothing physical . . . Against girls and their indirectness, their whisperings, he would be helpless" (166).

Over time, Elaine struggles with the blurred borderline between experience and reality. Consigned to silence, to live deceptively, out of relationship with what others perceive to be happening, never certain of her relationships with her friends, Elaine can no longer tell what is real. Saying nothing, revealing nothing, Elaine begins to feel nothing, to feel she is nothing.

What Elaine once knew she no longer knows: the pleasure of movement, the rapturous irregularity of her life, the embodied difference that once revealed the voices of her friends to be "wheedling and false" and their games to be tiring. These are the things that others threaten to leave Elaine for knowing and being. She cannot know these things and be in relationship with others. "You don't *have* to play with them," Elaine's mother says to her suddenly one day in the kitchen. "There must be other little girls you can play with instead . . . I look at her. Misery washes over me like a slow wind. What has she noticed, what has she guessed, what is she about to do?" (166). It becomes immediately clear to Elaine that her mother, too, is helpless. She, too, cannot tell, she would not be believed. She too is powerless against a force this great. Struck by this knowledge, Elaine pulls away from her mother. Convention, ever consistent and certain, overrides her own lively imagination, her mother's incongruity. And as she takes in Cordelia's watchful, critical gaze, Elaine begins to feel herself disappear, stands outside herself, apart from her movements, apart from her feelings. That no one, not her father, not even her mother, will respond to her unhappiness and suffering confirms to her that her friends are correct—that in her present imperfect state, she is nothing. Her rage and grief, buried under the silence, under the burden of her own shortcomings, under the force of the culture, find its hated object:

> In the endless time when Cordelia had such power over me, I peeled the skin off my feet. I did it at night when I was supposed to be sleeping . . . I would begin with the big toes. I would bend my foot up and bite a small opening in the thickest part of the skin, on the bottom, along the outside edge. Then with my fingernails . . . I would pull the skin off in narrow strips . . . It was painful to walk, but not impossible. The pain gave me something definite to think about, something immediate. It was something to hold onto. (120)

In the secrecy of her bedroom, Elaine strips away the outer layers of her nothingness. No longer sure what she feels, she speaks her sadness and rage into and through her body—her imperfection through bitten lips and fingers; her containment through her tight throat and clenched teeth and stiffened body; her desire to escape, to disappear, through illness and fainting: "I'm beginning to feel I've discovered something worth knowing," she says. "There's a way out of places you want to leave, but can't. Fainting is like stepping sideways, out of your own body, out of time or into another time. When you wake up it's later." Like sleep to the depressed, "time has gone on without you" (182). With the help of her precious cat's eye carried close in her pocket, her marble that holds the power of protection, Elaine retreats further and further until, she says, "I am alive in my eyes only"; until even her dreams are soundless. Further and further Elaine retreats, until an indelible scar is the only evidence of the emotional wounds she has sustained. Like her cat's eye, hers are "the eyes of something that isn't known but exists anyway" (67).

Elaine is partially shaken from this waking sleep when she overhears Mrs. Smeath and Grace's Aunt Mildred talking:

> "She's exactly like a heathen," says Aunt Mildred . . . "What can you expect, with that family?" says Mrs. Smeath . . . "The other children sense it. They know." "You don't think they're being too hard on her?" says Aunt Mildred. Her voice is relishing. She wants to know how hard.
>
> "It's God's punishment," says Mrs. Smeath. "It serves her right." (190)

The unfairness of Mrs. Smeath's condemnation bleeds into her consciousness until, drop by drop, a small underground pool of hatred grows. What Elaine "thought was a secret, something going on among girls, among children, is not one. It has been discussed before, and tolerated" (190–91). If Mrs. Smeath, slow and small-minded, has known, then who else? Her teachers perhaps, the other mothers? It must seep into Elaine's awareness that they all have known, they all have said nothing, done nothing. She cannot trust real women to save her and God the Father has failed. Elaine decides to do something "rebellious": she turns to Mary, "Virgin of lost things" in prayers that are "wordless, defiant, dry-eyed, desperate, without hope. Nothing happens" (210).

Until one snowy March afternoon; a day Elaine dares to feel "some of the euphoria [she] once felt in falling snow" (196). But for the sin of feeling genuine pleasure Elaine must suffer. Grabbing her hat, Cordelia runs to the bridge and throws it into the dreaded ravine. On a cruel dare, Elaine climbs down the steep banks of the river to retrieve her hat, and breaks through the icy water. Panicking, feeling the pull of her heavy wet clothes, she scrambles to the bank, where, exhausted and frozen, she lies on the snow looking up at the sky. Her friends have run away, but she sees the dark outline of a woman on the bridge, then feels her enclosed arms "like a small wind of warmer air." "*You can go home now,*" the woman says. "*It will be all right. Go home*" (200–201).

As Elaine slowly makes her way, it is the reality of her mother, frantic, half-dressed, coat open, walking quickly toward her, that pulls her back to herself. "When she sees me she begins to run . . . I see her eyes, large and gleaming with wet . . . She has no mittens on. She throws her arms around me, and as she does this the Virgin Mary is suddenly gone. Pain and cold shoot back into me. I start to quiver violently" (201).

Elaine's near death in the ravine stirs something deep in her, although it is not something she can name. In her dreams, however, there is sound, shouting; she dreams of rescue and of escape. Perhaps it was her mother's visible fear, her mother's anger, her final recognition of the cruelty Elaine had suffered; her certainty, in spite of Elaine's half-hearted denial, that the others had abandoned her daughter in the ravine; perhaps these things give Elaine the strength to resist Cordelia's rebuke when she returns to school, to walk away from the old familiar taunts and commands, to finally hear Cordelia's accusations for what they are, "an imitation . . . an impersonation, of someone much older." "It was always a game," Elaine realizes, "and I have been fooled" (205).

Although Cordelia fades with time; although Elaine makes new friends and life goes on, she is not free. She harbors the scars of feeling nothing, of feeling she is nothing. By thirteen, Elaine recalls, "I've forgotten things, I've forgotten that I've forgotten them. . . . Time is missing" (213).

> Nobody mentions anything about this missing time, except my mother. Once in a while she says, "That bad time you had," and I am puzzled. . . . I am not the sort of girl who has bad times. I have good times only. There I am in the Grade Six class picture, smiling broadly. *Happy as a clam,* is what my mother says for happy. I am happy as a clam: hard shelled, firmly closed. (213)

Recovery

That Elaine's dissociation and lapses in memory are the emotional residues of the trauma and loss she experienced as a child is perhaps not a revelation. Nor is the fact that these early experiences affect her feelings about herself and her relationships in later life. As Carol Gilligan emphasizes, it is a well-known psychological truth that "what is dissociated and repressed—known and then not known—tends to return, and return, and return" (511). What is most poignant about *Cat's Eye* is that Elaine's suffering is at the hands of her girlfriends, her "best friend," and perhaps what is most unnerving is that her suffering was known and condoned, or at least tolerated, by adult women, including her mother.

As Atwood follows Elaine through the years, we understand that in these childhood relationships are the seeds of Elaine's sharp tongue and "mean mouth" toward other girls in high school, her resentfulness toward her mother, her alliance with men and their power, her general mistrust of women and her distance from herself. Through this psychologically astute novel, Atwood maps the intricate and subtle nature of internalized oppression as it happens at the hands, not of the oppressors—that would be so easy to track—but of other subordinates. She alludes to the need of those without power to enact on each other what they themselves endure on a daily basis and thus, unconsciously, to secure at a very early age, through anger, pain, and loss, their proper place in the patriarchal order.

Cordelia, feeling the weight of expectations and images of proper or conventional femininity that her father will approve and unable to openly protest the loss of herself to someone who will listen and respond, acts out her frustration on Elaine. "It is always easier for a woman [in this case, a girl] . . . to take out her rage over her silence and her powerlessness on another woman than on that culture itself," Susan Griffin argues (207). For Elaine, too, the possibilities are limited: she can either struggle to stay with herself, to know and express her feelings and thoughts, and risk losing her relationship with Cordelia and the others, or she can remain silent and risk losing herself, dissociating from what she knows to be true from her experiences. Because she is all alone, because, although others see what is happening, they do not or cannot respond to her pain, Elaine remains silent. Over time, her silence and not knowing in the presence of her friends leads to a deeper silence—the repression of her feelings and her dissociation from herself.

Elaine is not alone. Research on girls suggests this is familiar territory, this loss, this unexpressed rage that turns inevitably to self-denigration and depression. "Little girls are cute and small only to adults," Elaine thinks, reflecting on this time. "To one another they are not cute. They are life-sized" (124).

But the process of acculturation is so slow as to be nearly imperceptible. First are the separate pieces—certain words associated with certain actions, tones, inflections; certain actions with a certain gender; a certain gender with, a certain gender without. Then the pieces begin to form a whole; a realization—but this means you, this means me; a fight breaks out—I cannot, I will not—resistance. But you will if you wish to be loved. (And remember this always, anger is never acceptable—it's one of those feelings that do not go with me, with us, with this gender. Anger is ineffective, disturbing, dangerous.) Split off the anger, the sadness. Move them underground, unseen and unheard. While "it is easy to slip into a parallel universe," Susanna Kaysen states in her book *Girl, Interrupted,* "most people pass over incrementally, making a series of perforations in the membrane between here and there until an opening exists. And who can resist an opening?" (5).

Cat's Eye implicitly warns women of the dangers of unconsciously passing on to girls what we, ourselves, have suffered at the hands of patriarchy. Like Mrs. Lumley, Elaine's teacher, who unreflectively prepares girls for their subordinate roles in the culture—who leads, in Madeline Grumet's words, "the great escape" from the maternal order to the paternal state (25)—Mrs. Smeath in her religious fervor, and, most tragically, Elaine's mother in her immobilized uncertainty in the face of her daughter's suffering, collaborate in Elaine's powerlessness through their own silence. But in the glare of this maternal lineage, we too often forget the wider picture, the culture in which such lessons, such losses, are nourished and rewarded.

Atwood alludes to the complicated reasons that adults turn away from girls. Fathers, men, she implies, do not fully see, cannot easily decipher the messages encoded in girls' relationships. Theirs is a blindness inherited from power and privilege. Mothers, women, too, may not see, may not hear, not because they cannot read the signs, but because girls' relationships bring to light the unresolved pain of their own childhoods, the tenuous compromises made for the sake of sanity and survival—the times when they spoke and were not heard, felt betrayed, excluded, all alone. Girls' voices interrupt and disrupt the precarious balance of women's lives and threaten to reveal to women what we once knew but have since forgotten. Girls' struggles and resistance, their anger and sadness, must not be seen or heard, for in them lie the dangerous memories of suffering and freedom (Harris 35).

Another psychological truth, says Gilligan: "The hallmarks of loss are idealization and rage, and under the rage, immense sadness. ('To want and want and not to have.')" (511). When we expect perfection, when we allow for only nice and kind thoughts and feelings, girls are forced to bury the complexity of their knowledge and experiences of the relational world: The dark underside of pink and sweet and innocent and perfect *must* be the whispering, the derisive laughter, the judgments, the exclusion, the rage. When there is no public space for genuine relationship, for the full range of feelings, for conflict, for voice and resistance, an underground thrives. And what remains underground, without the nourishment and fresh air of relationships, eventually dies or becomes grossly distorted and inhumane. "There is a danger," Adrienne Rich reminds us, "run by all powerless people: that we forget we are lying or that lying becomes a weapon we carry over into relationships with people who do not have power over us." And "to lie habitually, as a way of life," Rich suggests, "is to lose touch with the unconscious," to suffer amnesia (187).

But Rich also is certain "the unconscious wants truth" (187). Through her art Elaine speaks the truths she could not speak directly, could not even know fully. Through her art, she struggles to make something out of nothing: proves she is worthy. Elaine expresses through painting what she once expressed on the canvas of her body—her resistance, her suffering, her sadness and rage. Painting allows Elaine her resentment—allows her "to feel again" all that she once buried and lost. But if her psychological health depends on this outlet, for years so does her daughter's.

As women who care for girls, there are many questions we might ask ourselves. What do we do to girls when we ignore their pain, sanction their cruelty, and expect their smiling cooperation? What do we say when we say nothing, when we see nothing? We might ask ourselves, as teachers, mothers, therapists, as caretakers of girls, what do we want from them? The answers are difficult to know. Justification? Our own salvation perhaps; our desperate attempts to hang onto the last remnants of hope that they could become what we, in all our human frailty, could not?

More simply, perhaps, we might ask what do *girls* want? Elaine, we imagine, might answer: I want women, real women, not an imagined ideal—pure and all-loving, all-forgiving; not a model of perfection but a flesh and blood woman, a mother who will be enraged on my behalf, who will run to me in my pain and suffering, see and name what is happening, who will be loyal to me—above others, most of all above a culture that requires my silence and passivity, my dissociation and repression, for its smooth continuance.

Because this is Elaine's story, we cannot know fully, but only through allusion, the losses and psychological violence Cordelia sustains; over time, we hear of Cordelia's confusion and sadness, her futile attempts at resistance and her painful stabs at conformity, her suicide attempts and her stay in a mental hospital. What we, as readers, come to know in bits and pieces through Elaine is that Cordelia's treacherous and cruel behavior has its roots in her own suffering and powerlessness. And what the adult Elaine comes to know finally, standing on the bridge over the ravine, looking into the ghost of a child's eyes is that the

> shame, the sick feeling in my body, the . . . knowledge of my own wrongness, awkwardness, weakness; the . . . wish to be loved, the . . . loneliness, the . . . fear . . . are not my own emotions anymore. They are Cordelia's; as they always were . . . I reach out my arms to her, bend down, hands open to show I have no weapon. *It's all right.* I say to her. *You can go home now.* (443)

The real tragedy, Atwood implies in her novel, is that Elaine and Cordelia will never really know each other, that they will feel so totally separate, unable to see the common threads that tie them. Elaine and Cordelia's stories seem distinct and unrelated; their interdependence obscured because they are locked in battle against each other. Because the trauma they endure happens at the hands of different people, they cannot name its common source. They remain shadows, ghosts to each other—silent, ever present, haunted by a need to know and remember. They are, as Atwood says, "reflections" of each other; like "the twins in old fables, each of whom has been given half a key" (434).

I wish to suggest that, as women, our deafness and blindness to girls' active resistance to the debilitating and narrowing effects of conventional femininity—to the outward signs of a healthy resistance before it is pushed out of view, forced underground into girls' relationships with each other and feelings about themselves—is the legacy of our own trauma and loss. Elaine's memories of her childhood and Cordelia and her subsequent life speak to the costs of unwittingly passing on this pain, but also to the deep pleasure of what is possible. From her window seat on the plane home to Vancouver, Elaine, like the child on the top floor of an unfinished house, looks out ahead to the sun sinking "in a murderous, vulgar, unpaintable and glorious display of red and purple and orange" (445). She looks to the seats beside her, occupied by two "old women, each with a knitted cardigan, each with yellowy white hair and thick lens glasses with a chain for around the neck, each with a desiccated mouth lipsticked bright red with bravado." They are playing cards, "laughing like cars on gravel when they cheat or make mistakes . . . They're rambunctious, they're full of beans; they're tough as thirteen, they're innocent and dirty, they don't give a hoot" (446).

The danger of time travel for Elaine, and for ourselves, is that we may come to know what we once knew and then buried—the deep sadness, the great rage, the bitter disappointment, the gross injustice—that we confront demons, grown enormous from years of active not knowing. With the danger, then, comes the power of recovery, of remembering; the possibility that we will become whole, in Audre Lorde's sense, "erotic"; that we will heal the inner divisions, "feel deeply all the aspects of our lives" (57). But our memories make demands on us, call us to action, to the difficult task of acting differently. "An eye for an eye," Elaine decides, "leads only to more blindness" (427). With the danger and the power is the possibility of forgiveness and the capacity for passion, the promise of life fully lived in "a murderous, vulgar, unpaintable and glorious display of red and purple and orange."

Works Cited

Atwood, Margaret. *Cat's Eye*. New York: Doubleday, 1988.

Brown, Lyn Mikel. "A Problem of Vision: The Development of Voice and Relational Knowledge in Girls Ages 7 to 16." *Women's Studies Quarterly* 19 (1991): 52–71.

Brown, Lyn Mikel and Carol Gilligan. *Meeting at the Crossroads: Women's Psychology and Girls' Development*. Cambridge: Harvard UP, 1992.

Gilligan, Carol. "Joining the Resistance: Psychology, Politics, Girls, and Women." *Michigan Quarterly Review* 29 (1990): 501–36.

Gilligan, Carol, Annie Rogers, and Deborah Tolman, eds. *Women, Girls and Psychotherapy: Reframing Resistance*. Binghamton: Haworth, 1991.

Griffin, Susan. *Pornography and Silence*. New York: Harper & Row, 1981.

Grumet, Madeline. *Bitter Milk. Women and Teaching.* Amherst: U of Massachusetts P, 1988.

Harris, Maria. *Woman and Teaching.* New York: Paulist Press, 1988.

Kaysen, Susanna. *Girl, Interrupted.* New York: Random House, 1993.

Lorde, Audre. *Sister Outsider.* Freedom, CA: The Crossing Press, 1984.

Rich, Adrienne. *On Lies, Secrets, and Silence.* New York: Norton, 1979.

Rogers, Annie. "Voice, Play, and a Practice of Ordinary Courage in Girls' and Women's Lives." *Harvard Educational Review* 63 (1993): 265–95.

Rogers, Annie, Lyn Brown and Mark Tappan. "Interpreting Loss in Ego Development in Girls: Regression or Resistance?" *The Narrative Study of Lives.* Ed. Ruthellen Josselson and Amia Lieblich. Vol. 2. Newbury Park: Sage, 1994. 1–36.

3

In the "I" of Madness: Shifting Subjectivities in Girls' and Women's Psychological Development in *The Yellow Wallpaper*[1]

Annie G. Rogers

Ourself behind ourself, concealed
should startle most.

—Emily Dickinson

A shadow seemed to lie across the page. It was a straight dark bar, a shadow shaped something like the letter "I". One began dodging this way and that to catch a glimpse of the landscape behind it.

—Virginia Woolf

I have discovered something at last . . . The front pattern *does* move, and no wonder! The woman behind shakes it!

—Charlotte Perkins Gilman

My house is wallpapered with lies.

—Eliza, a ten-year-old girl

Ourself Behind Ourself: Startling Voices of Girls

I have taught Charlotte Perkins Gilman's *The Yellow Wallpaper* in both literature and psychology classes and noticed that women readers readily identify with its narrator, but do not commonly understand the strength of their emotional connection with her. As a developmental psychologist, I have also observed that adolescent girls in the late twentieth century struggle with the veracity of their perceptions in ways that remind me vividly of this short story, and through this work I have come to understand my own and many women's emotional responses to *The Yellow Wallpaper* in a new light.[2] Women's resonance to this short story, I believe, is rooted in the hazardous transition from late childhood into adolescence that characterizes women's psychological development.

Psychological researchers and clinicians have repeatedly noticed that adolescence is a time of heightened vulnerability for girls.[3] During this time in their development, many girls begin to change their self-conceptions and aspirations, and are particularly susceptible to depression, eating disorders, self-mutilation, and suicide attempts. My colleagues and I at the Harvard Project on Women's Psychology and Girls' Development sought an explanation for this developmental vulnerability in girls. In our longitudinal interviews, we saw young girls, ages eight to eleven or twelve, as self-confident, outspoken, and courageous. Girls at this age expressed a wide range of emotions, including anger and disappointment, and were surprisingly resistant to conventional dictates of feminine behavior. However, in early adolescence and throughout adolescence, we heard girls struggle to voice their feelings and experiences and begin to show signs of psychological distress. At the heart of this struggle, as girls come of age in early adolescence as young women in patriarchal cultures, they face an unyielding relational dilemma: they may either continue to speak authentically, living fully and freely in the world of relationships as they had in childhood, and in the process risk being dismissed, denigrated, or rejected as young women—or, alternatively, learn to silence their authentic voices in order to protect and preserve their relationships (Brown and Gilligan 265–295).

Like the narrator of *The Yellow Wallpaper* who becomes disconnected from some aspects of her experience, girls at adolescence begin to experience a profound disconnection with themselves—separating psyche and body, heart and mind, speaking and relationship—and begin to live in a tangle of confusing contradictions (Brown and Gilligan 273). Girls lose their "ordinary courage" and find that speaking authentically requires courage that is both "transgressive" and "extraordinary" (Rogers, "Voice, Play," 273–275). In adolescence, courage does not disappear from women's lives, but becomes transformed, and neither women nor the societies and cultures in which they live easily recognize it.

As teenage girls become self-reflective and capable of abstract thinking, they also become more acutely aware of the cultural ideals and expectations for women. The norms, ideals, and ideologies of prescribed femininity come into focus, and girls suddenly find themselves struggling for their own voices as they try to hold fast to what they once knew from experience.[4] What results is a doubling of their knowledge of their own experience and what is said to be "reality." I call this complex process "double-subjectivity," a pattern common in women's psychological development.[5]

Most women, however, do not clearly remember the intense struggle for voice during early adolescence, nor recall the strength and clarity of perception they knew as girls. This "lost time" in women's development is often repressed, covered over, forgotten.[6] What remains after adolescence are the characteristics of women's psychology—the tendency of women to become selfless or voiceless in their relationships, the inclination of women to use their gifts of empathy to cover over their own feelings and thoughts as they respond to others. These characteristics, in turn, become hallmarks of women's psychological distress in adulthood, particularly, but not exclusively, for white women. At the same time, a pattern of double subjectivity, used as a strategy of resistance in adolescence, remains strong in the organization of psychic life throughout adulthood, but is far less obvious because women find it commonly wise to conceal their strategies of resistance.

"Ourself behind ourself, concealed / should startle most" (250), Emily Dickinson wrote, touching on women's experience of concealing and revealing themselves. Charlotte Perkins Gilman's narrator in *The Yellow Wallpaper* also reveals a startling self—the woman she releases from the bars of the wallpaper near the end of the story is a fragmented self who speaks the truth of her experience. Putting her "madness" aside for a moment, I am reminded of preadolescent girls who speak the truth of their experiences in ways that adults—both men and women—find startling and disturbing.

Ten-year-old Eliza, sitting in the back seat of my car,[7] states unequivocally, "I know all about lies," in a heated argument about when it is and is not all right to lie. "My house is wallpapered with lies,"[8] she says succinctly, conjuring up for me the attic room in Gilman's story and its yellow wallpaper. This argument about lying goes to the heart of girls' desire for authentic relationships at this age. Their capacity to ferret out lies in relationships gives them, at times, an unwavering epistemological authority. Girls like Eliza do not doubt the veracity of the reality they live in, nor are they misled by lies into doubting themselves, as, for instance, the woman narrator of Gilman's story comes to doubt her reality and herself.

But their authority is eroded as girls learn to mask their feelings and change their voices in the face of cultural pressures not to know and speak what they see in their relationships. Tess, for example, at eleven, is outspoken about what she feels and thinks. She also notices that not everyone else is so open, that "people are always wearing masks."[9] She insists on honesty at eleven in ways that are not always easy to hear. At twelve, when she is a little taller and her breasts have begun to bud, she has learned to silence herself and mask her own feelings. In an interview with me, Tess tells a story of what she does when she is angry at her aunt:

> "Shut up, shut up, shut up," [I tell myself] and then I [she hits herself on the mouth] give myself a little bit [sic] hit on the mouth, and then I walk out with a smile [laughs]. And I kind of go like this through my hair, and I just kind of sit there like, "Yah." And I don't say anything . . . 'cause I know I would get in trouble and I would really hurt some people's feelings if I did.[10]

While Tess stops herself from speaking, at twelve she still knows what she feels and why she is doing this. We have repeatedly observed that girls at eleven and twelve stop speaking as a strategy of self-protection, as well as a way of not hurting others. Initially, this strategy is self-conscious; the girls know what they are feeling and their reasons for not speaking. After girls stop speaking more habitually, the strategy disappears. What remains conscious is only a selfless justification for not speaking: the wish not to hurt others.[11]

Tess's description of putting a bit in her mouth is strikingly similar to Dana Jack's portrayal of married women silencing themselves to placate or please their husbands (32). In the process of doing so, these women became clinically depressed, twentieth-century counterparts of Gilman's depressed narrator. At the beginning of her seventh-grade year, at thirteen, Tess appears depressed too—slumped over, quiet, sad. Even her shoulders cave in. After several weeks, Tess begins to speak about what has been bothering her: the girls in her class "like" a couple of boys, and this has created competition and deception among the girls, dividing her friends from one another. As Tess confronts the girls about this, she begins to regain her characteristic sprightliness and outspokenness.

Karen, at thirteen, finds herself feeling continually sad and feels frightened of her anger. She is a clinically depressed girl whose family has requested that I see her in therapy. She describes her father as a man she loves deeply, but as someone who traps her in his logic and reduces her to tears in arguments with him. As she watches him do the same thing with her mother, Karen fears that she, like her mother, will just "give in and collapse." "My dad is a really violent man," she says, looking to see how I am taking this in. "You wouldn't know it meeting him on the street, but at home he just crushes my mother down like an aluminum can that you, that you would just step on . . . and she is reduced to tears, she just does not fight him back." Karen is determined to resist and, if need be, to argue and get mad with her father about his "bossiness"—without being "reduced to tears."[12] Karen is consciously choosing a strategy of fighting back, using important relationships in her life as supports. To fight her sadness, she consciously rehearses getting angry with her father, with me, with her mother, and with her best friend at school. Karen's determination to speak honestly about her experiences of anger, unlike the indirect hints Gilman's narrator uses as she speaks to her husband, grounds Karen in her bodily feelings of anger and her own version of "reality."

Three girls, Eliza, Tess, and Karen, thus portray a struggle for knowledge and voice, for epistemological authority, that is vital to women's sanity and authentic relationships. Like the narrator of *The Yellow Wallpaper*, these twentieth-century girls acutely struggle with relational realities that are upsetting and disturbing. Eliza, at ten, takes in the lies of relationships in her house and succinctly comments on her stark observations. Tess, at twelve, learns to protect herself at times by silencing herself. She begins to live in a double-subjectivity—as an "I" who knows what she is feeling and thinking and as an "eye" who watches herself and stops herself from saying what she feels at times.[13] Karen, at thirteen, begins to separate what she knows about her feelings from what she will allow herself to speak in relation to her father. She finds a way out of her depression by learning to fight back without emotionally collapsing.

The Yellow Wallpaper speaks powerfully to women's experience of relational dilemmas about voice and silence, love and cruelty, sanity and madness. The voice of the narrator resonates with the doubling of subjectivity and struggle for voice characteristic of women's psychological development in adolescence. In the course of the story, the narrator moves from double-subjectivity into psychic splitting and dissociation and, finally, into fragmentation and madness. Her determination to free the woman imprisoned in the wallpaper, I argue, recalls a time of intense psychological struggle for voice and epistemological authority in women's lives at adolescence. Gilman's brilliant short story continues to warn women that nothing less is at stake for us and our daughters than our sanity.

Girls may provide women with cues about how and when to resist, how to sustain a difficult doubleness of knowledge about one's experience and what is called "reality" without going mad. In my analysis of Gilman's text, I will illuminate her struggle and her journey from double-subjectivity into madness. Gradually, I will introject the voices of girls into the turning points in the story, as if they were characters who could speak directly with Gilman's narrator, advising her, warning her, comforting her, accompanying her.

In the "I" of Madness: The Narrator's Dilemma

The woman who narrates *The Yellow Wallpaper* tells her tale in a first-person voice, revealing to the reader the process of leaving one's senses in order to come to terms with a senseless "reality." Located clearly in the genre of autobiographical fiction, this short story, published by Charlotte Perkins Gilman in January 1892 in *The New England Magazine*, is a psychological drama derived from the author's own treatment for a nervous breakdown (Hedges 41). The text portrays a young married woman who is suffering from "a nervous depression" in an interlude at a summer house, where she is taken by her husband, who is a physician, to rest and recover. Her stay is anything but restful, however; and rather than recover, she goes mad.

Who is the narrator of this story? She is a woman who tries valiantly to hold fast to her writing and her knowledge of her feelings; most centrally, she struggles to keep her sanity in relation to her husband. She has come to live in the country—an ideal place to rest, it seems—in the company of her husband, her sister-in-law, and her baby. We learn from the opening paragraphs of the story, however, that the house they have rented is "strange," and the woman discovers that her husband, John, does not believe she is really sick at all. Still, he imposes a "rest cure" on her, including the instruction that she is not to write.

The narrator is caught in an unyielding dilemma: to be in connection with her husband means to be out of touch with the knowledge of her own experience; yet to be in connection with herself means ultimately to be out of touch with what is taken to be "reality," to be driven unmistakably mad. The treatment she receives—isolation and inactivity—exaggerates her weariness and depression. This treatment creates what Judith Herman calls "a climate of coercive control" (83). In her isolation, the narrator hears only her husband's dictums and evaluations: required to rest, forbidden to write, she is deprived of the one activity that would enable her to express herself freely. The subtext of her "treatment" is not so much recovery as submission to the authority of her husband.

At the beginning of the story, the narrator doubts her husband's expertise and resists his treatment, albeit privately in her writing. But as she is constantly watched and checked on, her every hour and every activity accounted for, she must become more sly to resist her husband and his co-conspirator, her sister-in-law. Because it becomes exhausting to write secretly, it is not surprising that she writes less and less. Her captors make her tired, and her increasing fatigue is dangerous in itself. She begins to alternate between submission and resistance. Driven further into herself, she seeks freedom from constraint in an interiority she will later find difficult to escape.

Her complete isolation heightens the narrator's need for stimulation and interaction, and she learns what most political prisoners learn—to create a world of her own in relation to inanimate objects. She becomes particularly preoccupied with the disturbing patterns in the wallpaper of the room she inhabits. After trying to make sense of these haphazard patterns, she discovers a "subpattern" of bars and, behind them, a woman living inside the wallpaper. Identifying this woman's wish to get out, the woman frees her to speak unspeakable truths. And slowly, she identifies with and thereby becomes this woman. Thus, the narrator solves her dilemma in relation to her husband; through this identification she is able to tell him directly what she knows and feels, to be in an odd kind of connection with him and also authentically in connection with herself. But she is also starkly mad.

The physical details of this story function as warning signs of the downward course of the narrator's psychological journey. Confined to an upper room with a great bed nailed down to the floor, with grotesque and torn yellow wallpaper, "rings and things in the wall,"[14] and barred windows, the narrator guesses that this was once a nursery and, later, perhaps a gymnasium for boys. She fails to consider that another woman has lived here, too. Gilman hints that this is the case as the story unfolds. The narrator tells us that the wallpaper has been torn around the bed as far as she, an adult woman, can reach; that the bedstead itself has been chewed; and that there is a "long even smooch" all along the mopboard of the room, "as if it has been rubbed over and over" (29). The narrator unconsciously repeats the same sequence of actions. Once she discovers another woman barred into the yellow wallpaper, she begins to tear down the paper to release that woman, as far as she can reach. The narrator also bites the bedstead in frustrated rage. Finally, she crawls along the perimeter of the room and, as she moves, her shoulder fits perfectly into the mark along the wall left by her unimagined predecessor.

We, the readers, having understood the physical details of the "nursery" as warning signs, as markers perhaps of another woman's journey, are horrified, but not entirely surprised, by the narrator's descent into madness. The narrator herself, however, does not link the yellow wallpaper directly with the danger of her situation—so these physical details of the room haunt her, inhabit her body and psyche.

This short story has puzzled me for many years as a textured layering of voices that comprise a narrative "I" of a woman who is never named. Listening to her shifting voices as distinctive and overlapping "subjectivities"—culminating in the "I" of madness—we can begin to hear transformations in this woman's resistance to her patriarchal marriage and to the treacherous treatment of her illness. Listening to her story in the company of contemporary girls' voices, we can also begin to imagine those voices as a catalyst for a more sustained resistance.

A Divided Self: Splitting "I" into the "i" and "eye" of Double-Subjectivity

In *A Room of One's Own*, Virginia Woolf writes as a woman discovering the character of the "I" in patriarchal academic discourse—discerned in the writing of a certain "Mr. A":

> A shadow seemed to lie across the page. It was a straight dark bar, a shadow shaped something like the letter "I." One began dodging this way and that to catch a glimpse of the landscape behind it. Whether that was indeed a tree or a woman walking I was not sure . . . "I" was a most respectable "I"; honest and logical, hard as a nut, and polished for centuries by good teaching and good feeding. I respect and admire that "I" from the bottom of my heart. But—here I turned a page or two, looking for something or other—the worst of it is that in the shadow of the letter "I" all is shapeless as mist . . . But, I am bored. But why was I bored? Partly because of the dominance of the letter "I," and the aridity, which, like a giant beech tree, it casts within its shade. Nothing will grow there. (103–104)

This "I" casts a shadow over women's lives by making unceasing judgments about them with unquestioning authority, contradicting what women know from their own experience. In this respect, Woolf's observation of the masculine writer's "I" is uncannily similar to the character of John described by the narrator of *The Yellow Wallpaper*:

> John is practical in the extreme . . . He has no patience with faith, an intense horror of superstition, and he scoffs openly at any talk of things not to be felt and seen and put down in figures . . . You see, he does not believe I am sick. And what can one do? (9)

Overwhelmed by the rhetoric of this disbelieving "I," its dictums and prescriptions, the narrator creates one "eye" who accepts her husband's disbelief and another overlapping "i" who resists.[15] The barred pattern of the yellow wallpaper becomes a metaphoric space for these shifting "I's," as various subjectivities that create divisions within the narrator as they emerge in the course of her story.

The "I" Virginia Woolf characterized as dominant must be "crossed, perhaps double-crossed, before it can signal the trace of female subjectivity in an autobiographical text," Sidonie Smith writes in *Subjectivity, Identity and the Body: Women's Autobiographical Practices in the Twen-*

t*ieth Century* (2). In other words, the traces of a woman's subjectivity in an autobiographical text exist in relation and in resistance to a dominant "I."

Gilman has created such a subjective persona; the voice of her narrator crosses and double-crosses the arid, impermeable, dominant "I" of John. As the subjectivities of the narrator multiply, she crosses over into madness, and in her madness, she begins to know, embody, and speak truths she could not grasp in her "sanity." These truths transform her ultimately ineffective resistance into a courage that is both transgressive and extraordinary. Her courage breaks the mold of "good woman" and creates unusual realizations about herself and other women.

In order to cross the dominant "I," a woman moves from a sense of whole subjectivity into "double-subjectivity." She narrates her own experience as a truthful subject—her inner thoughts, feelings, and bodily responses (I mark this voice as an "i" in the following text). She also narrates herself as a spectator subject (noted as "eye" in the text)—as one who watches herself playing the part of a "good woman" to meet the demands of her husband. Dana Jack calls this internalized righteous voice of the culture, which tells a woman what she should think and feel, "the Over-Eye" (94). In naming this process an "eye," I want to emphasize the constructive and subjective process of embodying cultural dictates, including internalizing how one's body is watched without words, and how one should (and should not) respond under an internalized "eye." Living consciously in the double-subjectivity of the "i" and the "eye," Gilman's narrator has a remarkable capacity to see and know what lies behind a veil of appearances. She speaks two languages—her own and the language of her husband—and plays one against the other. In the following passage, the narrator speaks as an "eye" overlapping with the assessments of another "i":

> If a physician of high standing, and one's own husband, assures friends and relatives that there is really nothing the matter with one but temporary nervous depression—a slight hysterical tendency—what is one to do? My brother is also a physician, and he says the same thing. So I (eye) take phosphates and phospites—whichever it is, and tonics, and journeys, and air, and exercise, and I (eye) am absolutely forbidden to work until I (eye) am well again. Personally, I (i) disagree with their ideas. Personally, I (i) believe that congenial work, with excitement and change, would do me good. (10)

Epistemologically, this double-subjectivity gives the narrator tremendous freedom and authority to create, verify, and act upon different sources of knowledge. She is neither fully free nor is she fully subjugated to patriarchy; her authority over her own knowledge may be largely hidden, but it is not dismissed. She is complicitous with patriarchy and simultaneously brilliantly resistant.

Such a woman experiences a double-body too. She lives in the body of her felt thoughts—those moment by moment physical impressions that guide her knowing—and also lives in what Judith Butler calls a "cultural body"—a body shaped and controlled by men's dictates and desires (133). Marginally connected to her body, rather than fully dissociated or fully embodied, she creates a psychological interiority that protects her from being entirely subjugated. Her interiority exists in an only partially repressed body. Therefore, she is free to authorize a form of knowing based in her own sensations and bodily responses, albeit privately. If voiced, however, these perceptions are likely to be denigrated or dismissed, if not punished. Aware of this likelihood, the narrator protects herself further by controlling her feelings:

> There is something strange about the house—I can feel it. I even said to John one moonlit evening, but he said what I felt was a draught, and shut the window. I get unreasonably angry with John sometimes. I never used to be so sensitive. I think it is due to this nervous condition. But if John says I feel so, I shall neglect proper self control; so I take pains to control myself—before him, at least, and that makes me very tired. (11)

Even as the narrator controls her feelings, she begins to slip from her own language and accurate perceptions of her experience. She calls herself "unreasonably angry" and "sensitive" when her husband dismisses her perception that the house is strange and tells her to shut the window. She also attributes her anger to "this nervous condition" rather than a natural response to being dismissed and ordered about. In the face of "If John says I feel so . . ." it is hard for her to sustain her double-subjectivity. The very effort to control herself makes her more tired.

How, then, is a woman's double-subjectivity sustained? The resistance girls show at the end of childhood and in early adolescence may provide strategic cues to women struggling with a doubled sense of "experience" and "reality." What would any of the girls I introduced at the beginning say to our narrator at this point? I imagine that Tess might step in and tell her: "You can't go on wearing a mask. If you keep trying to control your feelings all of the time, you'll explode." Tess would understand what it means to "mask" feelings, and how often that strategy carries with it a false sense of security and leads to suppressed rage. By habitually adopting a strategy of self-control, one gives up the possibility of finding relationships in which it is possible to speak and to rely on being heard. As Tess stated clearly in an interview about an experience of being bullied by several girls, "At some point, you just have to say, 'This is it, this can't go on and on, this is really bad for me and I won't let it go on.' And, you know, when I finally said that, they listened. Of course, I threatened to knock them out if they didn't."[16] The threat Tess makes reveals her anger and underscores her determination to speak without censoring herself.

Yet voicing what one experiences is a complex act, particularly in a relational world where one has no visible allies. If allies do not exist, however, a woman might write, creating a relationship with a text, almost as if she were writing to another ear.[17] The narrator of this story has no means of verifying her own experience, after all, except for her own written text. She notices and records the contradictions of her situation. "I am glad my case is not serious," she begins, then adds, "John does not know how much I really suffer. He knows there is no reason to suffer, and this satisfies him!" (14). She also knows that writing can help her: "I think sometimes if I were only well enough to write a little it would relieve the press of ideas and rest me" (16).

But Gilman's narrator is forbidden to write and she writes only on the sly. Sensing that her intimate relationships are treacherous, finding no verification of her experience except in her surreptitious writing, reality itself wavers. She describes John as "careful and loving" (12), when he is controlling and cruel throughout most of the story. This distortion of John's behavior is an alignment with what he wishes her to think. Thus, Gilman's narrator is not only continually undermined and made to feel that her wishes are of no worth by her "loving" husband, she also participates in and becomes complicit in that perception in order to keep herself in "relationship" with him.

I can still hear Karen at thirteen noticing that, "When my dad says, 'I love you,' I feel crazy. Arguing with me until I am broken down in tears, until I am a wreck, that's not love."[18] At thirteen, her keenness of vision is steadfast; Karen has not yet practiced illusions of love for so long that she can believe them, and precisely because she has not, she might be good company for Gilman's narrator. Perhaps here, at this juncture, she might say to our narrator, "No, that is not love; a loving husband doesn't treat you this way."

But the narrator of *The Yellow Wallpaper* did not have Karen's company. As she is driven further into interiority, her thoughts and feelings grow out of proportion in relation to the events that gave rise to them. She becomes increasingly tired, irritable, preoccupied, filled with self-doubt and self-recrimination. She easily slips over into the "eye" of John's vision and loses her fine double-vision.

Double-subjectivity is a continual balancing act, difficult to sustain. The "rest cure" imposed on the narrator eventually makes this balancing act impossible. This treatment relies on isolation; it leaves a woman without verifying relationships with like-minded others and (largely) without a relationship to the "ear" of a written text. Watched carefully by her husband and her sister-in-law, "a perfect and enthusiastic housekeeper, who hopes for no better profession," the narrator struggles to write, but writing, under these circumstances, makes her feel both guilty (deceptive) and tired. Eventually, her writing seems futile: "I don't know why I should write this. I don't want to. I don't feel able" (21).

Again, I think of Karen, who, in the midst of her depression, began to keep a diary. "If I don't write, I start to feel like I'm losing myself—well, not myself exactly, my shadow—that's scarier than losing myself even." "Why is that scarier?" I ask her. "Because if you don't have a shadow, if you don't write down the shadow stuff, it will get bigger and bigger, and it will get so big you are scared of yourself, do you know?"[19] I did know, and perhaps Gilman's narrator initially knew this too.

As the narrator begins to slip away from herself, she feels the danger, as Karen did, and she tries to write, but even her writing becomes ineffective when she undermines herself in her own text. Writing about her wish to have the room repapered and John's response to her wish, she says:

> At first he meant to repaper the room but afterwards he said that I was letting it get the better of me, and that nothing was worse for a nervous patient than to give way to such fancies . . . "You know the place is doing you good," he said, "and really, dear, I don't care to renovate the house for a three months' rental." "Then do let us go downstairs," I said, "there are such pretty rooms there." Then he took me into his arms and called me a blessed little goose, and said he would go down to the cellar, if I wished, and have it whitewashed into the bargain. (14–15)

As her experience is dismissed in this way, the narrator increasingly sees herself as a culprit, as the cause of her "fancies" and her suffering. After the exchange with John quoted above, she comes to this conclusion about the wallpapered room: "It is as airy and comfortable a room as any one need wish, and, of course, I would not be so silly as to make him uncomfortable just for a whim" (15).

The subterfuge of her efforts to write gradually fatigues and wears her down so that it becomes difficult to hear her own voice, to discern her own experience, even in her writing. She becomes preoccupied with the yellow wallpaper in her attic room, at first disgusted and fascinated by it at once, and later, determined to solve a puzzle within it. During this part of the story, the narrator begins to experience visions of other women— both within and outside the wallpaper. These women represent increasingly dissociated and fragmented subjectivities in relation to a new text, the text of the wallpaper.

Inside and Outside the Yellow Wallpaper: The "i" and "eye" Fragmented

The discovery of another woman barred behind the wallpaper is a turning point in Gilman's story. This is where the narrator begins to leave what is taken to be "sanity." "I have discovered something at last," she says. "The front pattern *does* move, and no wonder! The woman behind shakes it!" (30). The narrator treats this woman as a separate person, not as part of herself. The doubleness of her experience has changed radically: rather than knowing herself in the double-subjectivity of the "i" and the "eye," she experiences double-consciousness, the term Freud and Breuer originally used to describe "dissociation." The "i" that holds her experience of truths about herself becomes fragmented, then split off from consciousness (Breuer and Freud 12).

At first it is not clear what is happening to the narrator. That is the brilliance of Gilman's story. Gilman has created a narrator the sensitive reader can ally with and trust. The voice of this narrator is wonderfully wry, perceptive, astute. She says "John laughs at me, of course, but one expects that in a marriage" (9), and "John is a physician, and perhaps—(I would not say it to a living soul, of course, but this is dead paper and a great relief to my mind)—perhaps that is one reason I do not get well faster" (9–10). And later, when John chides her for complaining about the house, she writes, "There is something strange about the house, I can feel it" (11). Clearly, this is a woman who can "talk back" to John—at least sometimes to herself, in her writing.

Despite this capacity, we see how she is driven into subterfuge in the face of continually being undermined and dismissed. Gradually, she comes to have little confidence in her wishes and knowledge. For example, when she argues that seeing relatives would be a great relief to her, the argument ends with her tears and John's insistence that this would not be good for her. "It is getting to be a great effort for me to think straight" (21), the narrator reports after this exchange. As she loses her epistemological authority, her willingness to trust her own knowing, reality itself begins to slip out of her grasp. At this point, she is unable to sustain her double-subjectivity, which depends upon the epistemological authority of the inner "i" in resistance to the cultural "eye."

This is the turn in the story where the narrator begins to experience disconnected states of consciousness or "dissociation." For example, she projects her depression and potential destruction onto the text of the wallpaper, and begins to create a conversation within herself about the wallpaper:

> I never saw a worse paper in my life. One of those sprawling flamboyant patterns committing every artistic sin . . . when you follow the lame uncer-

tain curves for a little distance, they suddenly commit suicide—plunge off
at outrageous angles, destroy themselves in unheard of contradictions. (16)

This seems a rather astute description of the wallpaper when we consider the contradictions this narrator experiences and the desperation of
her situation. In fact, the internalized "eye" of John, and of the culture
at large, dwells in the wallpaper and becomes fragmented in this part of
Gilman's story. The narrator, we must remember, is continually watched.
Unable to sustain the truths of her experience as an "i," she finds "eyes"
within the wallpaper proliferate: "Up and down and sideways they crawl,
and those absurd, unblinking eyes are everywhere" (13).

Here, at the edge of the narrator's madness, I imagine ten-year-old
Eliza, the girl who said, "My house is wallpapered with lies," coming
into that attic room, getting past every obstacle to find our narrator. Eliza's mode of discourse in an emergency is shouting. When a trip to the
Museum of Fine Arts was unexpectedly canceled and we did not tell the
girls ahead of time, Eliza shouted at me, "Stop lying to us. You said we
were going, and now we are not. You lied to us!"[20] At ten, her accusation
is stark, her voice unmodulated, and my explanations are not much help
or comfort. Eliza, like other girls in late childhood, is particularly sensitive to lying. I imagine her now shouting at our narrator, "Get a life! This
house is wallpapered with lies. There isn't any 'pattern'—just a pack of
lies. Listen to the walls and they will whisper all their lies to you. And,
you better believe it won't make any sense!"

The narrator decides that the wallpaper's patterns are "pointless,"
even without the shouted advice of Eliza, yet she is determined to "follow
them to some conclusion" (19), to make sense out of what is senseless.
This attempt to make sense of the wallpaper, ironically, is precisely what
pushes her further toward madness. She notices that just when she is
about to find some pattern or meaning in the wallpaper, "it slaps you in
the face, knocks you down, and tramples upon you" (25). Reading this
part of the story, we are reminded vividly of her interactions with John.
The narrator, however, instead of sensing a connection with her own
experience, becomes preoccupied with solving the puzzle of the wallpaper, watching it even at night. Her attitude about staying in the attic
room suddenly changes: "I am getting fond of the room in spite of the
wallpaper. Perhaps because of the wallpaper! It dwells in my mind so!"
(27), she writes.

Our trust in the narrator is a little shaken as she begins to see women
"creeping" in the lane outside by day and "barred" into the wallpaper at
night. She does not seem to know that these women are aspects of herself,
fragmented aspects of the "i" who struggled against John's dictates. Separated from her body and from consciousness, these fragmented "i's" are

treated by the narrator as independent beings. Projected onto what can be known, named, understood, they live in the world in her place, "troubling the space from which she has been banished" (Smith 95). The "i" of her experience, in fact, becomes a series of fragmented subjectivities who live in the wallpaper in relation to a watchful, disbelieving, fascinated "I." The narrator portrays this relation in the following way:

> A strange, provoking formless sort of figure . . . seems to skulk behind that silly and conspicuous front design. The dim shape gets clearer and clearer every day. . . . The faint figure seems to shake the pattern as if she wants to get out. . . . It changes so quickly I can never quite believe it. That is why I must watch it always. . . . I am now quite sure it is a woman. I think that woman gets out in the daytime! I'll tell you why—privately—I can see her. I see her out of every one of my windows . . . she is always creeping. (18–30)

The narrator begins to sympathize with the woman who creeps in the daytime and is again imprisoned in the yellow wallpaper at night. She works frantically to free this woman:

> As soon as it was moonlight and that poor thing began to crawl and shake the pattern, I got up and ran to help her. I pulled and she shook, I shook and she pulled, and before morning we had peeled off yards of that paper. . . . I don't like to look out of the windows even—there are so many of those creeping women and they creep so fast. (32–35)

The narrator continues to peel off wallpaper the next day; for as long as it sticks to the wall, women are imprisoned within it. After she releases these women, she no longer exists in relation to them. Rather, she identifies herself as a woman who has emerged from the wallpaper. She has moved from fascination with the wallpaper to fragmentation within it, to becoming one of the fragmented, projected aspects of herself. After this transition, she writes:

> I wonder if they all came out of the wallpaper as I did? It is so pleasant to be out in this great room and to move around as I please! Here I can creep smoothly on the floor and my shoulder just fits into that long groove on the wall so I cannot lose my way. Why there's John at the door! . . . I looked at him over my shoulder. "I have got out at last," said I. . . . "And I've pulled off most of the paper, so you can't put me back." (35–36)

Here the narrator slips completely into madness—where, ironically, it is possible for her to know, to feel, and to speak about what is real: her outrage at John's treatment plan and her ultimate freedom from his restrictions and dismissals. But in madness, she is grotesquely embodied as she crawls around the perimeter of the room and, though she speaks truthfully in her "mad-sane way" (Hedges 53), she is likely to be even more radically restricted, watched, imprisoned.

Conclusion: Connections between *The Yellow Wallpaper* and Women's Psychological Development

This exploration of *The Yellow Wallpaper* deepens my questions about women's relational experiences and women's development. Thinking and writing about Gilman's narrator leads me to reconsider earlier conceptualizations of girls' relational development. At the heart of the Harvard Project's analysis of women's psychological development is a struggle in girls' relational development. As girls come of age, they face an unsolvable relational dilemma: they may either continue to speak authentically, living fully and freely in the world of relationships or, alternatively, learn to silence themselves in order to protect and preserve their relationships (Brown and Gilligan 7; Rogers, "Voice, Play," 273). Thinking about this struggle in the text of *The Yellow Wallpaper* has led me to be more critical of our constructing girls' development in the stark terms of "either" and "or" and has raised new questions about a range of responses involved in women's psychological development in adolescence and adulthood.

The narrator's relational position, from the beginning of Gilman's story, places her in a terrible dilemma. Creating a parallel with the earlier analysis of girls' relational struggles in adolescence, I conceptualized this dilemma in the following way: How could she possibly know the reality of her own thoughts and feelings and also be in connection with her husband, who upholds a societal order that would have her not exist as a whole and sane subjective person? Given the nature of this conceptualization, as well as my analysis of the climate of control created in the "treatment" of her depression, including taking from her the one means of giving voice to reality (her writing), it makes sense that the narrator is driven mad.

What is missing from this construction, however, are the "grays" of the narrator's story, the turning points in her development in the face of an unyielding relational dilemma. In my analysis of *The Yellow Wallpaper*, I discovered a graduated continuum of responses, ranging from double-subjectivity to psychic splitting to dissociation and fragmented subjectivities,[21] that now allows me to recast the relational dilemma itself in terms that are no longer black and white. I would now ask: How can the narrator sustain the knowledge that connects her with a complex "reality" that includes the truths of her experience, the cultural dictates of the world in which she lives, especially in relationship with her husband, John, who upholds a societal order that would have her not exist as a complex and knowing subjective person? When her knowledge cannot be sustained, in herself, in the world in which she lives, and in her relationships, how does the narrator resist, and what transformations are evident in her resistance? Finally, what would sustain an effective resistance over time?

These questions, together with the analysis of Gilman's short story presented in this chapter, point toward new conceptions about the psychological processes involved in women's development, particularly during and after adolescence. Keeping an authentic inner voice alive appears to be a complex interplay of overlapping strategies, and double-subjectivity may be centrally important among these. Double-subjectivity involves a healthy capacity to see from at least two perspectives and to hold them in tension. This appears to be difficult to sustain in adolescence for many girls, who then become strikingly dismissive of a truthful inner voice because that voice would seemingly endanger their relationships. In early adolescence, girls are especially psychologically vulnerable, particularly in the absence of validating relationships. However, it may be that in adulthood this picture changes to some degree. Women's ability to appreciate the ambiguity of multiple perspectives and to consider them critically as a system may increase the likelihood of sustaining double-subjectivity and more effectively resisting the "toxins of the culture" (Kegan 96).

When this double-subjectivity breaks down, however, a woman's continued resistance requires psychic splitting: a division of the world into binary terms so that different aspects of our relational experience are seen as contradictory and irreconcilable—love is selfless or selfish; one must be wholly honest or completely withdraw from relationships; self perceptions are right or completely mistaken. These either/or constructions create a terrible vulnerability in women to the authority of others' judgments and assessments (whether these are validating or dismissing), particularly in close relationships.

In the face of chronic isolation and repeated dismissals, psychic splitting may lead one to doubt the very reality of one's actual experiences. This profound doubt opens the possibility for effectively "gaslighting" women's lived experiences so that one feels crazy when holding to the truths of experience and feels less crazy in moments of self dismissal. The process of relational "gaslighting" is in itself potentially traumatic. It may result in dissociation, a profound separation of one's thoughts and feelings from one's experience and memory.[22]

Gilman's story not only leads me to reconsider a range of responses and psychological processes used in an attempt to sustain resistance and psychological resilience in adult women, but also to highlight women's knowledge in relationships with girls. Gilman's story is by no means unique. Her courageous struggle for voice and sanity represents an extreme example of the ways other women fight for clarity in patriarchal societies and cultures. I found myself wishing that she had written an autobiographical accompaniment to *The Yellow Wallpaper*, the story of her return to sanity, a text for which we need to imagine new plots and possibilities. In the absence of such a story, I created a fiction within her story by having girls I have known interrupt and speak to Gilman's narrator. If the narrator reminds us of "ourself," and "ourself behind ourself," I intend for the girls to remind us of that truth-telling voice of courage and resistance, rooted in many of our experiences of girlhood.[23] As these young adolescent girls step into the narrative of a woman's life to comment and to intervene, can their startling voices potentially interrupt a process of cultural madness—for themselves as girls coming of age and for us as women? This is not what happens generally. Each of the girls, Eliza, Tess, and Karen, as well as girls we all know, girls we have been, at one point or another, learn to disconnect aspects of themselves in the face of cultural dismissal or shaming. As this process continues, these girls, like Gilman's narrator, are in danger of crossing the boundaries from double-subjectivity into psychic splitting and from psychic splitting into dissociation, fragmentation, and madness. Though relatively few young women step over the boundary into madness, a clear pattern of psychological repression repeats itself as generation after generation of stalwart and lively girls grow into women within patriarchy. Seeing how much is at stake in this process, however, may allow women to follow another course with girls and with one another. If girls' voices sometimes provide cues to women to resist a cultural process of madness, their voices are not enough. Girls depend on the strength and knowledge of women in their communities. Women's capacities to hold the ambiguity of double-subjectivity, and to consider different subjectivities systematically, may be crucial in helping one another and girls to sustain resistance and avert the edge of madness. The loss of women's lived "realities" might then become untenable and unnecessary for us and for our daughters.

Notes

1. A portion of this paper was presented at Trinity College, Psychology and Women's Studies Departments, Dublin, Ireland, April 25, 1995.

2. The research I draw from in this paper is part of a study I directed entitled "Strengthening Healthy Resistance and Courage in Girls." This project was cre-

ated in collaboration with Dr. Carol Gilligan, and the research was part of a coordinated series of studies conducted by the Harvard Project on Women's Psychology and Girls' Development in the late 1980s and early 1990s funded by the Spencer Foundation and the Lilly Endowment.

3. As a number of studies document, adolescence appears to be a time of psychological risk and vulnerability for girls, comparable to early childhood for boys. The move into adolescence affects girls' self-conceptions and marks a sharp drop in self-confidence, primarily, but not exclusively, among white and Latina girls. See, for example: Block, Elder, Nguyen, and Caspi 368–371; Greenberg-Lake Analysis Group 7–9; Petersen 594–596.

4. As girls progress from self-awareness in ego or self-development toward conscientious and more abstract thinking about self, relationships, and the social world, they lose a fine edge of resistance and resilience. See Rogers, Brown, and Tappan.

5. I distinguish double-subjectivity, the capacity to hold two contradictory voices or perspectives, from both psychic splitting—a tendency to describe experience in binary terms and to miss gradations and ambiguities—and from dissociation—a clear disconnection of feelings, conscious knowledge, and memory.

6. For a more complete description of this process, see Gilligan, Rogers, and Noel.

7. Eliza is a member of the Theater, Writing and Outing Club for Girls, an intervention designed by me, Carol Gilligan, and Normi Noel, to strengthen girls' courage and resistance at the end of childhood. She is a working-class, European American girl. In this scene, we are going to a forest for a walk in the rain.

8. Quotation of Eliza from my observation notes on the Theater, Writing and Outing Club for Girls, October 21, 1991.

9. Quotation of Tess from my observation notes on the Theater, Writing and Outing Club for Girls, November 9, 1991. Tess is a working-class, European-American girl.

10. Annual research interview with Tess, "Strengthening Healthy Resistance and Courage in Girls Project," Fall 1991.

11. Brown and Gilligan, 38; Rogers, Brown, and Tappan.

12. Clinical interview with Karen, February 1989. Karen is an upper-middle-class Jewish girl.

13. Dana Jack, in her study of depressed women, identified a voice of an "Over-Eye" as part of a two-voice inner dialogue with an "I" who attempts to speak authentically. The "Over-Eye" is the internalized voice of cultural standards dictating "good" behavior for women. Jack also ties the development of this voice with a "personal history of maternal submissiveness and paternal dominance" (114).

14. *The Yellow Wallpaper* (New York: The Feminist Press, 1973/1899), 12. All further references to Gilman's story correspond to this edition.

15. The voice of "i" is a quiet, inner experience of truthful subjectivity that preserves knowledge; it sometimes is spoken aloud in resistance and sometimes held in silence as resistance. The voice of "eye" is an internalized experience of a spectator subjectivity. Initially, I began to describe the "eye" and "i" as voices in

an inner dialogue, repeating Dana Jack's approach, but soon discovered that the binary nature of this conceptualization did not fit my analysis; the idea of an "i" and an "eye" as overlapping double-subjectivities allowed me to trace the ways they were often braided together in the same sentences.

16. Annual research interview with Tess, "Strengthening Healthy Resistance and Courage in Girls Project," Fall 1992.

17. In my research and clinical work with adolescent girls who have histories of trauma, I use a written text as "another ear." I engage the girls in creative writing with me, initially using associative language exercises such as word clustering and free-writing, and actively interpret their writing with them as if these texts could "hear" and then "speak" to us about what they actually feel and think and know but cannot allow themselves to acknowledge. Rogers, A. "Writing on Their Bodies I: Understanding Self-Destruction with Adolescent Girls through Creative Writing and Diaries." Presented at the Harvard Medical School Conference, "Child and Adolescent Self-Destruction," Boston, February 3, 1996, and at Trinity College: Psychology and Women's Studies Departments, Dublin, Ireland, April 25, 1996, submitted to the *Journal of Counseling Psychology*, 1996.

18. Clinical interview with Karen, March 1989.

19. Clinical interview with Karen, September 1990.

20. Quotation of Eliza from my observation notes on the Theater, Writing and Outing Club for Girls, November 23, 1989.

21. I also saw this pattern in an analysis of women's trauma narratives. Double-subjectivity serves the function of resistance in psychic life and does not involve dissociation. I distinguish this concept from dissociation, a radical disconnection of conscious thoughts and feelings from experience and memory. Resistance expressed as double-subjectivity and chronically met with social censor or punishment can, however, lead to dissociation. In my research with women who have trauma histories, I identified "exiled voices" in their interview narratives, i.e., voices driven out of their relationships became a "counterpoint of resistance and dissociation." See Rogers, "Exiled Voices."

22. This pattern was clearly evident in my study of women who had experienced chronic trauma in childhood. The women described attempts by family members and others to undermine their experience and sanity, a process I have called "gaslighting" because it led to a profound doubting of reality.

23. Emily Hancock has written about women's experience of "the girl within" as a vital resource for women throughout our adult lives. Hancock, E. *The Girl Within: A Groundbreaking New Approach to Female Identity*. New York: Ballantine Books, 1989.

Works Cited

Block, Jack. "Ego Resilience Through Time: Antecedents and Ramifications." *Resilience and Psychological Health*. Symposium of the Boston Psychoanalytic Society, Boston, 1990.

Breuer, Josef, and Sigmund Freud. 1895. *Studies on Hysteria.* Ed. James Strachey. London: The Hogarth Press, 1955.

Brown, Lyn Mikel, and Carol Gilligan. *Meeting at the Crossroads: Women's Psychology and Girls' Development.* Cambridge: Harvard UP, 1992.

Butler, Judith P. *Gender Trouble: Feminism and the Subversion of Identity.* New York: Routledge, 1990.

Dickinson, Emily. *The Complete Poems.* Ed. Thomas H. Johnson. Toronto: Little, Brown and Company, 1960.

Elder, Glen H., Tri Van Nguyen, and Avshalom Caspi. "Linking Family Hardship to Children's Lives." *Child Development* 56 (1985): 361–75.

Gilligan, Carol, Annie G. Rogers, and Normi Noel. "Cartography of a Lost Time: Women, Girls and Relationships." Harvard Project on Women's Psychology and Girls' Development, Unpublished manuscript, 1992.

Gilman, Charlotte Perkins. *The Yellow Wallpaper.* 1899. New York: The Feminist Press, 1973.

Greenberg-Lake, The Analysis Group. *Shortchanging Girls, Shortchanging America: A Nationwide Poll to Assess Self Esteem, Educational Experiences, Interest in Math and Science, and Career Aspirations of Girls and Boys Ages 9–15.* Washington, DC: American Association of University Women, 1991.

Hancock, Elizabeth. *The Girl Within: A Groundbreaking New Approach to Female Identity.* New York: Ballantine Books, 1989.

Hedges, Elaine. Afterword. *The Yellow Wallpaper.* By Charlotte Perkins Gilman. New York: The Feminist Press, 1973.

Herman, Judith. *Trauma and Recovery.* New York: Basic Books, 1992.

Jack, Dana. *Silencing the Self: Women and Depression,* Cambridge: Harvard UP, 1991.

Kegan, Robert. *In Over Our Heads.* Cambridge: Harvard UP, 1994.

Petersen, Anne C. "Adolescent Development." *Annual Review of Psychology* 39 (1988): 583–607.

Rogers, Annie G. "Exiled Voices: Dissociation and Repression in Women's Trauma Narratives." *Stone Center Collected Papers,* Wellesley College, Wellesley, 1994.

———. "Voice, Play and a Practice of Ordinary Courage in the Lives of Girls and Women." *Harvard Educational Review* 63 (1993): 265–295.

———. "Writing on Their Bodies I: Understanding Self Destruction with Adolescent Girls through Creative Writing and Diaries." Presented at the Harvard Medical School Conference: "Child and Adolescent Self-Destruction," Boston, February 3, 1996, and at Trinity College: Psychology and Women's Studies Departments, Dublin, Ireland, April 25, 1996, submitted to *Journal of Counseling Psychology,* 1996.

Rogers, Annie G., Lyn Mikel Brown, and Mark Tappan. "Interpreting Loss in Ego Development in Girls: Regression or Resistance?" *The Narrative Study of Lives.* Ed. Ruthellen Josselson and A. Lieblich. Vol. 2. Newbury Park: Sage, 1994.

Smith, Sidonie. *Subjectivity, Identity and the Body: Autobiographical Practices in the Twentieth Century.* Bloomington: Indiana UP, 1993.

Woolf, Virginia. *A Room of One's Own.* New York: Harcourt, Brace & World, 1929.

4

Fairy Tales, Feminist Theory, and the Lives of Women and Girls

Jerilyn Fisher and Ellen S. Silber

Engaging and familiar as "happily ever after" narratives for children and adults alike, fairy tales exert a noticeable influence on cultural ideals of goodness, images of evil, models of manhood and womanhood, and fantasies about "true love." A majority of the stories most frequently retold, such as "Snow White," "Cinderella," and "Rapunzel," feature a young girl's halting progression to royal marriage, her dream-come-true repeatedly threatened by the wicked deeds of a depraved stepmother, witch, or enchantress. The fairy-tale father, oblivious to his child's misery, never intercedes; nor is he reproached for being inattentive.[1] Ultimately, the prince delivers the heroine from women's wrath. His power to save her and her utter dependence on him seem key to their imagined future happiness.

In 1971, Anne Sexton published a series of poems called *Transformations*, her ironic revision of tales by the Brothers Grimm. She was among the first to expose the discrepancy between the Grimm's fairy land romance and real life, boldly ridiculing the bizarre script for female characters in the tales. Following Sexton's early poetic statement came other influential analyses of the stories' sexist fantasies and the restrictive training in gender roles effected through them (Dworkin, Lieberman, Gilbert and Gubar). No less truthful now than it was in 1979 is Karen Rowe's recognition that the potency of fairy-tale characterizations and plot in forming the female psyche is "awesome." Today, these stories and their messages still captivate young girls' minds and hearts with intriguing archetypal motifs that "effectively sabotage female assertiveness" (218).

Many parents, educators, and literary critics know that it remains impossible to read these charming tales and ignore their capacity for reinforcing limiting sex role stereotypes and conservative ways of thinking about family that act upon children when they are most impressionable. Reconstructing traditional theories to include the developmental experiences of women, and, increasingly, of culturally diverse women, feminist psychological theories offer effective tools for "resisting" male fantasies, which, when consumed uncritically, can narrow young girls' visions of their social roles in this culture.[2]

"What is needed," Jack Zipes writes in his introduction to *Don't Bet on the Prince,* "is a socio-psychological theory based on the recent findings of feminist investigations and critical reinterpretations of Freud that will help us grasp how fairy tales function . . . within the American and British socialization processes" (2). Our work attempts this kind of analysis. Reading stories by the Brothers Grimm through the lens of feminist psychological theory, we examine mothers and their daughters; female voices of deception and desire; and, lastly, the tales' "happy endings"— all thematic portraits that instill patriarchal values within a readership that is demographically heterogeneous, yet mostly female.

Mothers and Their Daughters

"Dear child, be good and pious, and then the good God will always protect you, and I will look down on you from heaven and be near you" (121).[3] With that message, Cinderella's birth mother dies and so ends the first sentence of the story. But Cinderella's birth mother—completely absent in both Charles Perrault's and Walt Disney's versions of the story—exerts a strong influence on her daughter in the Grimm's tale. This dying mother's words are few but loving, and it is her enduring magical presence (incarnated in the hazel bush and in the birds) that enables Cinderella to overcome her famous stepmother's wickedness. Finally, however, when Cinderella is "chosen" by the prince, she leaves behind the hazel bush, escapes the cruel world of women, and fully enters the patriarchal world, thus satisfying the conventions of women's proper role.

As the fairy tales readily show, and as other critics have amply demonstrated (Dworkin 35–41; de Beauvoir 573–5; Gilbert and Gubar 36–44), it is not angelic but demonic images of the mother that prevail. The good mother is completely eclipsed by the entrance of her vile antithesis, the renowned witch or stepmother. Proffering a psychological rationale for this demonic female presence, Bruno Bettelheim argues that the child needs and in fact thrives on destructive maternal figures in fairy tales (68–71). His psychoanalytic view posits children's exposure to images of women's malevolence as a curative, allaying their guilt by providing an acceptable outlet for unconscious, hostile fantasies about their mothers. Therefore, says Bettelheim, fairy tales assist the child in achieving the necessary maturational goal of separation. For example, girls can identify easily with an innocent heroine who enjoys the demise of "an older ill-intentioned female."[4] Bettelheim contends, to our disbelief, that the older woman's malicious deeds in the story allow the child to transfer more readily her ambivalent maternal attachment to the culturally sanctioned attachment of a young girl's affections: the handsome prince.

Thus, from Bettelheim's perspective, the wicked (step) mother's patently evil deeds let children constructively displace onto fictional female objects those hateful, fearful thoughts they would otherwise harbor toward their own mothers, who withhold as they provide. This analysis has been challenged by those who see its patriarchal assumptions that prize the (absent) father over the mother in the child's eyes (Barzilai 518) and its misogynist views about the inevitability of mother-hating and the desirability of having hateful mothers in children's literature (Zipes, "Breaking" 64). Still, it is not uncommon today for teachers and scholars to reference *The Uses of Enchantment* as a valid interpretation of and even justification for the preponderance of negative maternal portraits.[5]

Current feminist psychological studies elucidate Bettelheim's misreading of the basis for girls' fury with their mothers. Judith Herman and Helen Lewis, for example, explain that the Freudian interpretation of a young girl's anger toward her mother (resulting from the inferiority complex the daughter develops), entirely overlooks the male-dominated context in which a growing girl "first recognizes what it means to be female in a world where power and privilege are the province of men" (150). Disturbed and ashamed to observe that her mother and other women are devalued, the daughter expresses outrage at female subordination by "hating" her mother.

Missing from Herman and Lewis' interpretation is an account of the positive maternal feelings that researchers have documented in African American girls who grow up with mothers enjoying respect and positions of authority within their communities (Collins 49; Joseph, "Roles and Traditions" 94; Bing and Trotman Reid 193). For more than two decades, studies have shown that many African American girls are taught by their mothers' examples and words to become independent, self-supporting, and not too reliant on men. In personal reflections and responses to interviews, these girls voice tremendous admiration for their mothers' abilities to negotiate racist and sexist conditions (Collins 51–2; Guy-Sheftall 4; Joseph, "Perspectives" 95; Joseph, "Roles and Functions" 101). This research implicitly challenges both Bettelheim and Herman and Lewis by bringing into psychological theory recognition of positive relationships between strong mothers and their daughters. Moreover, African American girls would seem a notable exception to Bettelheim's theory of a split consciousness around the idea of "mother": for the daughter's image of the African American mother is both "tough and tender" (Joseph, "Roles and Functions" 101).

Yet, as these daughters of color enter adolescence and grow more sensitive to institutionalized prejudice, they eventually see that in the outside racist and sexist world their mother's status declines. From this perspective, Herman and Lewis contribute insightfully to our discussion of fairy tales when they maintain that "anger between mothers and daughters is often a displaced anger" (140), the hidden source of which is "the oppressed condition of women" (153). Their analysis, instead of implicating the fairy-tale stepmother for her terrifying acts of aggression toward the girl under her care, draws our curiosity to the untold story of this disruptive female character whose rebellion against the "feminine plot" of passivity and submission is repeatedly cast as the source of conflict in the tales (Gilbert and Gubar 39; Dworkin 41).

Inevitably, Grimm's evil stepmothers come to a much deserved, horrible end. Cinderella's stepmother's desperate attempt to royally wed her daughters—no matter what it takes—does not succeed. For "their wickedness and falsehood" (128) the stepsisters, whose identities are fused with the stepmother, are barbarously punished. In "Snow White," the stepmother also faces defeat: with "red hot shoes" on her feet, she is forced to dance "until she dropped down dead" (258). The morally corrupt and duplicitous mother of "The Juniper Tree" has a millstone thrown at her head and is "entirely crushed by it" (229); in "Hansel and Gretel," the wicked stepmother is dead, and the wicked cannibal-witch has been pushed into a hot oven, where she howls "quite horribly" and is "miserably burnt to death" (93). Within and across most tales, we find a horrible witch, cast in a corrupted care-taking role, who has replaced the ephemeral birth mother.

Clearly, our culture's dualistic images of maternity are perversely joined in coexistence; indeed, it has been well documented that the Mother in Western tradition is characterized above all by ambivalence (Caplan 2–4; Chernin, *Hungry Self* 36–7, 87–93; Rich, *Of Woman Born* 15–6; Ruddick 31). Simone de Beauvoir in *The Second Sex* speaks of the "respect that haloes the Mother," while at the same time, since the Middle Ages, the myth of the mother-in-law has allowed expression of the "masked horror of maternity." De Beauvoir sees an analogue in the figure of the stepmother, who, like the mother-in-law, incarnates the cruel and destructive aspects of motherhood (196–7) and whose contrasting presence in the fairy tales throws an aura of perfection around the fleeting image of the innocent birth mother.[6]

But this maternal contrast alone cannot sufficiently establish the birth mother's good standing: she must also be "killed off" or repressed so that her benevolence remains frozen in its purity. In "Cinderella," as well as in other stories, once the idealized mother dies without having caused anyone the least bit of trouble, her image is fixed, an embodiment of flawless love, not resembling much at all a human mother in dynamic relationship with her real-life daughter. In psychoanalytic terms, by leaving the story quickly—before any relational conflicts ensue—the birth mother in the fairy tale remains glorified like Freud's pre-Oedipal mother (the earliest mother who bestows food and love in abundance). By having the good queen die both naturally and prematurely (in effect, "killing her softly," never violently like the wicked queen), the tales allow the biological mother to leave the story adored, content to sit by a window and sew, contemplating her child-to-be. But in a tale derived from patriarchal values, should this woman live beyond the earliest narrative moments, she would inevitably become the interfering maternal presence of the Oedipal years (Chodorow 83). Hence, the quick and urgent dismissal of any good mothers in the stories.

While the fairy tales consistently polarize the characterization of motherhood, a profound imbalance in these opposing maternal portraits stands out: as a character, the bad mother is at the center, dominating not just the princess, but the plot. In contrast to the good mother (Cinderella's or Snow White's, for example), who has a barely perceptible part to play—appearing literally for a sentence or two before dying—the wicked stepmother assumes a starring role as the girl's tenacious adversary. In terms of narrative significance, a fiercely competitive, vicious, and pathological mother becomes the extant symbol of adult womanhood. But, for the preadolescent girl—be she protagonist or reader—emulating the witch (the only available, *living* "model" of feminine maturity) would surely incur severe social criticism, a fate unequivocally symbolized by the stepmother's demise. Thus, the dutiful daughter assumes instead the passive, feminine identity of the first queen. By the end of the story, the princess, betrothed or newly married, appears ready to replicate the good mother's domestic role and destiny, avoiding any identification with the active principle embodied in the characterization of the bad mother/witch.

One particularly engaging tale in our study offers a refreshingly different set of possibilities for its "good" mother and daughter, both of whom assert themselves in surprising ways. In "The Twelve Brothers," a loving queen secretly warns her twelve sons so that they can escape a death decreed by the king, their father, should a daughter come next from his pregnant wife's womb. Minutes after their infant sister is born, the twelve boys receive the queen's warning and run away, living together in the forest until many years later, when their grown-up, brave, and faithful sister comes in search of her lost brethren.

Shortly after the girl finds her brothers, an old woman, who typifies the evil enchantress, bewitches the princess: the twelve boys are changed into ravens and the girl is forbidden to speak or laugh for seven years lest her brothers die. Soon she meets a wandering, love-struck king and agrees—in silence, of course—to marry him. But once they make their home in his palace, the king's mother, "a wicked woman," repeatedly lies to the king about his bride, finally persuading her spineless son to sentence the woman he admittedly loves to death. At the last moment possible, the princess is saved, just as the sinister spell has run its course. Here the story ends, climaxing with the usual, ruthless vengeance toward the evil stepmother, who is put to death in "a barrel filled with boiling oil and venomous snakes" (64). The girl's father (that death-decreeing king) has long vanished. Although his barbarous proclamation was the plot's original catalyst, only the stepmother personifies evil in this story. Forgotten, too, by the end of the tale, is the noble queen. Yet, we can claim that it is her maternal daring that accounts for this daughter's unusual and consistent courage in stepping beyond the limits of conventional femininity: uncharacteristically, the princess leaves home by herself, then heroically and silently risks her own life to save her twelve raven-brothers.

In classical psychoanalytic theory, a girl does not favorably identify with her mother. Instead, a girl's hostility and distrust nearly wipe out positive association (Freud, "Female Sexuality" 227, 233–5, 241). In her longitudinal study of adolescence, Terri Apter captures the other, very real but rarely promoted side of girls' constructive desire for enduring attachment to their mothers: "What remains unwritten," Apter notes, "is the story about how connection between mother and daughter . . . remains a strength, not an immaturity" (1). Indeed, a daughter's attachment to her mother becomes extremely problematic when white culture repeatedly conveys the media-message that the service mothers give to their families is less valued than the work fathers perform in the public sphere. Without exception, the typical fairy-tale plot reinforces this cultural disregard by the majority for the developmental value of girls' positive feelings about their mothers.

Feminist psychological studies, however, have documented thoroughly the importance of a mother's positive role in her daughter's gender identity. Jessica Benjamin's persuasive response to the classical psychoanalytic view of female development shows that, in contrast to Freud's portrait of a young girl coming to femininity through attraction to her father, "girls sustain the primary identification with the mother . . ." achieving "their femininity through direct identification with [her]" (90, 91).

Yet Freud's analysis and the patriarchally molded fairy tale depict the mother as a wholly depriving (even castrating) figure with no recognition of the healthy emotional attachment and comfort that girls can experience in a close relationship with their mother. "Mother-blaming," in life and in theory, moreover, is as common as it is in fairy tales. Mothers have been blamed for being "controlling, intrusive, engulfing . . . narcissistic, abusive, crazy" (Debold et al. 21). Speaking from clinical experience, Janet Surrey of the Stone Center at Wellesley College observes that a girl's early "emotional desire to be connected to her mother" is often obstructed by culturally sanctioned mother-blaming—a strategy Surrey finds frighteningly acceptable in professional training and practice, easily achieved, she says, in "a patriarchal culture which encourages separation of mothers and daughters" (85).[7] In the fairy tales, the innocent female protagonist *must* reject identification with or empathy for her depraved maternal nemesis. The passive young girl, morally superior to the aggressive adult woman in whose care the daughter has been placed, thus illustrates Freud's theory that "good" girls' rejection of the women who mother them is only "normal." This justified rejection then creates the space (and *need*) for our princesses to seek the ideal romantic relationship with the patriarchal designee, a rich and handsome prince.

Each of the six heroines in the tales we discuss *does* have an evil, threatening mother figure from whom she must free herself. This recurrent portrait of the evil mother serves one of the main cultural purposes of the fairy tale—conservation of traditional gender roles in the patriarchal state and family (Zipes, *Fairy Tale as Myth* 36). For example, if Snow White's (or Rapunzel's or Cinderella's) stepmother were a "good mother," the young girl would have been far less motivated to flee the castle (or tower or home) and, more importantly, might not have fallen hypnotically into the prince's arms.[8]

Psychologist Jane Flax notes rampant maternal devaluation and mistrust as a "cruel twist" in girls' development, because it is "only through relationships with other women [that] women [can] heal the hurts suffered during their psychological development" (60). Interestingly, Flax sees that "women's unresolved wishes for the mother is the truth behind Freud's claim that what women wish for in a husband is their mother" (60). Mirroring values of the dominant culture that debase women's familial power, fairy tales depict young girls who grow up without suitable mothers and look only to men for protection and fulfillment. In effect, these fictions of virtual motherlessness warp the true story of girls' healthy development: the daughter is prevented from fully identifying with her mother by the loving woman's early death; yet, attachment to the living, treacherous mother would be destructive and unimaginable.

However meaningful mother-daughter attachment may be, maternal separation—when freed from its significance in male-centered developmental theory—has an important place in girls' growth toward adulthood. Arguing against Freudian views, Jessica Benjamin disputes the idea that innate striving for individuation is a predominantly hostile reaction against the mother's early care-taking role. Benjamin renders a feminist interpretation of the will to separate, clarifying that the girl's separation from the mother is not enacted out of disdain for the one from whom she separates, but rather out of a need and desire to see herself as "other." In her argument, Benjamin recognizes that both boys and girls "can make use of identifications with both parents, without being confused about their gender identity" (112). The challenge girls face is to synthesize within themselves desire for feminine identification, represented by their attachment to the mother—and their desire for agency, represented by identification with the father (122).

For a girl child who does not develop an identification with her father, the desire for separateness "later emerges as ideal love, the wish for a vicarious substitute for . . . agency" (121, 122). Typical fairy-tale princesses do just what Benjamin says: lacking a model of maternal agency, and having a weak or absent father, they find in perfect romantic love the only feminine role available from which to act, albeit passively, and the only source of feminine accomplishment. Offering only blissful fantasies of feminine helplessness, the best-known fairy tales stir readers to anticipate and even welcome miraculous masculine rescue. Once rescued, the young woman will be elevated by the prince's choosing her as bride. In marriage, she will remain dependent on her husband's will, as was her "good mother" before her.

As Gilbert and Gubar have said, there is no escape from the stifling reflection of the mirror in which fairy-tale heroines see their images (37). For "good mothers" and their daughters, freedom from domestic restriction is possible only through early death, while a female character who acts as her own agent becomes the hated witch, condemned to die. In either case, a woman is silenced. Because there are few outlets for creativity, a woman's "works" in these tales are limited to childbearing or the devising of nefarious, conniving plots. Either choice—"lying in" or "lying to"—will eventually kill her, revealing only dead-end possibilities for female destiny.

Women and Deception

In 1925, Freud wrote what he says he hesitated to express: that women, more than men, are "influenced in their judgments by feelings of affection or hostility"; thus, they show less of a sense of justice and abide by different—meaning "lesser"—ethical standards than do their male counterparts ("Psychical Consequences" 257–8). In short, women's words and deeds are suspect: hardly surprising, because in the Freudian universe, this untrustworthiness results from penis envy built into the female character, an emotional response a girl cannot control because she, unlike her brother, lacks the stern superego forged during his Oedipal experience and which serves as a moral guide. Freud reminds us that "critics of every epoch" ("Psychical Consequences" 257) have reported women's inferior ability to react with men's objectivity (read: "truth" or "honor"), an observation that the father of psychoanalysis makes without taking into account that almost all these critics of the past have been males living under patriarchy.[9]

When Adrienne Rich, on the other hand, discusses honor from a distinctly feminist perspective, she speaks of women's conditioned need and willingness to fabricate. She understands that lies of duplicity, complicity, and denial are among the weapons women learn to wield in their ongoing struggle against sexual subordination. "Truthfulness," writes Rich, "has not been considered important for women, as long as we have remained physically faithful to a man, or chaste. . . . Women have been forced to lie, for survival, to men. How to unlearn this among other women?" ("Women and Honor" 188–9). Lying in word or deed not only divides women from each other but, as Rich makes clear, the lies of the fathers also have perpetuated in daily life the fairy tales' romantic and domestic illusions.

Outsiders to the patriarchal power structure, women in Grimm's who have ambition, who show a desire for control and status, must attempt to secure their standing by misleading others. They can find agency only through fraud and manipulation (the stepmother in "Hansel and Gretel"), masquerade/spell-casting (Snow White's wicked queen), or fabrication (the mother-in-law in "The Twelve Brothers").[10] Meanwhile, the fairy-tale fathers' established authority, acquired from maleness alone, assures paternal figures control and status without their having to resort to deception.

Yet witch and stepmother alike lie, not to take over the seat of power but to move closer to the male figures, be they kings or simply fathers. These fairy-tale women defraud and betray children's trust in their quest to be appealing to men. Hansel and Gretel's stepmother deviously seeks to rid herself of her husband's children so she will have him and his resources to herself; Snow White's stepmother uses trickery to ensure that she be identified as the fairest of them all; the wicked queen in "The Twelve Brothers" plots her daughter-in-law's death to eliminate a powerful rival for her son's affection; and the stepmother in "Cinderella" works slyly to have one of her daughters wed the king's son (thus assuring she will become near-royalty herself). Using means to promote the self that are at once perverse and creative, they pursue power by association with power. Ironically, rather than advancing their cause, their lies result in vilification by the very men whose recognition they seek.

For ambitious women in fairy tales, coercive ruses to impose their own wishes ultimately prove futile as acts of empowerment. Women are not allowed to achieve real and lasting power. Instead, the stepmother's ill-fated reign serves as a cautionary message about what happens to women who dare to imagine having power over others. Possessing no respectable status in the patriarchal kingdom, the stepmother can only assert influence with lies and disguises that soon implicate her as wicked. But power derived from falsehood is false power; and deceit consistently results in the liar's own demise.[11]

Perhaps the most wicked woman among those studied here is the wife in "The Juniper Tree." Frightened after having beheaded her stepson, Hans, the stepmother says to herself, "If I could but make them think that it was not done by me!" (222). She then lies about Hans' cause of death and tricks her young daughter, Marlinchen, into believing that the girl, not the murderous woman herself, has whacked the beloved step-brother's head off. Throughout the rest of the story, the woman continues to lie cruelly, pretending to guard the secret that Marlinchen has killed her brother. This lie haunts the stepmother like a ghost, finally leading the diabolic woman to her crushing death beneath the millstone.

This odious mother forces Marlinchen into another form of falsehood, that of silence. The girl, imagining herself guilty of a horrid deed, dares not contradict the stepmother's lies about Hans' whereabouts, telling no one that the stepmother has cooked Hans' bones into black-puddings. Instead, she collects some of his bones and buries them under the juniper tree, from which Hans arises, transformed into a magical bird who is empowered to reveal the true story. Again and again in the tale he sings: "My mother she killed me / My father he ate me / My sister, little Marlinchen, / gathered together all my bones . . . laid them beneath the juniper tree" (224). The boy-turned-bird possesses the only voice authorized to tell the incriminating story that Marlinchen has partly witnessed, but is afraid to speak.

Hans in "The Juniper Tree" can divulge the horrific truth because he, unlike Marlinchen, has been transformed and was never intimidated—as was his sister—into silence. But his role as truth-teller can be read in another way: Hans has not imbibed the primary lesson of relationships that young girls quickly learn—that is, to disown ugly knowledge or bad feelings for the sake of avoiding conflict of any kind. Looking at the character of young Marlinchen and what she knows but won't reveal, we wonder, in the words of Lyn Brown, "What would it take for a girl at the edge of adolescence to tell the truth about her life, to speak openly . . . about what she sees and hears around her . . . ?" ("Telling" 71–2). In "The Juniper Tree" (as in the case of eleven-year-old Jessie, who is terrified "of saying the wrong thing"), it would seem to take a girl who is unafraid to admit what she knows by speaking truthfully ("Telling" 78). Studying adolescents in *Meeting at the Crossroads*, Brown and Gilligan notice that for many girls on the cusp of womanhood, self-silencing becomes the "right" way to behave: it is socially acceptable for girls to withhold negative feelings, "covering dislike with lies" (179). Honest reactions of anger or frustration would betray a girl as "mean" or "rude" or "selfish," posing serious risks to her being loved or even tolerated.

As Brown and Gilligan indicate, girls and women confront powerful cultural images and voices that convince them to consider their authentic negative responses to human relationships as improper and therefore "wrong." This moral imperative to hush unpleasant feelings outweighs the psychological danger of girls dismissing how they feel or what they see around them. But not speaking with authenticity soon turns into not knowing what one means, and not knowing one's self results in a loss of identity. Furthermore, not being sure of who they are leaves young girls specially vulnerable to a widespread, impossible standard of female goodness and unselfishness, almost always at the expense of acknowledging or expressing their true feelings.

In the fairy tales, even relatively strong female characters cannot escape entirely the injunction to remain silent. "The Twelve Brothers" provides an interesting example of two brave women's quiet attempts at rebellion against male authorities they cannot otherwise influence. After agreeing to her husband's demands for secrecy, the good queen surreptitiously reveals to her son Benjamin that he and his eleven brothers will die should their pregnant mother's thirteenth child be a girl. In collusion with her condemned boys, the benevolent queen subverts her tyrannical husband's intentions without his knowing, thus keeping their sons alive and saving this father from committing a dozen murders.

Contrast this quiet betrayal of a husband by his wife with the mother-in-law's blatant lie in the same tale, a lie designed to malign and sentence to death her son's new and beautiful bride. The jealous mother-in-law throws unfounded suspicions at the innocent princess, accusing her of witchcraft because the girl does not speak or laugh, a silence maintained to fulfill a vow taken for seven years lest her brothers be "evermore changed into ravens" (62). The princess, of course, cannot defend herself against the wicked woman's accusation: to speak would be to turn against her brothers. But not to speak is to condemn herself to death. This story's crisis—for a girl to decide either to speak the truth and hurt (twelve) others, or to not say what she knows and thereby hurt herself—

uncannily replicates Brown and Gilligan's observations about girls' "voice" dilemmas. It echoes the no-win quandary girls in these studies have described: whether to speak honestly and maintain their sense of self or to preserve relationships at the cost of personal authenticity.

The brave princess's predicament in "The Twelve Brothers" vividly illustrates the plight of "silent" women discussed in *Women's Ways of Knowing*, women who have come to see their own words as weapons that will be used against them by others with power (24).[12] But this fairy-tale princess, whose resourcefulness stands out as uncharacteristic of women who have been forced into silence, can do nothing herself to resolve the impossible "voice" dilemma. It is only through an external force—the perfectly timed expiration of the seven enchanted years—that the princess—in the nick of time—escapes the flames at the stake (which are already licking her clothing), saves her brothers, and, finally, absolves herself of malicious slander. Gratified to discover that his wife's voicelessness was not a sign of her practicing "wicked tricks," the king immediately sees to it that his calumnious mother is herself deservedly silenced, once and for all.

Apart from the many girls and women in Grimm's tales who seek agency through deception or silent complicity, there are also a few "good" women in the tales who directly name and even act on what they want. All good wives fervently express their wishes for a child; Snow White longs for the tempting apple; Marlinchen, too, wants an apple from her mother's chest; and Rapunzel's mother fixes her sights on sumptuous lettuce leaves that rouse her appetite beyond containment. Consistently, the desired objects of these fairy-tale women are concrete in nature—stays and a comb, an apple, lettuce leaves, even a baby. What expressive women want delineates their circumscribed universe of desire and emphasizes their concern with the physical. However, whenever a female character in the tales articulates physical craving, satisfaction of that appetite leads to her death or another's suffering.[13]

Early in the plot of "Rapunzel," a mother must choose between appeasing her sensual appetite or keeping the long-awaited child she is carrying. Her choice of lettuce over infant results in her giving up the baby to the enchantress who owns the vegetable garden. The enchantress also expresses desire: as paradox would have it, the witch covets the baby growing inside the pregnant woman, and the happily married mother-to-be longs for the crop that the witch grows. Interestingly, both women dare to speak of and demand what they want, a striking recantation of the Freudian construct that aligns femininity with "being the object of someone else's desire, with having no active desire of one's own" (Benjamin 87). In "Rapunzel," articulation of desire brings both the mother and the enchantress a degree of agency, in that each gets what she wants, but unhappy consequences result: the mother loses her child and the witch eventually loses Rapunzel, too, unable to keep the young girl from becoming seduced by a prince's desire for her.

To desire, according to Jessica Benjamin, is to assert one's sexuality and felt passion. Desire in this sense is a kind of truth-telling forbidden to women, because such assertiveness of the self challenges that feminine ideal which insists on a woman's inhibition of her impulses. A "good mother" must learn, Benjamin maintains, "to accept the abrogation of her own will" (89). Thus, a woman trained to femininity is "unable to say 'I want that'. . ." (88); instead, she duplicitously masks or "selflessly" stifles her desire for individual fulfillment.

Women's lies play an important structural role in the fairy tales. So fundamental to each tale is women's deceptiveness that every falsehood uttered is a crucial narrative marker in the story's development. In "Hansel and Gretel," for example, Gretel's trickery at the oven door, like the first deceptive exploits of the stepmother, moves the story toward its reassuring climax and denouement: the death of the witch/bad mother, followed by the children's return to the father. By foiling the recalcitrant witch, Gretel upsets the maternal reign of terror and so helps to restore patriarchal control.

Reading Grimm's stories, we see writ large a portrait of female duplicity that, if left unexamined, feeds Freud's fallacious assumptions about women's disingenuous nature. Ironically, the plethora of lies told by female characters reveals the social truth of women's experience unacknowledged by Freudian analysis: that women's only source of power in patriarchy may be found through their successful attempts to deconstruct, undermine, and distort someone else's reality. Reconsidered within the context of patriarchal power, female duplicity in the tales represents women's moral limitations, which Freudians say result from penis envy, but rather result from social limitations placed upon all women and upon mothers in particular for their attempts to gain power under patriarchy. Liars, writes Adrienne Rich, "live in fear of losing control. . . ." Lies are a "false source of power" ("On Lies" 187–8, 190). Indeed, the only seemingly powerful women in Grimm's tales use what "false" power they have to deceive and harm young children. Thus, the good mother who does not connive can exert no lasting potency, while the more powerful witch or stepmother can pursue her diabolic and most "unmaternal" aims only by misleading men and children.

In fact, we join many other feminist critics in saying that the triumphant "happily ever after" grand finale is itself a kind of lie endemic to fairy tales. Brown and Gilligan, for example, report that in making up their own stories, girls like to use "happily ever after" endings to resolve painful dilemmas. This, the authors note, is more like "wishful thinking on their part, something heard in a fairy tale, a pleasing and acceptable cover for experiences of feeling left out and fears of being abandoned" (47). The fairy tales' "happily ever after" seems to accomplish more than simply reassuring readers by bringing "rightful" stature to the romantic patriarch. Happy endings also seal behind their thin facade ineffable female anger, aggression, fear of powerlessness, fear of men not pronouncing them sexually desirable, and, most of all, women's fear of being condemned for having spoken authentically of their uncomfortable feelings and experiences. The Good and True Princess has learned to maintain silence, for she comes to see that her truths would be punished as disruptive.[14]

Losing their truths, girls lose their selves; what they are left holding onto is the seductive, tranquilizing myth of perfect marital happiness. In these fairy tales, the female character's "voice," the ability to make oneself felt and heard, can find form only in acts of fraudulence and vengeful deception. Perhaps the stepmother's voice of bitterness and frustration with limiting narrative and social conventions is "the roar" that lies on "the other side of silence" (George Eliot, *Middlemarch*, qtd. in *Women's Ways* 3).

"Happily Ever After"—the Fantasy of the Fathers: Only One Woman Allowed

In the romance story it inscribes for girls and women, patriarchal culture in the West creates a subplot, the separation of girls from women, especially their mothers. Carol Gilligan has observed in her studies that adolescent girls "have to give up their relationship with the world of girls and women, the world they have lived and loved in . . . for the sake of relationships that have been prescribed for them in male-led societies" (Debold et al. 13). For acceding to patriarchal demands, girls are promised a "happy ending" that will act like a "balm for the wounding losses inflicted." In response, girls learn to sacrifice all other relationships as they search "for true love, a perfect love that will never disappoint" (70).

This romance story, enshrined in fairy tales, divides girls from each other, from themselves, and from adult women, making them habitual competitors whose singular goal is to attract the man of their dreams.[15] The importance of pleasing a man and being chosen by him from among all others distorts women's relationships (Debold et al. 17), between contemporaries and among members of different generations. Reading fairy tale upon fairy tale, girl readers come to see that they must relinquish ties to other women so that all their energies can be harnessed in preparation for the fiercely competitive race toward men's approval. Trained to regard other women as adversaries, female protagonists in the tales never find contentment in the company of compassionate mothers, other female relations, or friends. Small wonder that the adolescent who yearns for "happily ever after" envisions in her fantasy no women at all— neither good mother nor stepmother, no sisters nor friends—only a handsome, well-born mate or (if she is prepubescent) a noble, protective father.

Through the pattern of idyllic endings that repeatedly separate girls from mother figures, characters and readers alike learn the patriarchal lesson that other women are not even remotely connected to the health and happiness of growing girls. Yet, Cinderella, Snow White, and Rapunzel all have "good" mothers at the beginning of their stories, women who wish for the birth of a long-desired child. In none of these tales, however, does the daughter find friendship or support from any other girl or woman once her original mother dies. Both Cinderella's stepsisters and her stepmother harass Cinderella as their mutual rival; moreover, the two sisters are themselves opponents for the same marital prize. Even more isolated is Snow White, for whom bonding with another female is impossible. Since her interactions with women are narrowed to frightening encounters with the wily queen, Snow White is left to find comradeship and guidance from seven diminutive men. Rapunzel, at her most wretched moment, cast out by the witch into the desert, has only the company of her newborn twin babes. All three fairy tales reach a proper patriarchal conclusion, each woman in the castle with her prince, shut away from mother and sisters alike: these tales offer readers no imaginable female ally. Indeed, the "triumphant" exclusion of adult female characters in the final narrative frame signifies a "happy" return to male dominion.

In what is essentially a male-centered genre, only boys can be allies to girls, notably to any sisters who take initiative in the face of treachery. For example, in "Hansel and Gretel," "The Twelve Brothers," and "The Juniper Tree," both female and male siblings experience ill-treatment. Support comes from the loving concern they show for each other from the start. In the adventure that befalls her and her brother Hansel, Gretel takes an active role in tricking the witch and then killing her. The children's cleverness effects their return to their father's house, a place made safe by the heartless stepmother's death. With witch and stepmother out of the way, heroic Hansel and Gretel join their father to celebrate victory over feminine evil. Thus, enterprising girls can contribute *with* their brave brothers to the demise of dangerous women, but should those girls remain cunning as they mature, they become witch or stepmother and suffer her same sorry fate.

A similar thematic pattern unfolds in "The Twelve Brothers": a brave sister bonds with her brothers to triumph over a witch's spell and a stepmother's murderous wishes. Likewise, Marlinchen in "The Juniper Tree" works together with the enchanted bird that is really her brother to bring Hans back to human form and to lure the stepmother to death. But even with the stepmother gone, "The Juniper Tree" does not end with the good mother's resurrection, which might, in this world of transformations, have easily followed the revivification of her son. For, as we have seen, a mother must not be part of the conventional "happy ending." The children's devotion to her and hers to them would challenge the patriarch's domestic reign, calling into question the tale's carefully crafted fiction, which maintains male supremacy. An active (and thus, by definition, evil) mother does not escape unchallenged when she exerts authority; instead, she is cut down at the hands of her stepchildren, who struggle courageously to defeat her. Thus, as "The Juniper Tree" ends, these two courageous children appear safe with a father who, after all, never seemed to respond to his son's sudden and prolonged absence from the household; nor did he even suspect his wife's apparent acts of malice toward his children. At the end of the tale, this useless man has been reconstructed: by virtue of his children's unquestioned forgiveness, he emerges, like many other negligent fathers in the tales, a "figure of male good . . . beyond moral law and human decency" (Dworkin, 41). Clearly, as representatives of patriarchy, immobilized fairy-tale fathers seem immune to serious criticism.

So it is that the weak, emotionally and physically absent fairy-tale father always wins out. In the six stories we have studied, not one of the fathers has a dominant role in the plot. Cinderella's father doesn't seem to see or protect his daughter from the stepmother's abuse and he disappears for most of the story—except for an odd scene in which he tries to chop down his daughter's pigeon house and pear tree because he suspects she is hiding within. The king in "Snow White" vanishes without notice before he can help his child survive her stepmother's terrible tricks. In "Rapunzel," the father gives in to his wife's desires even if this means giving their child away to the enchantress. In "The Twelve Brothers," the seemingly powerful father-king is tricked by his honorable wife, his daughter, and his youngest son, who successfully collaborate to keep the twelve boys alive. And in this tale, the royal husband of the young heroine allows his mother, the older queen, to make all the arrangements for a death by fire of the young bride he loves.

Why in a patriarchy, where the rule of men is law, are so many fairy-tale fathers portrayed as weak and ineffective? In a critique of Freud's essay "Some Psychical Consequences of the Anatomical Distinction Between the Sexes," Juliet Mitchell discusses the hold that patriarchy has on all of us. She describes "the way in which a patriarchal society bequeaths its structure to each of us . . . gives us, that is, the cultural air we breathe, the ideas of the world in which we are born and which, unless patriarchy is demolished, we will pass on willy-nilly to our children and our children's children" (231–232). "Whether or not the actual father is there does not affect the perpetuation of the patriarchal culture within the psychology of the individual," Mitchell continues. "[P]resent or absent," she emphasizes, "the father always has his place" (231–2).

These fathers in Grimm's, although ineffectual, do have an important narrative function. For if the patriarch were strong and influential, the witch, the stepmother, or the evil mother-in-law could not be a controlling force in the story. It is the father's powerlessness, or absence, that makes possible the temporary and threatening ascendance of the evil stepmother over the helpless, "feminine" ingenue. When patriarchy is menaced by the reign of an aggressive woman, her defeat ensures its reinstatement. Moreover, the resulting triumph of the royal couple (or the motherless family unit) strengthens patriarchy's hold on readers and characters alike, precisely because it has been momentarily endangered.

To demonstrate the power of male myths in shaping portraits of women's relationships with one another, we can turn again to feminist psychological findings about adolescent daughters. In fact, psychologists find that, unlike pubescent boys who respond to a strong imperative to separate from the mother and all that she represents, girls thrive on defining themselves in connection with their mothers (Apter 5; Chodorow 167; Gilligan, *Different Voice* 8; Surrey 55). Contradicting Freud's view that girls do and must reject their mothers, feminist research gives the lie to pervasive "happy endings" that systematically exclude enduring connections between girls and women.

Projecting male-centered myths of "normal" adolescent development, men craft tales in which maternal figures are absent in the ideal world of "happily ever after." The tales reinforce the story of a boy's journey toward autonomy in which the "good" mother of infancy dies—never to be resurrected. Perhaps, male fantasy warns, *that* mother's presence would "reduce" the boy to so-called regressive dependency. Or perhaps male fantasy creates stories in which the girl's "good" mother also necessarily dies; thus, she cannot hamper the boy in his pursuit of the heroine by creating a contest for attention that the hero (be he prince or father) might feel, unconsciously, that he cannot win.

Clearly, these stories enact a cycle of female disconnection. To forge a maternal bond, will the younger woman in the story have no choice but to imitate her birth mother, leaving the girl unable to imagine anything for herself but death or the familiar life script of helpless subordination recited by worthy queens? The growing girl in Grimm's tales, needing female models to empower her, is abandoned by women through early death or fiendish harassment. This cycle of female disconnection is perpetuated when the fairy-tale princess herself turns queen—and follows the only model available to her and in maturity becomes a good queen. Soon after childbirth, she either dies or lives to react jealously against her beautiful (step)daughter (Gilbert and Gubar 38–9).

For rebelling against society's rules for women, the willful, self-serving mother figure pays the ultimate price, revealing indisputably the vantage point from which these stories are told. But for whom is the ending happy? Given the aggressive mother's demise, it is no wonder that women and girls worry about overstepping the line of feminine conduct and incurring male rejection or social ostracism. The awful fate of the witch-mother, and the fact that *her* story is never told except as a subtext of warning to wayward young women and girls, sanctions girls' turning against "unfeminine" activity or models in pursuit of that dreamed-for "happy ending."

Encouragingly, contemporary feminist fairy tales, aimed at countering the stereotypes behind these stories' familiar conventions, avoid conclusions that feature only a princess and a prince, sometimes attended by the benevolent father figure.[16] These refreshing new stories dismiss male fantasy with its impossible standards of female goodness and "happy endings" that turn woman against woman, with each woman hoping to secure, at great sacrifice, the scarce rewards attainable only through slavish conformity to patriarchal ideals.

As Marcia K. Lieberman has pointed out, "happily ever after" comes right after courtship, a period "which is magnified into the most important and exciting part of a girl's life, brief though [it] is, because it is the part of her life in which she most counts as a person herself" (199). Women's real lives after marriage would not be written into fairy tales because, in ordinary life, modern adult women often defy male fantasy by eschewing total dependence on men and seeking gratifying relationships with women. But in the fairy tales, "happily ever after" means the prince and the princess alone. It means a young man enjoying dominance and the right to choose, which he inherits from his father before him; it means a young woman in the prime of her life who has lost not only a healthy relationship with her mother and all other women, but also her own identity and voice. Virginia Woolf reminds us in *A Room of One's Own* that women's relationships with one another in fiction are far too simply portrayed. Depicted rarely as friends or as mothers and daughters, they are almost always seen by and in relation to men (86). "And," Woolf adds with an almost audible sigh, "how small a part of a woman's life is that . . ." (86).

Conclusion

Renowned and full of charm, read or projected on a screen, fairy tales grasp the imagination of the individual consumer; on a broader, social level, the stories' repeated happy endings secure the hold of cultural archetypes and fantasies depicting chivalric love and women-in-waiting. Just as Freud's ideas about feminine development can be read not as "truth" but as an exposition of Victorian patriarchal ideology by which girls are prepared for womanhood, so fairy tales similarly reveal the deeply etched, subtle workings of entrenched, cultural artifice that indoctrinates boys and girls to accepted male and female roles.

While it may be true, as Marina Warner says, that fairy tales irresistibly create within the human imagination the utopian possibility that "anything can happen" (xx), it is no less true that the commonly retold stories severely limit girls' imagined selves, their ideas about adult relationships, and, ultimately, their destinies.

We believe that the fantasy of women rewarded for abiding mistreatment and waiting patiently for things to happen—wonderful "things" that in the stories eventually *do* happen, against all odds—hampers the initiative, will, and ambitions of girls: for they live in a real world replete with moral injustice, where "good" but long-suffering women often finish last.

While the power of fairy tales resides largely in intoxicating general readers with the image of a longed-for land of enchantment, the narratives can be said to cast a particularly potent, even poisonous spell on growing girls by molding their imaginations in much the same way as Cinderella's sisters' feet were cut—to fit the shape of male fantasy.

Time and again, the compliant, patient, lovely princesses-to-be in the tales are assured their handsome royal mates. But in real life, neither quiet endurance nor physical beauty nor aggressive pursuit succeeds in capturing the attention of whatever man a fantasy-smitten heterosexual girl might regard as her perfect "prince." Moreover, chasing that romantic illusion and the pain of its inevitable demise leaves young women little psychic space or time for other more creative endeavors. Looking for the one and only "Mr. Right" who does not exist and will not appear—except in fairy tales and cinema—can become, for middle-class girls, in particular, a full-time, doomed preoccupation.[17]

Holding this fantasy about men—ungrounded in real life relationships—seems more true for white than for black teenagers, whose mothers frequently tell their growing daughters that men are unreliable and that women need to remain independent and pursue self-sufficiency as well as education "through their own efforts."(Joseph, "Roles and Functions" 107). At the same time that the institution of marriage remains "ever-enticing" ("Roles and Functions" 112), Gloria Joseph hears in interviews with daughters recalling their mothers' teachings that African American women overwhelmingly give realistic, "sensitively coded messages and advice" to adolescents, ensuring that teenagers know that intimacy with men necessarily involves "inevitable problems that lie in waiting" (121).

Joseph contrasts these interviews with the responses of white, middle-class daughters to the same questionnaire. She observes that "there was more romanticism in the messages from white mothers. 'Marry for love' was a popular response" (125). Predictably, the responses of working-class white women were closer to those of black women, confirming that mothers who struggle every day with the realities of classism and/or racism are less likely to depict naïve, fanciful portraits of men and marital arrangements to impressionable daughters. Yet, two recent articles in *Ebony* magazine—"Plan the Perfect Wedding" and "Romance and the Single Mom" (June 1997)—perpetuate the myth of a "Mr. Right," as does HBO's advertisement in *Ebony* for the fairy-tale series "Happily Ever After" (May 1997). These titles suggest how great the challenge is to transcend media-promulgated cultural imperatives for all women to believe in and search out idyllic love.

The paradox is that fairy tales, clearly the stuff of fiction, portray a world of dubious magical circumstance that young readers often receive as a prescription for the way life should be. Thus, the many innocent glimpses of perfect heterosexual romance, of punishment deserved and dealt out, of handsome, winning heroes and of beautiful, obedient heroines, may actually increase girls' and women's daily anxieties. This is because real possibilities and conditions invariably fall far short of the tales' melodramatic intrigues, which typically end in blissful marriage with a prince. Matina Horner's early research reveals the extent to which many girls and women, limited, perhaps, by having internalized the tales' restrictive marriage plot, have feared the social costs of visible, ambitious achievement in the world. Competitive success against men is perceived as incompatible with femininity and too often leads to consequences of social rejection and acute discomfort (cited in *Different Voice* 14–15).

The other kind of competition that thwarts women's development—competition *between* women in the unrelenting contest for men's favor—affects women at least as negatively as does women's reluctance to show their true potential in contests with men. Louise Bernikow writes of the effect that the "Cinderella" story has had on her attitudes toward women:

> I carry [the story of Cinderella] with me for the rest of my life. It is a story about women alone together and they are each other's enemies. This is more powerful as a lesson than the ball, the Prince or the glass slipper. The echoes of "Cinderella" in other fairy tales, in myth and literature, are about how awful women are to each other. The girl onscreen, as I squirm in my seat, needs to be saved. A man will come and save her. Some day my Prince will come. (18)

Bernikow writes retrospectively as an adult. But one need look only at contemporary magazines directed specifically at teens to see how mired in fairy-tale fictions middle-class adolescents still are today. Articles such as "My Mom's Drinking Was Ruining My Life" (August 1996, *Seventeen*); "Quiz: Is Your Mom Driving You Crazy" (June 1996, *Seventeen*, cover story); and "A Home of Their Own" (September 1996, *Seventeen*)—an article about sexually promiscuous girls who come from families with dysfunctional mothers—"Toxic Friends: Are They Poisoning Your Life?" (October 1996, *Teen*); " 'Call of the Wild': Is Your Best Friend Bad News?" (February 1996, *Seventeen*) all resound with and thereby legitimize the distrust young girls are taught to feel for their mothers and their female friends through messages from popular culture.[18]

In addition, the editors of *Seventeen* and *Teen* magazines count on luring their readers with headlines recalling the fairy tales' obsession with females winning coveted male attention: "Find Out How to Get Guys to Notice You"; "Your Crush: How to Make the First Move"; "Guys to Drool over and Dream About"; "Are You Guy Obsessed?" Just as in Grimm's fairy tales where the handsome prince is the focus of the girl's attention, "hot new guys" shine forth today from the glossy pages of *Seventeen* and *Teen*, billed as modern day princes—"guys you love"— ideals who represent the possibility of absolute fulfillment and yet, in reality, will never be possessed by any reader no matter what she does to shrink, stretch, color, or cleanse her body.

Not only cultural sources, but psychological studies, too, confirm that warnings about female disobedience—such as those repeatedly implied in the tales—prevent girls from taking charge of their lives and breaking free from the restraints of conformity. In Grimm's, it is the "bad" women who express hateful jealousy or create conflict in relationships. Their rage shatters the fictional illusion of everlasting interpersonal harmony, a fantasy that is revived only when that disruptive woman's voice is, at last, silenced.

Meeting at the Crossroads by Brown and Gilligan tells of the many adolescent girls they interviewed who feel the best way to negotiate conflict is by declining to ever mention their hurt or angry feelings. The authors call these emotional facades "happy endings," like "something heard in a fairy tale . . . a pleasing and acceptable cover for experiences of feeling left out and fears of being abandoned" (47). This masked response to conflict is characterized in Grimm's by the countless heroines who are never disagreeable even in the face of emotional cruelty and abuse.

Aware that they must be polite to be included, girls willingly subjugate themselves to the "tyranny of nice and kind" (53): "'It's better to be nice than not nice—you get more friends . . . and relationships,'" one young girl confides (45). Most of the girls interviewed by Brown and Gilligan assess the social risk of speaking up and decide to sign a kind of Faustian contract: they sell their honesty and receive instead social acceptability, which, in fairy tales, includes having a man's protection from other, nasty women. Girls quickly learn, the Laurel School study shows, that if they speak about what they really think or feel, people will not want to be with them (218).[19]

The fantasies of the fairy tales are living today in the dilemmas girls face in school and at home. They are illustrated in and perpetuated by popular magazines that feature stories, advice columns, and regular quizzes to test knowledge of current beauty standards and successful flirting techniques for the contemporary dating marketplace. Easily consumed by impressionable adolescents, these publications resonate with images of princesses, princes, and stepmothers internalized at a tender age, before girls have acquired tools for questioning them. There can be no doubt that these myths learned in childhood continue to leave an indelible mark on girls' and women's identities. As Carolyn Heilbrun says, "the chief source of patriarchal power . . . is embodied in unquestioned narrative." Speaking of the stories that "come to us like the murmuring of our mothers, telling us of what conventions demand" (128), Heilbrun then asks: "Since the male plots, unchanged, will not do for women, and since there are so few female plots, how are we to make the new fictions that will sustain us?" (129).

We might answer Carolyn Heilbrun by saying that, before creating new fictions, we must deeply understand the old ones and their hold over us. As co-authors, we have studied Grimm's fairy tales, rereading, talking, and writing about them with images of the real girls we know in mind. Not surprisingly, we come across a reflexive sort of problem: once girls, the two of us internalized the stories' sexist messages long ago, hearing them read by our mothers, who had in turn learned their scripts from their mothers before them. In fact, we would venture to guess that these stories are kept spinning mostly by women, who take pleasure in returning, along with their children, to visions of perfect love, sweet revenge, and wondrous transformation.

But to free our daughters, our students, our young women friends, we must first free ourselves from the delicious fictions that have held us captive in subtle and penetrating ways. Perhaps through a new, woman-centered sociopsychological understanding of the tales, accomplished through the lens of feminist theory—the work of Terri Apter, Jessica Benjamin, Lyn Mikel Brown, Nancy Chodorow, Carol Gilligan, Jean Baker Miller, and others—we can begin to transform our expectations for ourselves and for our daughters and therein sow the seeds for new and liberating fictions and realities.

Notes

Our gratitude goes to Wendy Goulston and Kathy Klein for the substantive and stylistic suggestions they made that helped us to sharpen our essay.

1. In male-dominated cultures, children are taught to see the father as more worthy of respect than the mother, whom the children typically consider less authoritative. Often in literature and in life, however, it is the mother who serves as parental scapegoat, culturally assigned blame for "her" children's failings (Caplan 65; Chodorow and Contratto 80). Polarized fantasies about male and female parents show a kind of psychological splitting. As Jessica Benjamin writes, "The myth of a good paternal authority that is rational and prevents regression purges the father of all terror and . . . displaces it onto the mother, so that she bears the badness for both of them. The myth of the good father (and the dangerous mother) is not easily dispelled" (136).

2. The concept of "the resisting reader" comes from Judith Fetterley's book of the same title. It refers to a critical posture that feminist readers reading male-centered literature can take to overcome the pervasive influence of the male viewpoint on their reading, their thinking, and their identities. Writes Patrocinio Schweickart: this process (called "immasculation" in Fetterley's work) can be "disrupted . . . by exposing it to consciousness, by disclosing the androcentricity of what has customarily passed for the universal" (Schweickart 41–42).

3. *The Complete Grimm's Fairy Tales* (New York: Pantheon, 1972), 121. All further references to fairy tales by the Brothers Grimm will be to this edition, followed by page numbers in the text.

4. Gerda Schulman notes in her article about stepmothers and clinical practice that stepchildren commonly and quite naturally project their feelings of loss and anger onto any woman who plays the original mother's role and thus represents for them the family disruption. Yet these projections, writes Schulman, do not resolve the children's emotional pain, nor are they constructive for the child in negotiating the new family constellation. Schulman's clinical experience and conclusions cast doubt on Bettelheim's interpretation that the child's disdain for the stepmother in fairy tales is "healthy."

5. Reference to Bettelheim's ideas (though not necessarily with attribution) appeared as recently as July 30, 1995 in *The New York Times Book Review*, 17. The reviewer, Barbara Thompson, in writing about *The Lion's Whiskers, An Ethiopian Folktale* by Nancy Raines Day (New York: Scholastic, 1995), notes, "Psychologists tell us that the splitting of mothers into the good "real" mother and the bad "false" mother is the child's way of seeing his own powerful mother as uniformly accepting and benevolent, all negativity displaced to the Other One."

Furthermore, our own observations reveal that Bettelheim's ideas about fairy tales and an individual's early "normative" maternal experience are frequently disseminated (without being deconstructed) in college courses concerning child development and children's literature.

6. We recognize these representations of angelic and demonic motherhood as male fantasy, particularly of men living in a patriarchy and formed by its ideology and culture. As early as 1932, Karen Horney saw that men frequently "objectified" and thus projected their dread of women, deeply rooted in distrust and resentment of maternal biological powers, as artistic expressions. They thus transform their own inner fears of women into "the very personification of what is sinister" (135). The evil women in fairy tales, for example, stand as projections of male rather than female-originated fantasy. See Freud, "Female Sexuality" 227, 234–5, 241.

7. Presumably, Surrey's reflection is based on her practice of predominantly white women and girls. However, studies indicate that African American daughters view their mothers with less contempt and more admiration than their white counterparts (Joseph, "Roles and Functions" 92; Lewis 128). This would suggest that mother-blaming is less prevalent in the African American community.

8. Clearly, it is impossible and fallacious to offer a definition of "good mothering" given the diversity of cultural norms, personal style, situation, and individual children's needs. Yet the evil stepmothers in Grimm's seem to defy any reasonable assumptions about what mothers do constructively and responsibly in raising their children. See, for example, Sara Ruddick's description of "maternal practice" as "works of preservative love, nurturance, and training" (17).

9. In her work on Freud, Juliet Mitchell describes his 1935 essay, "Some Psychical Consequences of the Anatomical Distinction Between the Sexes," as distinctively revealing the pervasive power of the father. She establishes that Freud's theories, inarguably rooted in male paradigms, offer "a key to the understanding of the oppression of women under patriarchy" (232).

10. Interestingly, however, the harmful spells that evil women cast in fairy tales provide only a temporary means of their effecting agency. As literary critic Nancy Walker points out, these evil spells and wicked transformations do not lead to lasting, beneficial change in these female characters' circumstances (46).

11. Ruth Bottigheimer reminds us that Eve was "the first to be deceived and led astray" (72). This biblical foremother of sinfulness is widely recognized by scholars from different disciplines and persuasions as a symbol of warning against women's deceitfulness altogether. In *Grimm's Bad Girls and Bold Boys*, Bottigheimer points to a 1497 German tract about women's guilt in paradise, a source from which she indicates that female characters in Grimm's replicate Eve's original "misuse of her voice" in consorting verbally with the serpent and then deceiving Adam. According to Bottigheimer, the "mother of us all" is the literary progenitor for widespread images of women's dishonesty in fairy tales.

12. In their recent collection of essays, *Knowledge, Difference and Power*, the authors of *Women's Ways of Knowing* reconsider the name of their first category of knowers used in their original research, "silence." They have determined now that a more apt term would have been "silenced." Their distinction draws attention to the difference between those upon whom silence is imposed by threat or force and those who choose silence as a strategy for listening and knowing (Belenky 427; Goldberger 346).

13. Girls and women in our culture, in fact, are likely to be reprimanded or even stigmatized when they acknowledge and communicate their own physical longings. As the authors of *Mother Daughter Revolution* write, their "expressions of desire—curiosity, outspokenness, pleasure—are seen as sexual or are sexualized by the adults around them" (50). This insight helps explain the punitive consequences of female characters' expressions of desire in fairy tales.

14. Marina Warner cites the many traditions that have regarded silence, along with submissiveness and restraint, as the feminine ideal. Like Bottigheimer (see note 14 above), Warner goes back to Eve's moral transgression, after which "even fair speech becomes untrustworthy on a woman's lips" (30).

15. Mothers or women in care-taking roles who advocate the sacrifice of female relationships in the competitive race for romantic success with men unwittingly collude in their daughters' loss of empowerment. However, studies show African American girls, in particular, identifying with and respecting, not competing with, their mothers and other women in their communities (Joseph, "Roles and Traditions" 94–107; Robinson and Ward 92). Specifically, Robinson and Ward explain the socializing influence in the black community toward "human interdependence," which they distinguish from "Eurocentric principles of excessive individuality and autonomy" (92) that underlie competitive female relationships. Observing mutuality and sisterhood between and among generations of African American women, Joseph concludes that "It was and still is necessary for Black mothers and daughters to collaborate in their fight against powerful societal conditions . . ." ("Roles and Functions" 94). African American mothers empower their daughters by serving as role models in their neighborhoods: They are "women who share with, look out for, and help each other" (101). In this way, they foster connectedness, not competitiveness, with others, including girls and women. Patricia Hill Collins adds to this analysis in her discussion of "othermothers" who, in women-centered families in the African American community, "foster an early identification with a much wider range of models of Black womanhood, which can lead to a greater sense of empowerment in young Black girls" (54).

16. See Jack Zipes, *Don't Bet on the Prince* and *The Outspoken Princess and The Gentle Knight*; Angela Carter, *The Bloody Chamber*, New York: Harper and Row, 1979; *Tatterhood and Other Tales*, ed. by Ethel Johnston Phelps, NY: The Feminist Press, 1978; and Nancy A. Walker's literary analysis of feminist fairy tales, "Twice Upon a Time," in *The Disobedient Writer*.

17. *The Rules: Time-Tested Secrets for Capturing the Heart of Mr. Right*, the 1996 best-seller designed for middle-class women's consumption, underscores the never-ending pursuit of Prince Charming that restricts and derails women's intellectual and creative drives. An example of the rewards to be expected from following its counsel: "What can you expect when you do *The Rules*? The answer is total adoration from the man of your dreams." Ellen Fein and Sherrie Schneider, 155.

18. While the scope of this essay cannot encompass a comparative study of different messages that popular culture sends to ethnically diverse young women, there are apparent distinctions that can be made upon casual review of several

women's magazines. In *Ebony* and *Essence*, as examples of publications directed at African American women, we see content and advertisements that perpetuate fantasies of romantic heterosexual love, but there are, on balance, noticeably fewer articles that highlight antagonism between girls or between young girls and older women. Additionally, these two magazines seem not to feature—in their headlines or in regular columns—tactics for "capturing" men and offer instead more coverage of real, unromantic complexities in the lives of heterosexual couples: divorce, infertility, single parenthood. Yet, it is important to note that *Seventeen* and *Teen* are produced and marketed exclusively for high school women (albeit with predominantly white models and "cover girls"), while *Ebony* and *Essence* are aimed at the young to middle-aged African American woman. Youth magazines (such as *Vibe*), directed to African American teens in particular, extend to an audience of both sexes. A substantive comparison of popular culture messages that middle-class teenage girls in different racial groups receive from the magazines that entertain and guide them requires more research than is appropriate to our study, thus suggesting interesting directions for future work in this area.

19. In the Laurel School study, Sonia, an African American girl, stands out from many of her eleven-year-old classmates as being "confident and clear" (73). An outsider in a white society, she has felt "unfairness and exclusion" (70), yet she has remained connected to her feelings and what she knows. Unlike many of the girls in the study who are tyrannized by "nice and kind," Sonia, say the authors, "tells a story of courage and resistance in bold straightforward terms" (73).

Works Cited

Apter, Terri. *Altered Loves: Mothers and Daughters During Adolescence*. New York: St. Martin's Press, 1990.

Barry, Rebecca. "My Mom's Drinking was Ruining My Life." *Seventeen*. August 1996: 222 + .

Barzilai, Shuli. "Reading 'Snow White': The Mother's Story." *Signs: Journal of Women in Culture and Society* 15.3 (Spring 1990): 515–534.

Belenky, Mary. "Public Homeplaces: Nurturing the Development of People, Families and Communities." *Knowledge, Difference and Power: Essays Inspired by Women's Ways of Knowing*. Ed. Goldberger, Tarule, Clinchy, and Belenky. New York: Basic Books, 1996. 393–430.

Belenky, Mary, Blythe Clinchy, Nancy Goldberger, and Jill Tarule. *Women's Ways of Knowing*. New York: Basic Books, 1986.

Benjamin, Jessica. *Bonds of Love: Psychoanalysis, Feminism, and the Problem of Domination*. New York: Pantheon Books, 1989.

Bernikow, Louise. *Among Women*. New York: Harper and Row, 1980.

Bettelheim, Bruno. *The Uses of Enchantment: The Meaning and Importance of Fairy Tales*. New York: Alfred A. Knopf, 1976.

Bing, Vanessa and Pamela Trotman Reid. "Unknown Women and Unknowing

Research: Consequences of Color and Class in Feminist Psychology." *Knowledge, Difference and Power: Essays Inspired by Women's Ways of Knowing*. Ed. Nancy Goldberger, Jill Tarule, Blythe Clinchy and Mary Belenky. New York: Basic Books, 175–202.

Bottigheimer, Ruth B. *Grimms' Bad Girls and Bad Boys: The Moral and Social Vision of the Tales*. New Haven: Yale UP, 1987.

Brown, Lyn Mikel. "Telling a Girl's Life: Self-Actualization as a Form of Resistance." *Women, Girls & Psychotherapy: Reframing Resistance*. Ed. Carol Gilligan, Annie G. Rogers, and Deborah L. Tolman. New York: The Haworth Press, 1991. 71–86.

Brown, Lyn and Carol Gilligan. *Meeting at the Crossroads: Women's Psychology and Girl's Development*. Cambridge: Harvard University Press, 1992.

Caplan, Paula. "Making Mother-Blaming Visible: The Emperor's New Clothes." *Woman-Defined Motherhood*. Ed. Jane Price Knowles and Ellen Cole. Binghamton, NY: Harrington Park Press, 1990. 61–71.

Chernin, Kim. *Reinventing Eve*. New York: Harper and Row, 1987.

———. *The Hungry Self: Women, Eating and Identity*. New York: Times Books, 1985.

Chodorow, Nancy. *The Reproduction of Mothering: Psychoanalysis and the Sociology of Gender*. Berkeley: U of California P, 1978.

Chodorow, Nancy and Susan Contratto. "The Fantasy of the Perfect Mother." *Feminism and Psychoanalytic Theory*. Nancy Chodorow. New Haven: Yale UP, 1989. 79–96.

Collins, Patricia Hill. "The Meaning of Motherhood in Black Culture and Black Mother-Daughter Relationships." *Double Stitch: Black Women Write about Mothers and Daughters*. Ed. Patricia Bell-Scott, Beverly Guy-Sheftall, Jacqueline Jones Royster, Janet Sims-Wood, Miriam DeCosta-Willis, and Lucie Fultz. Boston: Beacon Press, 1991. 42–60.

De Beauvoir, Simone. *The Second Sex*. New York: Alfred A. Knopf, Inc., 1953.

Debold, Elizabeth, Marie Wilson and Idelisse Malave. *Mother Daughter Revolution*. Reading: Addison-Wesley, 1993.

Dworkin, Andrea. *Woman Hating*. New York: E.P. Dutton, 1974.

Fein, Ellen and Sherrie Schneider. *The Rules: Time Tested Secrets for Capturing the Heart of Mr. Right*. New York: Warner, 1995.

Flax, Jane. "The Conflict Between Nurturance and Autonomy in Mother-Daughter Relationships and Within Feminism." *Women and Mental Health*. Ed. Elizabeth Howell and Marjorie Bayes. New York: Basic Books, 1981. 51–69.

Freud, Sigmund. "Female Sexuality." *The Standard Edition of The Complete Psychological Works of Sigmund Freud*. Ed. James Strachey. Vol. 21. London: Hogarth Press, 1961. 225–243.

———. "Some Psychical Consequences of the Anatomical Distinction Between the Sexes." *The Standard Edition of The Complete Psychological Works of Sigmund Freud*. Ed. James Strachey. Vol. 19. London: Hogarth Press, 1961.

Gilbert, Sandra and Susan Gubar. *The Madwoman in the Attic*. New Haven: Yale UP, 1979.

Gilligan, Carol. *In a Different Voice: Psychological Theory and Women's Development*. Cambridge: Harvard UP, 1982.

Gilligan, Carol, Annie Rogers, and Deborah L. Tolman. Eds. *Women, Girls and Psychotherapy: Reframing Resistance*. Binghamton: Haworth Press, 1991.

Golberger, Nancy. "Cultural Imperatives and Diversity in Ways of Knowing." *Knowledge, Difference and Power*. Ed. Nancy Goldberger, Jill Tarule, Blythe Clinchy and Mary Belenky. New York: Basic Books, 1996. 335–371.

Grimm's Brothers. *The Complete Grimm's Fairy Tales*. New York: Pantheon, 1972.

Guy-Sheftall, Beverly. "Mothers and Daughters: A Black Perspective." Unpublished address given at Marymount College, Tarrytown, NY, 1986.

Heilbrun, Carolyn G. "What was Penelope Unweaving?" *Hamlet's Mother and Other Women*. New York: Ballantine Books, 1990. 120–130.

———. *Writing a Woman's Life*. New York: Ballantine Books, 1988.

Herman, Judith Lewis and Helen Block Lewis. "Anger in the Mother-Daughter Relationship." *The Psychology of Today's Woman: New Psychoanalytic Visions*. Ed. Toni Bernay and Dorothy Cantor. Cambridge: Harvard UP, 1980.

Horney, Karen. "The Dread of Women." *Feminine Psychology*. Ed. Harold Kelman. New York: Norton 1967. 133–146.

Joseph, Gloria. "Black Mothers and Daughters: Their Roles and Functions in American Society." *Common Differences: Conflicts in Black and White Perspectives*. Ed. Gloria Joseph and Jill Lewis. New York: Doubleday, 1981. 75–126.

Joseph, Gloria. "Black Mothers and Daughters: Traditional and New Perspectives." *Double Stitch: Black Women Write About Mothers and Daughters*. Ed. Patricia Bell-Scott, Beverly Guy Sheftall, Jacqueline Jones Royster, Janet Sims-Wood, Miriam DeCosta-Willis and Lucie Fultz. Boston: Beacon Press, 1991. 94–106.

Keresy, Maggie. "Toxic Friends: Are They Poisoning Your Life?" *Teen,* October 1996: 32.

Lewis, Jill. "Mothers, Daughters, and Feminism." *Common Differences: Conflicts in Black and White Perspectives*. Ed. Gloria Joseph and Jill Lewis. New York: Doubleday, 1981. 127–148.

Lieberman, Marcia K. "'Some Day My Prince Will Come': Female Acculturation through the Fairy Tale." *Don't Bet on the Prince*. Ed. Jack Zipes. New York: Routledge, 1989. 185–200.

Livers, Eileen. "'Call of the Wild': Is Your Best Friend Bad News?" *Seventeen,* February 1996. 108–111.

Miller, Jean Baker. *Towards a New Psychology of Women*. Boston: Beacon Press, 1975.

Mitchell, Juliet. "On Freud and the Distinction Between the Sexes." *Women, the Longest Revolution*. New York: Pantheon, 1966. 221–232.

"Quiz: Is Your Mom Driving You Crazy?" *Seventeen,* June 1996.

Rich, Adrienne. *Of Woman Born*. New York: W.W. Norton, 1976.

———. "Women and Honor: Some Notes on Lying." *On Lies, Secrets and Silence*. New York: W.W. Norton, 1979. 185–194.

Robinson, Tracy and Janie Victoria Ward. "'A Belief in Self Far Greater Than Anyone's Disbelief': Cultivating Resistance Among African American Female

Adolescents." *Women, Girls and Psychotherapy: Reframing Resistance.* Ed. Carol Gilligan, Annie G. Rogers, and Deborah L. Tolman. Binghamton, NY: Haworth Press, 1991. 87–103.

Rowe, Karen E. "Feminism and Fairy Tales." *Don't Bet on the Prince.* Ed. Jack Zipes. New York: Routledge. 209–226.

Ruddick, Sara. *Maternal Thinking.* New York: Ballantine, 1989.

Schulman, Gerda. "Myths that Intrude on the Adaptation of the Stepfamily." *Social Casework* 3 (1972): 131–139.

Schweickart, Patrocinio. "Reading Ourselves: Toward a Feminist Theory of Reading." *Gender and Reading.* Ed. Elizabeth A. Flynn and Patrocinio P. Schweickart. Baltimore: Johns Hopkins UP, 1986. 31–62.

Sexton, Anne. *Transformations.* Boston: Houghton Mifflin, 1971.

Solin, Sabrina. "A Home of Their Own." *Seventeen,* September 1996. 252.

Surrey, Janet. "Mother-Blaming and Clinical Theory." *Woman-Defined Motherhood.* Ed. Jane Price Knowles and Ellen Cole. New York: Harrington Park Press, 1990. 83–87.

Thompson, Barbara. "The Lion's Whiskers, An Ethiopian Folktale." *The New York Times Book Review.* 30 July 1995: 17.

Walker, Nancy A. *The Disobedient Writer: Women and Narrative Tradition.* Austin: U of Texas P, 1995.

Warner, Marina. *From the Beast to the Blonde.* New York: Farrar, Straus and Giroux, 1994.

Woolf, Virginia. *A Room of One's Own.* New York: Harcourt, Brace Jovanovich, 1929.

Zipes, Jack. *Breaking the Magic Spell: Radical Theories of Folk and Fairy Tales.* Austin: U of Texas P, 1979.

———. *Don't Bet on the Prince.* New York: Routledge, 1987.

———. *The Outspoken Princess and the Gentle Knight.* New York: Bantam, 1994.

II

Epistemology: Women Developing Knowledge through Connection and Separation

The Western tradition of epistemology, with origins in Plato and Descartes, does not accept claims to knowledge which are based on impressions of the senses. The fact that we are embodied beings, according to this view, leads us toward confusion rather than to certainty. Such a perspective has produced an approach that is "virtually exclusively normative and staggeringly androcentric" (Duran 8), in which a knower believes herself or himself to be free of subjective experience, able to look at an object from nowhere in particular (Code 16) and so meet criteria for rationality and objectivity in knowing.

Although epistemologists in the Western tradition are almost always white and male, they do not appear to consider the impact on them as knowers of their claims to privilege based on gender, race, culture, and class. Nor do they ponder the influence of the historical moment in which they live. As Lorraine Code recognizes, these knowers assume that they represent an ideal of "pure objectivity and value neutrality" (16), which presupposes a human nature that stands for all people and allows knowers to be interchangeable. Such an epistemology implies that one can get beyond subjectivity in the quest for knowledge (Code 16).

Many thinkers in the Western tradition—Aristotle, Aquinas, Kant, Hegel, and Neitzsche among them—have cast doubt upon women's ability to reason (Tuana and Tong 1). Plato makes it clear that knowledge production is the undertaking of privileged men. Evelyn Fox Keller finds the source of women's exclusion from knowledge acquisition in *The Symposium* where Plato's "model for spiritual begetting is the love of man for man" (24). Since female nature is defined as Other, closer to nature, and more influenced by the senses through specifically female biological functions, women are not envisioned as producers of meaningful knowledge. Neither has the family—so often seen as women's sphere—been found worthy of philosophical reflection.

Feminist work in epistemology began as a critique of the tradition described above. Feminists sought (and continue to seek) answers to questions that had not been considered by mainstream epistemologists: Who is the subject (knower) of knowledge? Who should that subject be? How does the gender, race, culture, and class of the knower affect what is known and determine the processes considered appropriate for knowledge acquisition by that knower? How can we maximize objectivity, understanding that any subject will have a particular perspective? How can we best recognize the politics involved in knowledge? What are suitable objects of knowledge (Alcoff and Potter 13)?

In an effort to answer these and other questions, feminist epistemologists seek, in the words of Lorraine Code, a "remapping [of] the epistemic terrain" (20). Giving up the search for a disembodied perspective from an unspecified time and place, the new perspective means recognition of the personal and political investedness of knowers and groups of knowers in what they seek to know. It means doing away with the idea of gender neutrality and understanding as well as the notion that the race, culture, class, and other characteristics of knowers also influence their quest for knowledge. It requires that epistemologists take seriously the ideas that the world looks different depending on the particular perspective of the knower, and that there is no one privileged location (Code).

Feminist epistemologists do not envision one single ideal woman subject as the exemplary source of knowledge. Rather, as Sandra Harding says, "one must turn to all the lives that are marginalized in different ways by the operative systems of social stratification" (60). A feminist, gynocentric model of knowledge acquisition must be, according to Duran, "a context- and culture-related process" (185), one that is fluid enough to relate sensitively to people from a variety of backgrounds.

Some feminist scholars have focused specifically on women's "ways of knowing." Indeed, the most widely read study in the field of feminist epistemology—both by those inside academe and by the general public—is entitled *Women's Ways of Knowing*, written not by philosophers but by three psychologists and a professional in the field of education. Like feminist philosophers, they found that notions of truth and methods of discovering it have been formulated by the dominant white male culture, which continues to legislate norms of classroom interaction and the core of curricular content. Moreover, they observed that abilities rewarded by the academy and the society at large have been those "intellectual capacities most often cultivated by men" (7).

In the face of this evidence, the authors of *Women's Ways of Knowing* sought to "describe epistemological perspectives from which women view the world" (15), some of which are often ignored and disparaged in accepted models of intellectual development. They conducted a research study based on lengthy interviews with 135 women of diverse ages from a variety of ethnic backgrounds and social classes; living in rural, suburban, and urban locations; attending different kinds of institutions of higher education; or using the services of family agencies. In these conversations, the authors heard many examples of the metaphor of voice and silence. Women talked about " 'speaking up' " and " 'speaking out,' " being " 'silenced' " and " 'not being heard.' " They found women using the image of voice over and over, its meaning deeply intertwined with the development of mind and self (18).

In 1986, the authors of *Women's Ways of Knowing* chose to focus primarily on gender. However, in their most recent book, *Knowledge, Difference and Power: Essays Inspired by Women's Ways of Knowing*, Nancy Goldberger in "Cultural Imperatives and Diversity in Ways of Knowing" expands her view from recognition of how male models of knowing influence women to a realization of how whole cultures impose their ways of knowing on people in their midst who are defined as being outside the majority. Emphasizing the importance of culture and class in understanding both gender and epistemology, Goldberger adds significantly to the variables considered by her and her colleagues in their previous collaboration.

Three of the essays found in this book contain themes that relate to questions feminist epistemologists ask. Kathleen Gregory Klein describes "Truth, Authority, and Detective Fiction: The Case of Agatha Christie's *The Body in the Library*" as "an attempt to articulate the epistemology of detective fiction simultaneously with the subject of women as knowers." Because the *whodunit* has always been a "gendered genre"—the detective is by definition male—Miss Jane Marple, Christie's elderly, unmarried lady sleuth, subverts the conventions of the form when she "retains the experiences and perspective of the spinster while simultaneously gaining the authority and control of the detective." This double vision is what marks her as "transgressive."

Taking as her categories of analysis the epistemological positions developed by Belenky, Clinchy, Goldberger, and Tarule in *Women's Ways of Knowing*, Klein finds that the detective's way of knowing fits most closely into the categories of procedural and separate knowing, in which the knower applies objective procedures for obtaining knowledge, remains separate from the object, and seeks mastery over it. She argues that Agatha Christie is no less transgressive than her female detective by making Miss Marple a procedural thinker—giving her a way of knowing appropriate for a detective who, up until this point, has been defined as quintessentially male.

In "Reading Silence in Joy Kogawa's *Obasan*," Betty Sasaki calls attention to the meanings given to silence and voice in various cultures and, more specifically, to their differing interpretations by American feminist epistemologists/psychologists and two generations of women of Japanese descent living in Canada. Sasaki finds that some feminist studies interpret silence negatively, as a "defensive response" or a retreat from connection and communication. For Sasaki this view results in "a polarization of voice and silence that privileges the former and pathologizes the latter in an ironic analog of the either-or logic of Western thinking." It illustrates the limitations of feminist psychological theory when applied "wholesale" to writing by and about women of color whose race and culture may give meanings to silence and voice that differ from those of the white "majority."

As Kogawa shows through her female characters, Naomi, her mother, and her two aunts, silence for a Japanese woman is a complex language that must be carefully attended to by the reader. In addition to an inability to speak, silence can signify denial and pain or an "act of agency, a choice to withhold oneself and resist the invasive gaze of those who have historically held the power to interpret both the speech and silence of the 'other.'" In her analysis of an interaction between Naomi and her mother, Sasaki describes a style of communication in which silence and an averted gaze do not connote lack of empathy, and where "*knowing* itself is developed through the complex interaction of wordless languages, meaningful silences, and visual exchanges."

Sasaki's essay is a striking example of the need emphasized by feminist epistemologists to consider the historical and cultural context in describing and understanding people's ways of knowing.

So, too, is "Motherlands and Foremothers: African American Women's Texts and The Concept of Relationship," in which Sally Kitch acknowledges the limitations of feminist developmental theory based on the object relations model to adequately analyze the experience of the women characters in Paule Marshall's *Praisesong for the Widow* and *Mama Day* by Gloria Naylor. Because that theory assumes the primacy of the individual's identity and its tie to a nuclear family unit, it cannot adequately explain the interconnection between characters' "individual identities and their identification as members of a race whose history and values give meaning to their lives."

Kitch finds that French feminist psychoanalytic theory, however, provides a way of explaining the relationship between the protagonists of the two novels and a "collective history now knowable primarily through its vestiges in [their] unconscious minds." Inscribing the pursuit of truth through dreams, visions, ghosts, magic, ritual, and natural processes, these texts, Kitch demonstrates, are examples in which "the *feminine* becomes a powerful and disruptive voice in Western discourse."

In concluding her essay, Kitch ponders the relationships between the two texts she has analyzed and the appearance of some similar phenomena—particularly representations of the supernatural—in the works of a number of African American women writers. Perhaps processes described in African American women's quests for identity—ways that are antithetical to the Western tradition—will encourage us to question further the dominant objectivist epistemology and show us the fruits of embracing a multiplicity of ways of knowing.

Works Cited

Alcoff, Linda and Elizabeth Potter, eds. "Introduction: When Feminisms Intersect Epistemology." *Feminist Epistemologies.* New York: Routledge, 1993. 1–14.

Belenky, Mary Field, Blythe McVicker Clinchy, Nancy Rule Goldberger, and Jill Mattuck Tarule. *Women's Ways of Knowing.* New York: Basic Books, 1986.

Code, Lorraine. "Taking Subjectivity into Account." *Feminist Epistemologies.* Ed. Linda Alcoff and Elizabeth Potter. New York: Routledge, 1993. 15–48.

Duran, Jane. *Toward a Feminist Epistemology.* Lanham: Rowman and Littlefield, 1991.

Goldberger, Nancy. "Cultural Imperatives and Diversity in Ways of Knowing." *Knowledge Difference and Power: Essays Inspired by Women's Ways of Knowing.* Ed. Nancy Goldberger, Jill Tarule, Blythe McVicker Clinchy, and Mary Belenky. New York: Basic Books, 1996.

Harding, Sandra. "Rethinking Standpoint Epistemology: What is 'Strong Objectivity?'" *Feminist Epistemologies.* Ed. Linda Alcoff and Elizabeth Potter. New York: Routledge, 1993. 49–82.

Keller, Evelyn Fox. *Reflections on Gender and Science.* New Haven: Yale UP, 1985.

Tuana Nancy and Rosemarie Tong, eds. "Introduction." *Feminism and Philosophy: Essential Readings in Theory, Reinterpretation, and Application.* Boulder: Westview, 1995. 1–4.

5

Truth, Authority, and Detective Fiction: The Case of Agatha Christie's *The Body in the Library*

Kathleen Gregory Klein

> Q: What is truth?
> Q: What is authority?
> Q: To whom do I listen?
> Q: What counts for me as evidence?
> Q: How do I know what I know? (3)

More overtly than any of its literary or popular counterparts, detective fiction provides another context for exploring these five central questions raised in the first paragraph of *Women's Ways of Knowing*. The popular tag for the genre—*whodunit*—embodies all the questions raised above. One classic example of the form, Agatha Christie's *The Body in the Library,* is an unexpectedly female-centered text. This novel grants roles to women not found in other detective fiction or in real life of the time; it allows women to claim forms of knowledge and self-knowledge in the midst of a popular formula.

The formula or conventions of detective fiction manipulate both the writing and the reading of the text. And so, this essay is an attempt to articulate the epistemology of detective fiction simultaneously with the subject of women as knowers. It demonstrates how the genre establishes the centrality of the same five questions that Belenky, Clinchy, Goldberger, and Tarule raise, except that detective fiction is not concerned with women's ways of knowing, but has universalized what are recognizably men's knowledge patterns.

Q: What is truth? Unlike daily life where murders often go unsolved, serial killers attack without being caught, and trials raise more questions than they answer, detective novels end with the assurance of truth. The murderer has been identified and the innocent relieved of suspicion. The satisfaction offered by such conclusions is typically in direct opposition to the uncertainty of the less tidy reality that surrounds the rest of the reader's life.

Q: What is authority? In this predictable delivery of truth, the single and singular figure of the detective stands as the sole authority. Not only does the sleuth discern the precise truth among competing alternative narratives but, in making the mystery's solution clear to the reader in the novel's climax, the detective quite literally authors the story's end.

Q: To whom do I listen? The reader who hopes to solve the fictional mystery ahead of—or, at least, along with—the official sleuth, listens as well to the witnesses, the suspects, and the victim, weighing the evidence. Discarding apparent falsehoods and assembling the pieces of the truth, the reader-detective engages with the actual detective in search of the truth.

Q: What counts for me as evidence? Through careful investigation of all the clues, detectives compile the evidence, weigh the suspects, and arrive at the only explanation that accounts for all that is known.

Q: How do I know what I know? With the assurance of detective characters throughout the history of the genre, the protagonist (the hero, the sleuth, the 'tec) unfolds the case and its solution through the only narrative that makes sense of all the clues and statements. This narrative neatly sweeps away all competing stories and alternative murder suspects to stand alone as the authoritative version. Even a skeptical reader can retrace the pattern of the investigation to find again the mystery solved by the brilliant-by-definition detective.

Still, it cannot be said with any confidence that all readers, writers, and detectives share the same set of experiences. Detective fiction has always been a gendered genre. In its defining moments during the nineteenth century, the battle was fought between the sensational female-oriented fiction associated with such writers as Mary Elizabeth Braddon and the more male-focused ratiocinative tales of Edgar Allen Poe. In the end, the novels of domestic intrigue and women's perceptions of their world gave way to stories that valorized logical, rational, intellectual pursuits by amateur sleuths—men about town—and their police counterparts.[1] And so, in the early period, male writers, men's ways of thinking, and disproportionate numbers of male detectives were in a position to articulate both the gender and the genre of detective fiction. Women's ways of seeing the world and knowing life-as-it-is-lived were subordinated as the work of the much disparaged "scribbling women."

The 1920s and 1930s seemed to add geography to the terms of engagement in a conflict that was most often defined as pitting the classical British mystery against the hard-boiled American novel. But, as I have argued elsewhere, gender also played its part in this oppositional struggle.[2] Although men wrote the classic British mysteries, this fiction during the so-called Golden Age was most closely associated with five women writers (Agatha Christie, Dorothy L. Sayers, Ngaio Marsh, Margery Allingham, and Josephine Tey). As women came to master the nineteenth century's logical and ratiocinative form, men had to find a way to wrest control back into their own hands. They did. No women writers joined John Carroll Daly, Dashiell Hammett, and Raymond Chandler in the American's hard-boiled hall of crime. In "The Simple Art of Murder," Chandler explains why: "The detective . . . must be a complete man and a common man and yet an unusual man. He must be . . . a man of honor . . . the best man in his world and a good enough man for any world . . . The story is this man's adventure in search of a hidden truth, and it would be no adventure if it did not happen to a man fit for adventure" (21). Chandler and his cohorts insisted that the mean streets were not women's territory: women detectives could not walk the walk; women writers could not talk the talk. They attempted to relegate women writers and women's perspectives to the margins of the genre.

Given how little Chandler thought of the Golden Age, British mystery fiction, and classical detectives, he must have been more than a little frustrated by having to share his space on bookstore and library shelves with the more widely published and more popular, quintessentially classic, British, Golden Age detective novelist Agatha Christie. In fact, any mystery writer might look longingly at Christie's record: Her ninety-seven books have sold over a billion copies in English alone. She has been translated into virtually every written language, and her play, *The Mousetrap,* holds a production record for English theaters. And, among her contemporaries at the peak of the genre, she alone created several women detectives. Miss Jane Marple, gentlewoman and cynic, spinster and sleuth, is arguably her greatest and most subversive creation.

In her second Jane Marple novel, *The Body in the Library,* Christie takes the classic formula of the detective novel and turns it over to women. Her detective, the principal murderer, and both the victims are female. And, more to the point, they think like women. All four of them know the world in terms identified by Belenky, Clinchy, Goldberger, and Tarule as female. This articulation of female epistemology through popular fiction reveals the range of roles for women-as-knowers, in addition to demonstrating the adjustments Christie makes in generic conventions to accommodate her remarkable cast.

What follows is my interrogation of the figures of the detective and Miss Jane Marple, the murderer and Josie Turner, and the victim, plus Ruby Keene and Pamela Reeves through multiple lenses. First, the conventions of the detective role, apparently gender free but actually code male, are explored in the context of the five questions that opened this essay. Secondly, Christie's use of the role and the character whom she creates to fill it are examined. Thirdly, female epistemology as set out in *Women's Ways of Knowing* is connected with the specific genre roles of conventional detective fiction. Finally, Belenky, Clinchy, Goldberger, and Tarule's analysis is applied to Christie's characters in *The Body in the Library*. This interweaving of the epistemology of both the conventions of the genre and the women Christie places within her formula novel conveys the rich analytical field of what is often dismissed as merely popular reading.

The figure of the detective at its center sets the detective novel apart from the mystery, suspense, or crime thriller. The latter three can operate with an undifferentiated cast of characters; the main character can as easily be the victim or the criminal as the sleuth. And the narrative in those cases is not directed, as it is in all detective novels, on uncovering the criminal after the fact of the crime. By contrast, in a detective novel, the frequently employed plot device of a second or third murder that narrows the group of suspects and increases the urgency of the detective's task points up the degree to which solution dominates over prevention in this form. The detective may bemoan the increasing numbers of victims, but, by eventually solving the cases—almost always interlocked, usually directly connected—he restores the luster to his heroic image.

By custom and convention, the detective rewrites the plot of crime into the narrative of detection and solution. To the reader, the former is an apparently unending morass of information; one might even call it chaos. In the classical novel, a victim is placed by the author where a body is designed to provoke the greatest amount of shock. The unexpected sight of a bloodied body crumpled on the greens of a golf course, slumped over in a railway carriage, or arranged on the hearth rug in front of the fireplace in a country house library is intended to jolt the reader in ways that killings among criminals generally do not. This early disruption of an otherwise ordered and safe world cannot be undone by its members who, by the nature of their position in it, have become suspects. The detective, whether amateur or police, is something of an outsider who can return this world to its Edenic innocence not only by identifying the criminal and removing him or her from society but also by certifying the innocence of those suspected. The detective's role is, then, apparently one of omnipotence: like God Almighty, he or (until the 1970s, less frequently) she points the accusing finger at the guilty, damning for all eternity, especially in societies that still practice capital punishment. The innocent are cleared with a sweep of the all powerful hand, and society returns to the status quo of before the crime. If it is too far-fetched to equate the often all too human detective with god, it can at least be argued that this role in the novel—not the fictional character who occupies it in any given book—is granted godlike powers.

Beyond resolving the crime, the detective rewrites the narrative of the novel, quite literally claiming authority over the text. Reconstructing the case either in fact by bringing the suspects together to reenact their movements at the time of the murder or by verbally recapitulating the events as they must have happened, at the end of the novel the detective takes isolated and disjointed pieces of information from the preceding chapters and refashions the plot to provide a clear and coherent narrative of detection. This narrative then supersedes the narrative of crime which had previously controlled the flow of information to the reader. With this gesture, the detective controls all the elements of crime and consequence: the investigation, the clues and the suspects, the innocent and the guilty, the novel's climax, and denouement. The genre is set up at every juncture to reinforce the detective's eventual dominance.

Nothing in the culture of Christie's time or our own has defined women—especially unmarried elderly women—as figures of dominance and authority. Jane Marple is introduced to the readers of *The Body in the Library* (should they be unfamiliar with her) in the most unauthoritative terms:

> Miss Marple's telephone rang when she was dressing. The sound of it flurried her a little. It was an unusual hour for her telephone to ring. So well ordered was her prim spinster's life that unforeseen telephone calls were a source of vivid conjecture. "Dear me," said Miss Marple, surveying the ringing instrument with perplexity. "I wonder who that can be?" (13)

From such an inauspicious beginning, it takes only one hundred forty pages for the more familiar Miss Marple to emerge. As she begins her recapitulation of the crime and detection, three of the four police officials unsuccessfully working on the case acknowledge her position:

> Sir Henry Clithering said, "Speaking as Watson, I want to know your methods, Miss Marple."

> Superintendent Harper said, "I'd like to know what put you on to it first."

> Colonel Melchett said, "You've done it again, by Jove, Miss Marple. I want to hear all about it from the beginning." (153)

In fact, there has been no change in Miss Marple, no character development presented by the author, not even a dawning respect growing on the part of the police. Instead, the spinster becomes a detective; one role overwrites another. The resulting palimpsest, where the character retains the experiences and perspective of the spinster while simultaneously gaining the authority and control of the detective, marks Miss Jane Marple's transgressive nature.

In the final chapter, where the detective's opportunity to author the truth is greatest, she speaks from the spinster's knowledge. Like Lysistrata using domestic metaphors of spinning and weaving to describe the process of peacemaking in a warring society, Miss Marple exposes the killer through village parallels and a Victorian "mind like a sink" (154). Who else would have noticed "a schoolgirl's bitten nails" and "teeth that stuck out" (158)? And how reasonable that her mind should query suitable marriages—"the most obvious thing in the world. Somerset House! Marriage!" (155). Her method, as she tells her audience, is simple: "I always like to prove a thing for myself" (153). And so she not only claims the authority of her role but deserves it.

It should come as no surprise that in the sequence of ways of knowing that Belenky, Clinchy, Goldberger, and Tarule studied, the detective displays the most developed capacity for knowing among the characters in a detective novel. The conventions of the genre require that the detective outwit the criminal who has, in turn, outwitted the victim. The role of the detective fits most fully into the stage of knowing called procedural and separate knowing.[3] Separate knowers "assume that everyone— including themselves—may be wrong . . . [T]hey feel a special obligation to examine such ideas [those that feel right] critically" (104). Like a detective, they are suspicious but develop analytical and evaluative techniques; they listen because they are not threatened by the information they receive. *Women's Ways of Knowing* describes separate knowing in much the same terms as classical detective fiction: "an adversarial form . . . games" (106). In competitions between unequal opponents, as detective fiction eventually proves the detective and murderer to be, the less powerful player needs to be wary of her or his opponent.

Separate knowers, they continue, accept the standards of authorities— like the police in a detective novel—and even as they must accept criticism, they often "move toward a collegial relationship" where they can "criticize the reasoning of authorities" (107). Authority in this case is separate from the people who occupy positions of authority; it is "laws, not men" (107), *the* law, not the individual, often a flawed police officer. The conclusion of a detective novel, in which the protagonist describes for police and suspects how the crime was committed and by whom, corresponds to the claim by Belenky, Clinchy, Goldberger, and Tarule that separate knowers "speak a public language . . . and they see the listener as a potentially hostile judge" (108) as the detective argues the first version of the prosecution's case. This leads directly to the separate knower's attempt to remain dispassionate and "adopt a perspective that [her/his] adversaries may respect, as in their own self-interest" (109); separate knowers value "disinterested reason" (110). This knowledge— procedural knowledge—is "oriented away from the self . . . and toward the object the knower seeks to analyze or understand" (123), and it sometimes leads to what in individuals may be felt as a liability but is for detectives of the Golden Age a working principle: they are not personally connected to the knowledge they gain. In turning murderers over to the state for punishment, they feel satisfaction in having solved a puzzle, justification in having apprehended a criminal, and absolute confidence in having revealed the truth.

To her status as a separate knower, Jane Marple brings one essential quality of the subjective knower: the desire to know things for and through herself. In detective fiction, the main character always fails when she or he relies on someone else's investigation, questioning, research, or analysis. Miss Marple knows this instinctively and insists on subjecting all information to her own tests. In *The Body in the Library*, she combines what are her signature ways of knowing: detective investigation (the logical, careful examination of clues, evidence, suspects) and village parallels (looking for patterns between old experience and new). The detective and the spinster join forces. In this novel, her relationships with authority—the police—are separated into two categories: the skeptical Inspector Slack is reluctant to see the detective in a spinster's guise, although he also mistrusts all nonofficial investigators. By contrast, the three senior men have come to appreciate her reputation and, in general, provide assistance and accept her advice or conclusions. This seesawing relationship between the police and an amateur detective is another convention of the genre that Christie uses first to challenge and then to reaffirm the authority and the knowledge of her detective, absolute definer of the novel's final truth. And so, the detective in the character of an elderly spinster answers the questions posed by the authors of *Women's Ways of Knowing*; she is, explicitly, a woman-as-knower/detective and a knower/detective-as-woman.

But what a detective knows revolves around a crime and for this she requires a criminal, a murderer. Although it is a basic law of detective fiction that the detective reveals the truth (and can be relied on by the reader to do so when he or she is speaking *ex cathedra*), ironically, the murderer is the character actually in possession of the truth throughout the entire novel. Logic would suggest that in the battle which is engaged between the two they should be evenly matched.[4] But, unlike the detective who is the final arbiter of truth, the murderer is defined as a liar. Because the conventions of detective fiction do not allow for the criminal simply to disappear into the next county or the criminal underworld after committing a murder, in an attempt to evade discovery, he or she continues a normal routine of activities, engaging with the same community in which the victim was also a member. Thus, the murderer is first cast as a suspect who must lie for self-preservation.

Detective fiction plays on the likelihood that most people have some secret they would prefer to keep out of the public eye. And it furthermore assumes that no matter how insignificant the secret might be to the authorities engaged in the serious business of finding a killer, people are likely to lie when questioned in such a way as to open their private lives to official scrutiny. The function of suspects in a detective novel is to obscure the search for the truth. Most of them lie deliberately or by omission, in large matters or small. The truths they hide are not irrelevant, for when finally uncovered, each of them contributes to the picture in which a single damning lie—the murderer's lie—is spotlighted.

But, as the detective sorts out lies from truth, the murderer often plots or even kills again to protect his or her truth. Second or third victims in detective novels are often those characters who also know the murderer's truth, but refuse to share it with either the reader or the detective. Sometimes they, like the detective, value the power of knowledge. Other times they try to use the knowledge for their own gain. Even the detective is vulnerable when he or she knows the truth but has not yet revealed it; a dead detective (a clear-cut violation of the rules of the genre) is no threat to the murderer's truth.

In the climax of the novel, the detective and the murderer exchange positions. The murderer who has hid the truth is overtaken by the detective who reveals the truth. All lies fall away in the service of the truth—as the detective states it, for here his or her power and knowledge are absolute.

There are two murderers in *The Body in the Library*: a secretly married wife and husband. The woman, Josie Turner, is clearly identified as the brains and the executioner of the plan. Mark Gaskell, according to Miss Marple's reconstruction of the crimes, plays a secondary role, although he is also a killer. In her first scene, Josie Turner Gaskell blends truth and lies to tell the police the story of the previous evening when her cousin disappeared. The single lie that sets the police investigation moving in altogether the wrong direction is her deliberate misidentification of the victim. At this point, only she knows that two young women have been killed to provide a misleading chronology of events. In the novel's climax, the truth of murder and marriage, both damning secrets for Josie, are revealed.

Another truth about Josephine Turner makes her a plausible suspect in the class-conscious world of Agatha Christie's novels. She is, according to the cast of characters, a "professional dancer and hostess at the Majestic Hotel," where she mingles with the guests as more than staff but less than an equal. As a working-class woman, employed slightly above her social class, Josie has married even higher up the social ladder. She has imagined a social mobility that does not exist in the world of the novel and predicated her actions on a social acceptance that—even without murder or a secret marriage—she is unlikely to receive. She is clearly the other transgressive woman in this novel. As Miss Marple appropriates another gender role—the spinster detective—while maintaining her own, Josie tries to claim another class despite being continuously forced back to her original one. In the competition between the detective and the murderer that lies at the heart of detective fiction, it might be fair to say that Miss Marple's success and Josie Turner's failure to go beyond society's limitations signal the more conventional triumph of the detective over the criminal. Optimistically, one might then argue that the novel is not punishing female transgressiveness (manifest in either gender or class) but dividing the credit and blame down traditional fictional lines of protagonist versus antagonist.

The clearest definition of the murderer's position as a knower is found in Belenky, Clinchy, Goldberger, and Tarule's description of women functioning with subjective knowledge. In this position, "[t]ruth now resides within the person and can negate answers that the outside world supplies" (54). Rejecting law and social custom, the murderer justifies her or his actions from a personal understanding that outweighs all alternatives. No doubt the co-authors would be disturbed to find this movement toward "an inner source of strength" leading to murder when they describe the "repercussions in her relationships, self-concept and self-esteem, morality, and behavior" (54). One would like to think of all such growing in strength as having a positive impact not only on the woman but on her social community. But, inevitably, when "[w]omen become their own authorities," they acquire choices, not all of them wise, as Josie's decision to murder clearly demonstrates. *Women's Ways of Knowing* positively describes this sequence: "For women, the freedom from social conventions and definitions . . . represents a move toward greater autonomy and independence"; in the case of Josie Turner, autonomy and independence lead to double murder (55). Like the other subjective knowers in the study, the murderer comes "to disregard the knowledge and advice of remote experts . . . [T]hey argue against and stereotype those experts and remote authorities whom social institutions often promote as holding the keys to truth—teachers, doctors, scientists, men in general" and, I might add, police and lawyers (68, 71). Gaining an interior voice moves these subjective knowers toward a sense of "self . . . agency and control" (68).

Josie Turner has taken subjective thinking to one end of its logical spectrum. Defining the world from her position—she demonstrates a kind of solipsism that accepts that other points of view exist, but she cannot enter into them—she knows what she wants and refuses to accept the possibility that she might not get it. Even before the novel opens, she has risked a great deal by secretly marrying a man who pretends to be a widower in order to ingratiate himself with his first wife's father, Conway Jefferson. But Josie had seen her chance and, refusing to consider negative consequences, pressed forward. The marriage precipitates the murder as surely as does Conway Jefferson's announced plan to adopt Ruby Keene and provide for her in his will. Miss Marple strongly believes that Josie, not her husband, has planned the murders, producing two victims. As a subjective thinker, Josie has assumed agency, taken control, and acted on her own best judgment—however flawed—to get what she wants. Her partial and temporary success is overbalanced by her final and total failure to gain her desires. Her incomplete epistemological development limits her ability to deal fully with the five questions posed at the opening of this essay.

In the detective fiction triad, detective and murderer require a third party: the victim. In classical novels up through the Golden Age, the victim is often a sketchy figure, a stereotype: the nice girl, the young gentleman, the old soldier, the eccentric widow. Critics believed that to personalize the victim encouraged readers to identify too closely, and their subsequent empathy would impede their appreciation for the cool, intellectual, ratiocinative investigation of the crime. Even in the 1990s, traditionally constructed novels withhold the secrets of the victim for later in the novel at the center of the investigation.

The first consequence of the classical structure is that the victims never speak for themselves. Often they are not encountered alive by the reader, so they lack literal speech. They have been silenced by the murderer. More importantly, what they have concealed or might know unaware that resulted in their being murdered in the first place is revealed through the detective in a kind of ventriloquism where the victim has no opportunity to disagree. They are silenced a second time by the detective. These silencings are one reason among many for my argument elsewhere that whatever the sex of the victim, symbolically the victim is always female. In the power relations among the detective, the murderer, and the victim, the latter is always in the subordinate position.[5]

The second consequence of the classical structure for the construction of the victim emerges in comparing traditional novels with hard-boiled ones. In the latter, especially during the developmental years of the subgenre, the victim was likely to have ties with Chandler's "mean streets." By contrast, in the Golden Age novels, so far as anyone in the novel knows, the victim is a blameless innocent because the function of murder in these novels is to shock the reader by its unexpectedness. If one thinks of fictional characters as having independent will and making choices, it might be argued that the victims of hard-boiled novels have accepted a way of life in which violence is a possibility. By contrast, the victims of classical novels are plucked out of an apparently stable community in the service of the plot. Their fate is structural and functional rather than character-driven. To this extent—also seen in the fact that they are usually stereotypes—the characters themselves may be said not to exist; only their roles are significant.

The two young women murdered in Christie's *The Body in the Library* are such stereotypes. Miss Marple comments that the sixteen- and eighteen-year-olds are "both healthy, rather immature, but muscular girls" (156). Ruby Keene first comes to the Majestic Hotel to replace the injured Josie Turner as a demonstration dancer. She is murdered because a wealthy older man wanted to adopt her to replace his dead daughter, Rosamund. This plan would have foiled the hopes for inheritance of Josie and Mark Gaskell, Rosamund's widower. To construct an alibi for themselves in Ruby's murder, they kill Pamela Reeves and substitute her body for Ruby's. Apparently, all women are eternally interchangeable. And the three dead young women are even more so.

When the first unidentified body is found in the library of Gossington Hall, a country house near Miss Marple's village, Colonel and Mrs. Bantry remark several times that such things happen only in books: "You know, Lord Edgbaston finds a beautiful blonde dead on the library hearth rug. Bodies are always being found in libraries in books. I've never known a case in real life" (11). The victim is repeatedly characterized as "a blonde," effectively dehumanizing her. Mrs. Bantry insists that the blonde is not real and, despite the presence of a body, " '[i]t just isn't true' " (17). And Miss Marple concurs, speaking of yet another platinum blonde young woman: "And all these girls, with their make-up and their hair and their nails, look so alike" (21). The significance of this interchangeability has already occurred to the murderers, who callously lure young Pamela Reeves with the offer of a screen test, dye her hair the requisite blonde, and kill her.

Belenky, Clinchy, Goldberger, and Tarule describe the experience of voice for the silent—or the silenced—woman. These least-developed knowers, like the victims in a detective novel, find themselves out of the picture or on the outside of their community, one by fear of communication, the other by dying. They are erased by silence and silencing. Even as the character who is killed in a specific novel is overtaken by the killer, the role of victim in detective fiction is overtaken by the role of murderer. In this consistently dichotomous pairing, the terms always arrange themselves as murderer/victim: The murderer always occupies the dominant first or "a" position, while the victim is in the subordinate "b" slot. This subordination when matched with the usual male/female pair makes clear that the victim is always constituted as female. Thus, the connection with silent women who feel and act "passive, reactive, and dependent" and who perceive external authority—which might be construed as the murderer always constituted in this pairing as male—as arbitrary and all-powerful. The silent learners, say the co-authors, were conditioned not to engage in dialogue with either self or others, validating the passivity that society often ascribes to the female role. Like women who took the next step toward finding their voice—listening to others—the silent/silenced women were almost completely vulnerable to judgments of those in power. "If someone in a powerful position tells such a woman that she is wrong or bad or crazy, she believes it" (49), as victims are, by definition, vulnerable to their killers. . . . The women who remain silent never find the authority figures who help them see their capacity for learning and self-knowledge; they never get past their status as victims.

Age makes the victims of *The Body in the Library* particularly vulnerable: Ruby Keene is eighteen, Pamela Reeves only sixteen. Both want something that authority figures in their lives would have denied them. Ruby wants to be adopted and cared for by Conway Jefferson, thus ruining Josie's prospects for inheritance. Pamela wants the screen test for a film that both her Girl Guide leader and her mother would probably have quickly identified as a scam. Ruby is murdered because she must be silenced, Pamela because she has kept silent about her plans. They trust authority implicitly. Josie has gotten Ruby a job dancing at the Majestic, taught her how to act in this new world, and introduced her—ironically—to the wealthy Conway Jefferson. In Ruby's limited experience, Josie is the one whose knowledge and experience give her authority. Similarly, Pamela has accepted Mark Gaskell as a film director and Josie Turner as his make-up assistant; she is willing to follow their instructions about secrecy and the necessity of transforming her appearance. Unable to assert themselves, to speak up, to think their way out of dangerous situations, both girls are murdered in the cause of a subjective thinker who sees the world through her own needs and wants. In general, they have not yet begun to think about the questions that Belenky, Clinchy, Goldberger, and Tarule articulate as the basis of female epistemology. Because these two young women do not yet think of themselves as active knowers, they can be manipulated and eventually silenced.

To conclude, Agatha Christie's *The Body in the Library* demonstrates in itself and as a representative of its genre a range of the epistemological realities for women as revealed in the research of Belenky, Clinchy, Goldberger, and Tarule in *Women's Ways of Knowing*. However, neither Christie's characters nor their counterparts in the genre of detective fiction during the Golden Age proceed to the level of "integrated knowledge." The conventions of the genre insist that truth exists independently and objectively, that its discovery by the detective is a matter of superior intelligence and investigative skills. But, the rules of the genre insist that the solution that the detective provides in the climax of the novel be seen as unassailable, even independently verifiable. Thus, the idea that *"the knower is an intimate part of the known"* violates the genre's understanding of itself (137, italics in the text). Ironically, the experienced reader or critic of detective fiction recognizes the extent to which the detective has chosen the evidence, assembled the statements, examined the suspects, and decided upon the truth. In the absence of a murderer's confession—and widespread belief in its truthfulness—the detective's conclusions are not independent and objective but constructed. Its refusal to acknowledge the interplay of the investigator and the investigation in the announcement of the final truth is a hallmark of the traditional ratiocinative detective novel.

This examination of how authority, knowledge, and truth are constructed in detective fiction—especially a novel in which the three principal roles of detective, murderer, and victim are taken by women—cannot end without acknowledging the woman responsible for *The Body in the Library*: Agatha Christie herself. Although this is only the second Jane Marple novel, Christie was already a well-established novelist when it was published in 1942; thirty-one novels preceded it. She was then, as now, acknowledged as the master of the genre; in fact, her name is synonymous with the genre. By the time Christie created Miss Marple, the spinster detective was already a feature of detective fiction.[6] Christie contrasts the expectations of Jane Marple's society about harmless old ladies with the automatic belief of detective fiction readers that the detective always solves the murder. It might be argued that in this pairing of incompatible expectations, she proposed—even insisted upon—a reevaluation of the status of women. Putting a woman in the role of the procedural thinker—a style of analysis suitable for a detective that is, in turn, a role up to that point considered most suitable for a man—Agatha Christie joined Jane Marple among the ranks of the transgressors.

Notes

1. For further discussion, see my introduction in *Great Women Mystery Writers*.

2. See "Women Times Women Times Women" in *Women Times Three: Writers, Detectives, Readers*.

3. In fact, the sub-genre of detective fiction generally credited to Hillary Waugh's invention is known as "the police procedural."

4. See two articles by Keller and Klein for a further discussion of the interplay between the detective and the criminal.

5. See "*Habeas Corpus*: Feminism and Detective Fiction."

6. In several chapters in *The Woman Detective: Gender and Genre,* I analyze the function of age in women private eyes; Miss Marple, like her age-cohort, is one of Margaret Mead's "honorary men," the post-menopausal women for whom the gender restrictions of society have altered because of their age.

Works Cited

Belenky, Mary Field, Blythe McVicker Clinchy, Nancy Rule Goldberger, and Jill Mattuck Tarule. *Women's Ways of Knowing: The Development of Self, Voice, and Mind.* New York: Basic Books, 1986.

Chandler, Raymond. "The Simple Art of Murder." *The Simple Art of Murder.* New York: Ballantine, n.d. 1–21.

Christie, Agatha. *The Body in the Library.* New York: Pocket, c. 1942.

Keller, Joseph, and Kathleen Gregory Klein. "Deductive Detective Fiction. The Function of Tacit Knowledge." *Mosaic* 23 (Spring 1990): 2.

Klein, Kathleen Gregory. "Introduction." *Great Women Mystery Writers: Classic to Contemporary.* Westport: Greenwood, 1994. 1–9.

———. "*Habeas Corpus*: Feminism and Detective Fiction." *Feminism in Women's Detective Fiction.* Ed. Glenwood Irons. Toronto: U of Toronto P, 1995. 171–189.

———. *The Woman Detective: Gender and Genre.* Urbana and Chicago: University of Illinois Press, 1988; rev. ed., 1995.

———. "Women Times Women Times Women." *Women Times Three: Writers, Detectives, Readers.* Bowling Green: Popular Press, 1995. 3–13.

Klein, Kathleen Gregory, and Joseph Keller. "Deductive Detective Fiction: The Self-Destructive Genre." *Genre* 19 (1986): 155–172.

6

Reading Silence in Joy Kogawa's *Obasan*

Betty Sasaki

"**M**y name is Betty Sasaki, and I am a Spanish teacher." This is the line I was tempted to write on a sign and hang around my neck shortly after arriving at the small New England college where I currently work. Except for my colleagues in the Spanish department who had hired me, each person I met invariably assumed that I was the new person in East Asian Studies. Each time I would respond, "No, I'm the new person in Spanish." And each time, with varying degrees of embarrassment or unconsciousness, they would laugh and say something like, "Oh! Isn't that funny—you're Japanese but you teach Spanish."

In the summer following my first year of teaching, I was invited to a potluck by a colleague from another department. The table was loaded with an assortment of scrumptious looking dishes, including a tray of sushi, one of my favorite foods. As I was reaching for the sushi, I heard a voice behind me say, "You might not want to try that. I'm sure it's nothing like *real* sushi, nothing like yours. I really don't know how to make it." It was the hostess, humbly and anxiously disclaiming the inauthenticity of her culinary experiment in the face of what she believed to be my inherent expertise on the matter. "Inherent" because I was Japanese, or because I was a woman who cooks? Probably both. "Don't worry," I assured her, trying to diffuse the awkwardness between us, "I don't know how to make sushi, I only know how to eat it." After our brief bout of laughter, however, we found ourselves standing around that table of food starving for something to talk about. She finally smiled uncomfortably and excused herself. I proceeded to enjoy her sushi, wondering, as I ate, whether I had offended her somehow, whether she had believed me, and whether, after our short exchange, she would be willing to give me the recipe.

In the four years that I have been here, I've compiled a collection of such anecdotes, in part, because they are both humorous and telling examples of the complexities of racial and gender dynamics. They are also disturbing, not only because they reflect how I am perceived by others, but because they have made me question how I perceive myself. To what extent have I, in my own silences, participated in the circumscription of my identity as both a woman and an Asian American? Is it fair to expect them to understand my indignity and frustration which I try, and mostly succeed in, balancing with collegiality and amiability? At what point do I refuse to absolve the ignorance, however unconscious, of those who assume to know me because of my slanted eyes and straight black hair? And how might my silences be also an act of resistance to the barrage of well-meaning requests from white colleagues and students, anxious and uncomfortable around questions of race and difference, to tell them what to do? While I sense the sincerity of the question, I also see the privilege behind it, which gives them the choice of coming down to my level, like a parent crouching before the crying child, as a way of making me seem more equal.

Joy Kogawa both raises and responds to similar questions in *Obasan* (1981), an autobiographical novel narrated by Naomi Nakane, a Sansei, or third-generation Japanese-Canadian, whose family, like my father's, was relocated and interned during World War II. As a Sansei woman myself, I was both moved by and drawn to Naomi's personal struggle as she attempts to reconcile the paradox of her own identity as both a woman and an Asian American living in a culture that has historically marginalized her on both levels. In the character of Naomi, the development of self is complicated by questions of cultural and political history, gender, and ethnicity that cannot be compartmentalized into discrete categories of identity. It is at this intersection of the personal, cultural, and historical where we first find Naomi in the fictional present of 1972 (on the day she finds out that her uncle has died), many years after the traumatic events of the War. A thirty-six-year-old, single elementary school teacher, Naomi finds herself hopelessly out of place in the small, white middle-class town of Cecil, Alberta. On an uncharacteristic date with a widower father of one of her students, she is confronted with the "one surefire question [she] always get[s] from strangers" (9): Where do you come from? Despite her careful explanations, her companion's curiosity about her ethnicity and origin does not abate:

> The widower was so full of questions that I half expected him to ask for an identity card . . . I should have something with my picture on it and a

statement below that tells who I am. Megumi Naomi Nakane. Born June 18, 1936, Vancouver, British Columbia. Marital status: Old maid. Health: Fine, I suppose. Occupation: Schoolteacher. I'm bored to death with teaching and ready to retire. . . . Personality: Tense. Is that present tense or past tense? It's perpetual tense. (9)

In this brief, self-mocking passage, Naomi establishes the conflicted dynamic of her own identity, parodically intertwining the "official" categories of bureaucratic discourse with the voice of her own frustration, as she tries and fails to move the widower's perception of her beyond her appearance. Despite the innocence of the widower's interrogation, Naomi is cornered into a position of self-justification that leaves her little or no room to be more than a stranger in her own country. This is one of many experiences that has taught Naomi to anticipate the assumptions of her white community, leading her to forge a strategy of reticence in her interactions with and responses to its members. Thus, when in the same chapter the principal of her school informs her that her uncle has died, she reveals no emotional response: "Be still," the voice inside is saying. "Sift the words thinly" (11). Yet, ironically perhaps, it is the death of her uncle that both occasions Naomi's return to the town of her adolescence to care for her now widowed Obasan, and leads her to reconfigure, for herself and for her readers, the varied meanings of her silence. Told as a series of memories and flashbacks, Naomi's story unfolds as a journey, alternating between past and present and creating a narrative tension that underscores her struggle to reintegrate those parts of herself and her life that were fractured and lost during the traumatic events of her childhood. From a psychological perspective, the death of her uncle seems to converge with all the other losses Naomi has suffered in her life, producing an emotional crisis that shatters her silence and compels her to speak. Yet, Naomi's apparent gesture toward autobiographical confession is not merely a question of overcoming silence, but also of maintaining it.

Theoretical Reflections on Women's Silence

Feminist criticism from across the disciplines has generated a varied body of important work about women's voice and silence. In her groundbreaking study, *In a Different Voice*, Carol Gilligan underscores the need to read women's responses to the world through a different theoretical lens, demonstrating that female attachment, traditionally pathologized in male-centered psychological studies, forms the basis for an alternate but equally valid moral and ethical stance. In her formulation of a female "ethics of care," Gilligan places interpersonal connection at the center of women's sense of self, stressing the primacy of "voice" as a fundamental tool in the development of intimate relationship. At the same time, however, subsequent feminist psychological studies, based on Gilligan's earlier work, have tended to interpret the silence of girls and women as a "defensive response" (Saltzman 139) or a place to which women retreat when "words are perceived as weapons . . . used to separate and diminish people, not to connect and empower them" (Belenky et al. 24).[1] The result is a polarization of voice and silence that privileges the former and pathologizes the latter in an ironic analog of the "either-or" logic of Western thinking, which Gilligan so rightly cautions us against ("Preface," *Making Connections* 18). Such a contradiction points out, among other things, the limitations of feminist psychological theory when it is applied "wholesale" to texts written by and about women of color, whose "different" cultural context may assign very distinct values to silence and voice. Without the careful assessment and ongoing consideration of racial, cultural, and historical differences that inform the female experiences under analysis, the application of feminist psychological theories runs the risk of eliding differences under the generalizing rubric of gender.[2] Such is the case in recent studies on gender and reading which, influenced by Gilligan's work, presume a shared intimacy between the female reader and writer by virtue of their being women.[3] This elision of differences among women becomes even more problematic when we talk about works by female writers of color. The multicultural project, in its commitment to respond to the very problem of exclusion, runs the risk of overlooking the new questions it generates. At what points do efforts toward inclusion become acts of appropriation? To what extent are works written by the Other read through a homogenizing lens that ultimately reshapes differences to better fit into existing paradigms of universal selfhood or womanhood? For women, the will to speak is postulated as both a political and personal act. Yet, oddly, in certain feminist and multicultural readings, the political imperatives that distinguish the experience of a particular group or individual often take a back seat to, or are all together obscured by, the desire for a shared, and often spurious, intimacy. The possible results of this pseudo-intimacy are that, on the one hand, differences will be overlooked and, on the other, that the validity of the Other's life will be reduced to "an index of someone else's experience, subject to a seemingly endless process of translation and transference" (duCille 622). The question arises as to how one maintains the specificity/ integrity of one's experience in the face of her readers' well-meaning gestures toward empathy and intimacy.

In the case of Kogawa's narrator-protagonist, it is impossible to trace

Naomi's psychological development from childhood to adulthood without acknowledging the cultural and historical context in which she has lived. When Naomi is only four, at the onset of the war, she is separated from her mother, who goes to Japan and never returns. Raised by her Obasan, her uncle, and, to a lesser extent, her Aunt Emily, Naomi is caught not only between two cultures (North American and Japanese) but also between two generations of Japanese-Americans. On the one hand, her Obasan is Issei, a first-generation Japanese immigrant who speaks little English and is steeped in the cultural traditions of Japan. On the other, Aunt Emily is Nisei, a second-generation Japanese-American, born in Canada and highly identified with, and assimilated to, Western culture. While Obasan is quiet, self-contained, and seemingly disengaged from the external world, she is also the strongest and most constant female presence in Naomi's life, the figure that gives the novel its title. In contrast, Aunt Emily is an outspoken political activist, whose commitment to rectifying the injustices suffered by her community during the war take her into the world and away from Naomi. Where Naomi must work to have the semblance of a dialogue with her Obasan, she works even harder to keep her Aunt Emily's impassioned political discourses from completely overwhelming and invading her precarious sense of self. At the same time, neither of her aunts is willing to tell her what happened to her mother and why she never returned, transforming the maternal absence into a constant and underlying presence in Naomi's narrative.

The dilemma Naomi faces in telling her story concerns her bicultural, inter-generational viewpoint, and is alluded to in the strangely evocative passage that precedes the autobiographical narrative:

> There is a silence that cannot speak. There is a silence that will not speak. Beneath the grass the speaking dreams and beneath the dreams is a sensate sea. The speech that frees comes forth from the amniotic deep. To attend its voice, I can hear it say, is to embrace its absence. But I fail the task. The word is stone. / I admit it. /. . . Unless the stone bursts with telling, unless the seed flowers with speech, there is in my life no living word . . . If I could follow the stream down and down to the hidden voice, would I come at last to the freeing word? I ask the night sky but the silence is steadfast. There is no reply. (i)

Spoken across the first page with no introduction to the speaking subject, the novel's opening lines seem to emerge out of nowhere, from a disembodied voice, un-locatable in time or space. Before grounding her story in the familiar terrain of narrative convention, Kogawa's narrator purposefully leads her readers into an ontological darkness, where they are momentarily confused by the evasive identity of their speaker-guide.

What this ethereal voice invokes is both a yearning for speech and an honoring of silence; thus, speech and silence, like the images of stone and water in the opening page. They alternately posit speech as water, words as stone, voice as absence, and, ultimately, they converge and diverge, making it difficult to distinguish them from, or define them against, one another. In order to hear the "hidden voice," it is necessary "to embrace its absence," to acknowledge its silence. Thus, Naomi recognizes and honors the paradox of her own life as a Sansei woman living between two cultures and two temporal moments in a struggle to follow what Carol Gilligan has termed "the both-and logic of feelings" (*Making Connections* 19), which will allow her to connect the fragmented and conflicted parts of herself.

To read the novel as a testimony of the pain and courage required to break the silence of shame, which has been maintained by the majority of Nisei survivors of the internment, is as valid as reading Naomi's life as the story of a woman who struggles with and succeeds in finding her lost voice. Yet, besides and beyond the tension between silence and speech/voice, Kogawa explores the more subtle distinction between different kinds of silence. As the two first sentences of the above passage suggest, there is, on the one hand, the silence that arises from the inability to speak and, on the other, the silence grounded in the unwillingness to speak. It is the various configurations of silence that I want to problematize in this essay, suggesting that, just as silence can be read as a symptom of denial and pain, it also can be interpreted as an act of agency, a choice to withhold oneself and resist the invasive gaze of those who have historically held the power to interpret both the speech and silence of the "other." By this, I do not mean to undervalue either the power of speaking or the pervasive ways in which women and men and women of color are socialized to protect themselves in silence.[4] I do, however, want to suggest that silence is not always a negative state that must ultimately be overcome.

Naomi defines herself in the context of relationship and attachment, but not always along the same developmental lines followed by many feminist psychological theorists. Naomi's relationships with Obasan, her mother, and Aunt Emily, figured at the center of this study, are charged with a multiplicity of culturally inflected ways of responding, knowing, and caring. By examining not only what Naomi says about her relationships with these three women but also the ways in which she chooses to tell them, I will show how Kogawa deploys silence as a narrative strategy. Seemingly designed to evoke the pain of her protagonist's experience, silences also appear to subvert her readers' expectations of establishing an easy intimacy with the narrator. The implicit moral question for Naomi is how to tell her life without giving away either herself or those

she loves in the process. The larger but equally moral question that Kogawa poses to her readers is how to read another's life without appropriating that "other's" experience as one's own. The silence that "will not
speak" is not just the absence of speech or a refusal to communicate; nor
is it simply an evasive tactic that "bespeaks a self uncertain of its strength,
unwilling to deal with choice" (Gilligan, *In a Different Voice* 68). Silence
itself can be a language that tells its own story in such a way that readers
must attend to it with care and concentration, scrutinizing, in the process,
themselves and their own assumptions about women's voice and silence.
A beautiful and telling analogy for this narrative strategy is invoked in
the third chapter, when Naomi finds her dead grandfather's boat-build-
ing tools in her Obasan's attic and remembers how he once used them.

> I can feel the outline of the plane with the wooden handle which he worked
> by pulling it toward him. There is a fundamental difference in Japanese
> workmanship—to pull with control rather than push with force. (28–29)

Rather than having her narrator turn to the confessional mode of self-
revelation, Kogawa pulls her readers in closer so that they can hear the
wordless voices of Naomi's narrative. With the same subtle and evocative
language of this passage, however, she controls how close they can come.
Through her narrator and the carefully drawn cultural portraits of the
women in Naomi's life, Kogawa teaches her readers to read silence
through the racially charged and culturally inflected lens of Naomi's experience as a Japanese-Canadian woman.

Issei Silence: Obasan

The central female figure in Naomi's life is Obasan, who first appears in
the novel when Naomi returns to her house on the day of her uncle's
death. Despite Obasan's constant and caring presence throughout Naomi's childhood and adolescence, Naomi, as an adult, experiences an increasing ambivalence around Obasan's silence that is construed as both
a barrier and a bridge, paradoxically separating and linking their differences and similarities. When Naomi enters the house, she describes Obasan as the literal embodiment of silence. Her aunt is so deaf she does not
hear her niece calling out. "Her eyes are unclear and sticky," the result
of clogged tearducts; and "her mouth is plagued with a gummy saliva"
(14), causing her tongue to stick to the roof of her false palate. It would
seem for all practical purposes that Obasan herself is dead or at least
emotionally wounded to such an extent that her capacity for self-expression is cut off.

In order to "read" Obasan's silence as something more than a psychological symptom of her individual experience as a woman, however, it is necessary to sketch out the cultural and historical context that has shaped it. Whatever critical cultural or feminist perspective we might bring to bear on the situations described in the novel must be mediated by an acknowledgment of the historical context in which it is situated and the cultural differences between North American and Japanese value systems.

Obasan raises and cares for Naomi through the traumatic events of her mother's leaving, the separation of the family at the onset of the war and the relocation of the Japanese-Canadian community. She becomes for Kogawa a representative portrait of the Japanese female immigrant quietly struggling for the survival of her family. Born in Japan and immigrating to Canada when she is in her early twenties, Obasan is Issei, a first-generation Japanese-Canadian who embodies many of the cultural values from Japan and has not "assimilated" Western values. Her attachment to Japanese values and to her Japanese American community forms an intimate part of her identity, even though such attachment is often misread by members of the dominant white society. During the war years, the Issei were the community leaders, strongly emphasizing, in accordance with their Japanese values, group harmony and the avoidance of conflict. As O'Brian and Fugita point out: "To most Westerners, the extent to which Japanese culture demands that individual needs and interests should be submerged to meet collective goals would be totally unacceptable" (106).[5]

Within this social structure, which privileges the extended family and the community over the individual, Issei women were both the preservers and transmitters of cultural tradition and values (Nakano 48; Glenn 38). Morally and psychologically sensitized to the concepts of duty and obligation to the family, these women practiced and passed on the Japanese cultural values of "*gaman* (perseverance in the face of adversity), *giri* (sense of duty and obligation), and a kind of fatalism that decreed the acceptance of conditions that 'couldn't be helped' *Kodomo no tame ni* (for the sake of the children) . . . became almost a moral imperative for these immigrants" (O'Brian and Fugita 37–38). Not surprisingly, this phrase is repeated throughout the novel by Obasan, Uncle, and other Issei members of Naomi's community as an explanation for their unwillingness to speak about the confusion and injustice to which they are submitted during the war years. As a result, many of Naomi's childhood questions about why her mother does not return, why they must leave their Vancouver home, and when they will be allowed to come back, go unanswered and become submerged deep within her. "The memories were drowned in a whirlpool of protective silence. Everywhere I could hear the adults whispering 'Kodomo no tame. For the sake of the children . . .' Calmness was maintained" (26). Yet, even as she identifies the silence of the adults with the silencing of her own memories, the calmness of that silence often comforted Naomi as a child through the hardship of relocation and now characterizes the tone of her narrative. Despite Naomi's ambivalence toward her aunt as representative of the past, it is the cultural legacy of Obasan's silence that is both the "stone" and the "seed" from which Naomi's own telling originates. Her return to Obasan upon her uncle's death marks the beginning of her journey into that "amniotic deep" from which the "speech that frees comes forth" (i).

Naomi's initial description of Obasan without further context recalls the opening chapter on silence in *Women's Ways of Knowing.*[6] According to Belenky et al., the group of "silent women" often described themselves as "deaf because they assumed they could not learn from others, and dumb because they felt so voiceless" (24). Emphasizing the power of words to express thought, the authors privilege language as the primary means by which persons "can enter into the social and intellectual life of their community" and, ultimately, into connection with themselves (26). Yet, lest we be tempted to see Obasan only as a victim of voicelessness, Naomi acknowledges another understanding of her aunt's silence: "The language of her grief is silence. She has learned it well, its idioms, its nuances. Over the years, silence within her small body has grown large and powerful" (17). While Naomi underscores the pain associated with her aunt's silence, she neither pathologizes it as a mere symptom of trauma nor glorifies it as a culturally inherited characteristic. Obasan's relationship to silence is forged both by her (she learns it) and in spite of her (it grows within her), alluding to both her unwillingness and inability to speak.

To assume that Obasan's lack of voice is only a product of her pain and isolation is to conclude, as Belenky et al. do, that language holds the key to accessing the self in denial. Throughout the novel, however, Obasan rarely speaks, nor does Naomi presume to speak "for" her as a way of letting readers into her aunt's thoughts or feelings. Instead, she relies on detailed descriptions of her aunt's actions and surroundings, allowing the figure of her aunt to emerge in a series of contiguous relationships to the tangible things around her.

The house is indeed old, as she is also old. Every homemade piece of furniture, each pot holder and paper doily is a link in her lifeline . . . The items are endless. Every short stub pencil, every cornflakes box stuffed with paper bags and old letters is of her ordering. They rest in the corners like part of her body, hair cells, skin tissues, tiny specks of memory. This house is now her blood and bones. (18)

In purely rhetorical terms, Kogawa's narrator establishes a metonymic relationship between her aunt and her aunt's house. As a narrative strategy, however, this metonymy allows Naomi to invoke a deep and subtle image of Obasan without betraying the privacy of the self. Here we see how rhetorical silence deflects the potentially invasive gaze of readers away from the figure of Obasan, while at the same time obliging them to "read" her silence from a different perspective. In this case, each object described becomes another nonverbal sign in the silent but consciously "ordered" language of Obasan's text, signs that connect her intimately and visibly to the world she inhabits and the world that inhabits her. This sense of connectedness is made even more explicit when Naomi, watching Obasan clean her dead uncle's boots, compares her to "every old woman in every hamlet in the world. . . . The bearer of keys to unknown doorways . . . [t]he possessor of life's infinite personal details" (18–19). Like Naomi, readers also watch Obasan at a distance from which they perceive the personal details of her character through the smallest gestures of her body. This respectful attentiveness is the basis for understanding that Obasan's silent act of pushing uncle's shoes to the side and placing Naomi's neatly beside them is a gesture of connectedness and care.

In contrast to Obasan's careful and deliberate ordering of her life within the closed "text" of her house, the world outside those walls (which is also the world of the readers) is large and dissonant. Yet even as Obasan tells Naomi about the circumstances of her uncle's death in the hospital, her perception of the event is lucid and direct.

"There was no knowing," she says. She did not understand what was happening. The nurses at the hospital also did not understand. They stuck tubes into his wrists like grafting on a tree but Death won against medical artistry. She wanted to stay beside him there, but, again, "There was no knowing." The nurses sent her home. (16)

Most striking about this passage is the quiet display of the confusion brought on not only by Obasan's inability to communicate, but also by the nurses' inability to understand. Probably (white) women, dedicated to a caretaking profession, the nurses are, nonetheless, unable to establish a connection with this old Japanese woman, silently watching their efforts to accommodate her dying husband—efforts which, from her particular perspective, are as unnatural and artificial as a tree-grafting. The evocative and ambiguous phrase, "There was no knowing," refers less to Obasan's confusion than to the nurses' and readers' ignorance of her life. At this point in the novel, neither they nor we know that Obasan has already been separated from, and lost, almost every member of her family. Throughout the description of this scene, Naomi withholds any information or detail that would overtly invite readers' empathy, holding them, instead, at a measured distance. As a narrative strategy, her reticence counters readers' desire to identify with the feelings or experiences of Kogawa's characters, not because there is a lack of affect on the part of the narrator, but because the affect expressed is not "translated" into the cultural forms, words, or gestures that would make it easily recognizable to a white, middle-class reader. Thus, Kogawa maintains the cultural integrity of her character, configuring Obasan's silence with a variety of narrative strategies that call upon readers to "listen" to the experiential nuances of difference.

Nisei Silence: Mother

The cultural values Naomi inherits from her mother, like the ones embodied by the figure of Obasan, emphasize Japanese aesthetics of restraint and understatement, aesthetics of conduct which it would be mistaken to simplistically equate with patriarchal oppression. Although Naomi's mother is Nisei, born in Canada, she was raised in Japan. Thus, her cultural values, the ones she passes down to Naomi, are more sharply drawn from Japanese behavioral norms such as *enryo* (self-restraint, reserve), *oya koh koh* (filial piety), and social concepts of being *majime* (serious, honest) and *sunao* (gentle, obedient).[7] Although these values are rarely named explicitly, their presence and importance in Naomi's childhood are persistent and compelling influences that shape the way she sees the world, and the way the world sees her. Thus, seeing and being seen take on a complexity of cultural meaning that is often communicated silently, a process exemplified in Naomi's childhood recollection of riding on a streetcar with her mother. As she prepares to de-board, four-year-old Naomi notices a male passenger looking at her "quizzically":

> When our eyes meet, he grins and winks. I turn away instantly, startled into discomfort again by eyes. My mother's eyes look obliquely to the floor, declaring that on the streets, at all times, in all public places, even a glance can be indiscreet. But a stare? Such a lack of decorum, it is clear, is as unthinkable as nudity on the street. (58)

Naomi's ability to read both the gaze of the man and the oblique look of her mother exemplifies her understanding of what she terms "the language of the eyes," in which "a stare is an invasion and a reproach" (58). Like Obasan's silent "language of grief," the "language of the eyes" constitutes another wordless, cultural dialect, which Naomi and her mother "speak" fluently. While her mother's downcast eyes may denote deference, they do not in this context denote an inability to connect, nor are they a sign of evasiveness.[8] Neither Naomi's nor her mother's looking away arises out of fear or submissiveness, but rather from a deep sense of social impropriety. From this cultural standpoint, communication and connectedness take place in the context of exchanged glances, which, as the above passage indicates, is full of unstated emotional and psychological responses. While they perceive the man's gaze as invasive, their shock and discomfort arise primarily from their belief that he has exposed himself publicly. Their subtle gestures and silence are acts that belie both a resistance to his gaze and a polite consideration of his and their personal, private space, which he has, in their eyes, unwittingly invaded.

The public and private spheres of interaction have been closely examined by feminist theorists, many of whom distinguish the public as a primarily male domain, while the private, often equated to domestic space, is relegated to women. Within this scheme, many groundbreaking cultural critiques on the "institution" of mothering have emerged, resulting in a more complex understanding of mothering as a social construct of patriarchy rather than a biologically, essentialist "instinct."[9] At the center of these studies, however, is the important role of the mother in the moral and psychological development of her daughter as a gendered individual. Yet, how do we read the role of the mother in a predominantly non-Western culture? Stressing the connection between the development of girls' knowledge and education and the development of their relationships with others, Gilligan rightly observes the importance of adult female role models in teaching girls to cultivate and maintain their voices. Paraphrasing Virginia Woolf, who asks "why mothers do not leave more of a legacy for their daughters, and why . . . mothers do not endow their daughters' education with greater comfort" (cited in *Making Connections* 25), Gilligan encourages women "to stay in the gaze of girls so that girls do not have to look and not see," and to "sustain girls' gaze and respond to girls' voices" (*Making Connections* 26). In Naomi's relationship with her mother, this gaze is clearly sustained, but the silences that characterize many of the "languages" shared between them do not quite fit the model of responsiveness proposed by Gilligan and others.[10]

A telling example of the cultural differences in mother-daughter responsiveness occurs in a specific memory where Naomi, playing in the garage of her house, observes that a white hen in a cage is separated from her chicks. She automatically assumes that the family should be together and proceeds to put the chicks in the cage. To her horror, the mother hen begins to peck her children to death, prompting Naomi to run and find her mother, who is visiting with a neighbor, Mrs. Sugimoto. When her mother sees her, she responds immediately, "without a word and without alarm" (70):

> With swift deft fingers, Mother removes the live chicks first, placing them in her apron. All the while that she acts, there is calm efficiency in her face and she does not speak. Her eyes are steady and matter-of-fact—the eyes of Japanese motherhood. They do not invade and betray. They are eyes that protect, shielding what is hidden most deeply in the heart of the child. She makes safe the small stirrings underfoot and in the shadows. Physically, the sensation is not in the region of the heart, but in the belly. This that is in the belly is honored when it is allowed to be, without fanfare, without reproach, without words. What is there is there. (71)

Naomi's sense of connectedness to her mother arises from the calmness and matter-of-factness communicated without words, suggesting a culture-specific definition of empathy that underscores a certain emotional distance between mother and child. Contrary to Surrey's definition of mutual empathy as a shared experience of " 'feeling seen' and . . . sensing the other 'feeling seen' " (55), the empathic connection between Naomi and her mother relies upon the seemingly disaffected gaze of the maternal eyes, which do not "invade and betray." This is not to deny that there is a "mirroring process" that takes place between the mother and daughter, but rather to emphasize that such a process, within the frame of Japanese culture, is more deflective than reflective in nature. Naomi knows that her mother understands her feelings and needs because her mother protects those feelings by not overtly or explicitly recognizing them. The feeling of safety she experiences is the product of her mother's silence and "matter-of-factness," which allows Naomi the private, emotional space to keep "what is most hidden" in her child's heart.

In contrast to her mother's protective distance, Naomi juxtaposes a description of Mrs. Sugimoto, who has followed them out to the garage. "Her face is not matter-of-fact like Mother's. Her eyes search my face. Her glance is too long. She notes my fear, invades *my knowing*" (emphasis mine, 71). Without the cultural context, it would be easy to read Mrs. Sugimoto's response as empathic and concerned. The visible emotional expression of her face and the look of concern are, from a Western psychological view, signs of relatedness and recognition. Yet, read in conjunction with her mother's response, the description of Mrs. Sugimoto's gaze points to the potential invasiveness of the well-meaning, but overcurious gaze.[11] Naomi's discomfort is a reaction to what she perceives as an assumed intimacy on the part of the adult woman whose glance, despite their common gender and ethnicity, invades the young girl's "knowing" precisely because it exposes her fear.

By implication, this episode problematizes the position of readers, whose own empathic connection is mediated and in a sense resisted by the narrative distance maintained throughout this passage. The clipped sentences, the unadorned descriptions, and the "matter-of-fact" tone are powerful in their understatement, never giving over to inflated idealizations of her mother, or underhanded vilifications of Mrs. Sugimoto. This distanced and resistant position is, perhaps ironically, the result of Naomi's intimate connection to her mother. Shortly after the incident with the chicks, her mother speaks with her about it:

> "It was not good, was it?" Mother says. "*Yoku nakatta ne.*" Three words. Good, negation of good in the past tense, agreement with statement. It is not a language that promotes hysteria. There is no blame or pity. I am not responsible. The hen is not responsible. My mother does not look at me when she says this. . . . She has waited until all is calm before we talk. . . . There is nothing about me my mother does not know, nothing that is not safe to tell. (72)

By translating and breaking down each particle of the Japanese sentence uttered by her mother, Naomi locates the culturally specific grammar of simplicity and emotional restraint that characterizes her own narrative language in English. Her mother's voice, when she does speak, remains measured, even, and unobtrusive in the brevity of its statement. Her apparent lack of emotion and the aversion of her eyes from her daughter are not signs of evasiveness, withholding, or failed empathy, but rather culturally inflected responses of care and connection. That Naomi understands this is clear in the feeling of safety and of being known, which she experiences in relation to her mother. As we have seen throughout these passages, *knowing* itself is a culturally defined concept, developed through the complex interaction of wordless languages, meaningful silences, and visual exchanges.

Such a complex web of communication and connection requires a reconsideration of the dichotomizing metaphor of voice and silence that Belenky and her co-authors privilege as the link in the development of "women's ways of knowing and of the long journey they must make if they are to put the knower back in the known and claim the power of their minds and voices" (19). At the same time, the notion of the gaze must be taken beyond questions of gender to include those of race and culture.[12] While Gilligan clearly identifies the power of the "male gaze" as a means of subordinating and objectifying women, she does not acknowledge that her own analytical gaze is informed by her position as a white, middle-class member of a social order that has historically oppressed both men and women from "other" cultures. What occurs is a sidestepping of racial considerations that posits gender as "a variable of human identity independent of other variables such as race and class, that whether one is a woman is unaffected by what class or race one is" (Spelman 81).[13] Through the narrator's memories of her mother, Kogawa counters such projections and assumptions by carefully contextualizing her female characters' silences and behaviors from the perspective of Japanese American cultural and social values. By amplifying the interpretive lens through which the non-verbal, but often visible, language of her characters is read, Kogawa encourages her readers to examine their own critical positioning so that they, like Naomi, might learn to be "visually bilingual" (58). Aware of the objectified position in which Asian Americans, in general, and Asian American women, in particular, have been historically placed as passive, reserved, selfless, and blindly obedient, Kogawa, through the detailed chronicling of Naomi's relationship to her mother, underscores the importance of both silence and seeing in the construction of Naomi's multicultural knowledge of herself as both a woman and an Asian American.

Nisei Voice: Aunt Emily

"How different my two aunts are. One lives in sound, the other in stone. Obasan's language remains deeply underground but Aunt Emily . . . is a word warrior" (39). Thus, Naomi recalls the figure of her Aunt Emily, her mother's younger sister, when Obasan brings her a package of documents, letters, and personal writings saved by Aunt Emily before and during the war. Although Emily is, like Naomi's mother, a Nisei, she was raised exclusively in Canada and insists on her political identity as a Canadian citizen. Consequently, she is an outspoken defender of the rights of her Japanese American community, and it is largely through her words, both written and spoken, that the historical dimensions of racial injustice are exposed and critiqued in Kogawa's novel. As a political activist for her people, Aunt Emily's voice stands in apparent opposition to Obasan's and Naomi's mother's silence, creating in Naomi a split view of her aunts, the two living female forces in her life. In contrast to Obasan, who accumulates and orders the personal history of their family in the infinite odds and ends that clutter her house, Aunt Emily gathers and organizes the collective history of her people. While Obasan constitutes the central figure of constancy and stability in Naomi's life, Aunt Emily is always on the move and rarely present.[14] After the war, during infrequent visits to Obasan, Aunt Emily encourages her reluctant niece to remember the past as a way of recovering what she perceives to be the lost voices of her victimized community.

> "We're gluing our tongues back on," Aunt Emily said. "It takes a while for the nerves to grow back. . . . We have to deal with all this while we remem-

ber it. If we don't, we'll pass on our anger down in our genes. It's the children who'll suffer." (43)

Like the dominant metaphor of feminist psychology, voice, Aunt Emily's image of the disconnected tongue reflects her own privileging of voice as the primary means of processing the traumatic events of the war. To rebuild a "healthy" community necessitates an externalization of what she assumes to be the silenced and buried anger of its members. From a feminist psychological viewpoint, which often equates unspoken anger with "being out of relationship," (*Making Connections* 16–17). Aunt Emily's insistence on voice and memory are both compelling and justified. Yet, as one of the many "voices" that populates Naomi's inner world, her aunt's well-intentioned command that she remember and speak runs counter to the earlier messages that she has received from both Obasan and her mother. Here, Aunt Emily's warning that continued silence will engender the suffering of future generations recalls and opposes the cultural imperative of the Issei that silence be maintained "for the sake of the children." Caught in the middle of these contradictory voices, Naomi struggles to mediate this conflict by maintaining an ambivalent position. For her Aunt Emily, however, there is no middle ground, and she perceives both her niece's and her community's reticence and ambivalence about the past as their unwillingness to take a stand. Thus, when Naomi tries to suggest that the cautious, post-war attitude of many Japanese Americans might be based on the belief that "the welfare of the whole is more important than the welfare of the part" (42), her Aunt responds sharply, "Some people are so busy seeing all sides of every issue that they neutralize concern and prevent necessary action" (42).[15]

Although Aunt Emily clearly possesses a voice, one that is compelling in its moral authority and urgency, it neither recognizes nor affords space for the personal and cultural conflicts of Naomi's life experiences. Like Naomi, Aunt Emily is caught between two cultures, but where Naomi travels inward toward the "hidden word," Aunt Emily travels outward toward the world. Always speaking in the "we" rather than the "I," Aunt Emily transforms the pain of her personal experiences into political indignation for her community. Her assimilation to the dominant Western culture in which she lives has gained her access to a voice, but at the expense of losing her "ear"—she cannot hear the subtle, cultural registers of silence that characterize Naomi's, Obasan's, and her sister's languages. As a result, her capacity "to know" and to empathize with her niece is limited by her inability to listen, making it difficult for her to sustain an intimate connection to Naomi and her family. Thus, even while Naomi admires her aunt's activism and acknowledges the moral imperative behind it, she questions that moral imperative by asserting her own:

People who talk a lot about their victimization make me uncomfortable. It is as if they use their suffering as weapons or badges of some kind. From my years of teaching I know it's the children who say nothing who are in trouble more than the ones who complain. (41)

Naomi's wariness of Aunt Emily's indignation, which she hears as complaining, could be interpreted pathologically: a symptom or denial of her own fear and shame around being perceived as a victim. Further, Naomi's view of "suffering as weapon" echoes the assessment made by Belenky et al. on how silent women view "words as weapons," suggesting that silence is the best strategy of protection in a hostile and uncaring world. Yet, even while denial may be part of Naomi's resistance, she is careful to contextualize her unwillingness to engage in the political battle her Aunt Emily so insistently pushes her toward. Naomi's reference to her own perceptions as a teacher who "reads" the silence of her young students as a sign of their trouble once again configures silence as a language whose meaning can only be discerned through careful listening. Although they are not explicitly invoked, her mother's and her Obasan's wordless languages resonate below the surface of this passage, speaking to those readers who have listened attentively to episodes described earlier. From this perspective, responsibility as the ability to respond becomes Naomi's moral imperative, which she posits as a dialectical process—one that both amplifies and complicates the role of the listener and the speaker. This is not to deny the significance of Aunt Emily's voice in Naomi's life or the legitimacy of Emily's position among the others presented by Kogawa, but to suggest that the psychological development of voice is both complicated and informed by specific cultural and historical contexts.[16] Aunt Emily's voice, like Naomi's silence, is the product of both internal and external factors that have shaped each woman's position in relation to herself and the world.

As Naomi begins to read the packet of Aunt Emily's documents left in the care of Obasan, she finds Emily's wartime diary, which is full of unsent letters to Naomi's mother in Japan. It is through these letters, written in the midst of relocation, that we hear the private voice of Emily's pain and confusion, which gradually turn to numbness.

Nothing affects me much just now except rather detachedly. Everything is like a bad dream. I keep telling myself to wake up. There's no sadness when friends of long standing disappear overnight—either to Camp or somewhere in the Interior. No farewells—no promise at all of future meetings or correspondence—or anything. We just disperse. It's as if we never existed. We're hit so many ways at one time that if I wasn't past feeling I think I would crumble. (105)

Read in conjunction with her impassioned activist voice, this passage un-covers the "silenced" sources of pain and powerlessness that inform Aunt Emily's angry and defiant stance against the world. To feel, as Naomi and Obasan do, the depth of loss incurred by the war would be for Emily "to crumble" and die. It is Aunt Emily's detachment from her personal pain that Naomi senses in the vehemence of her voice, which has become her primary weapon of resistance to the underlying helplessness she once felt. Her hard-fought and heroic efforts "to tell the lives of the Nisei . . . to make familiar, to make knowable the treacherous yellow peril that lived in the minds of the racially prejudiced" (49) have paradoxically taken her so far from her family that, in their eyes, she becomes increas-ingly unfamiliar.[17] Thus, even as Aunt Emily exhorts Naomi to express her memories and feelings because "denial is gangrene," her own voice is full of silences which Naomi's attuned ear picks up. Despite the seem-ing clarity of Aunt Emily's voice, which certainly nudges Naomi toward the personal conflict that initiates her own narrative, Aunt Emily alone does not possess the "living word" that Naomi seeks. As we have seen, Naomi mediates that conflict by refusing to take sides, by listening care-fully to both the voices and the silences that have shaped her life, and that she now reshapes for herself and her readers in her own telling.

Conclusion

The resolution to Naomi's story occurs when all the living members of her family (Obasan, Aunt Emily, her brother Stephen) gather at Obasan's for her uncle's funeral. It is then that her mother's disappearance is finally explained in a series of letters included among the many documents saved by her Aunt Emily. The letters are dated 1949 and are sent from Naga-saki by her grandmother, who describes in detail the mortal wounding of Naomi's mother in the atomic bombing of the city and how, before she died, she requested that her children never know the truth of her death. This unspoken secret is at the center of the "silence that cannot speak" invoked by Naomi in the opening line of the novel, and is intimately connected to the other "silence that will not speak." For even as Naomi is filled with grief as she hears her mother through the words of her grandmother, her expression of loss is to listen to the "powerful voice-lessness" of her mother which cannot hide her pain from her daughter: "Beneath the hiding I am there with you" (290). The painful recovery of her mother's silent voice, spoken across time, is what allows Naomi "to know" her mother's absence, "though [she is] not here" (292). And it is this knowing that transforms the stasis of her ambivalence into the free-ing movement of her acceptance as she embraces the myriad voices that live within her: "the voices pour down like rain but in the middle of the downpour I still feel thirst. Somewhere between speech and listening is a transmutation of sound" (295). It is in that transformative space between "speech and hearing" that Naomi locates her own voice, inflected with the sadness and longing, the hope and compassion of all her wordless and word-filled languages as she tells her own story and the history of her community.

To read Joy Kogawa's novel requires an ear tuned to the rich and meaningful nuances of silence and speech, which take their shape both within and against a culturally specific and historically inflected narrative frame. Within this frame, Kogawa posits silence as both a language of connection and a strategy of resistance, revealing in the process an ethic of care constructed on a notion of responsiveness that is often unvoiced. Rather than privilege the reader, as one would expect from an autobiographical narrative that typically promises to disclose the inner life of its subject, Kogawa's narrator often holds her readers at arms length, obliging them to attend, like Naomi, to the hidden voice beneath the words. To the moral question raised earlier as to how one tells one's life to another without giving oneself away in the process, Kogawa answers with silence, but a silence that is full of meaning for those who know how to listen. As a result, silence, which is traditionally associated with passivity, resignation, fear, and repression, takes on the deeper dimension of agency, resistance, courage, and insight.

Notes

1. The importance of voice in the "self-in-relation" theory of women's development is grounded in Gilligan's work on female voice. See also *Women's Growth in Connection*, Eds. Judith V. Jordan et al.

2. In *Inessential Woman*, Spelman points to the problematic dimensions of Western feminist theory, which fails to account for the racial and class differences among women. The result is the illusion of equality based on an elision of those differences, which Spelman compares to Kenneth Stampp's argument for "racial equality"—an argument founded on the belief that all African Americans are white men underneath: "Western feminist theory has in effect used Stampp's argument whenever it has implicitly demanded that Afro American, Asian American, or Latin American women separate their 'woman's voice' from their racial or ethnic voice without also requiring white women to distinguish being a 'woman' from being white. This double standard implies that . . . Blackness and womanness or Indianness and womanness are discrete and separable elements of identity" (13).

3. One of the important early studies toward a feminist theory of reading is Fetterley's *The Resisting Reader* (1978), which develops feminist reading strate-

gies of canonized, male-authored texts. According to Fetterley, women must learn to overcome the male-identified training they received in graduate school in order to resist becoming "immasculated." In her article "Reading Ourselves: Toward a Feminist Theory of Reading," Schweickart expands Fetterley's theory to include strategies of reading works by female authors. Incorporating Gilligan's emphasis on female voice and responsibility, she suggests that women readers can read themselves in works by women writers: "In the dialectic of communication informing the relationship between feminist reader and female author/text, the central issue is not control or partition, but of managing the contradictory implications of the desire for relationship . . . and the desire for intimacy, up to and including a symbiotic merger with the other" (55).

4. Joy Kogawa participates in a growing movement among Asian American writers who, in Traise Yamamoto's words, "see silence [as] something to be broken, shattered, shredded; it is something solid through which one must pass in order to join one's voice to the voices on the other side. It sits stone heavy in the body, or is a stifling enclosure within which the body suffocates. The act of writing becomes the broadest stroke toward speech" (131).

5. In their article "Asian-American and Pacific Islander Patients," psychologists Chien and Yamamoto discuss in detail the influence of Confucianist philosophy in the social and moral values of most Asian cultures. From within that culturally drawn frame, they observe that in "most Asian and Pacific cultures, family is the important unit, not the individual" (134).

6. It is worth noting that the authors' opening statements to the chapter on silence belie a certain ambivalence as to the importance of silence and silent women who are relatively few among those women interviewed. The authors consider silence the "simplest way" to begin their description of women's ways of knowing. Further, although they note that the absence of voice is salient in some women, they offer a quasi apology for this category because "it is not parallel to the terms [they] have chosen for the other epistemological positions" (24), in a sense, ranking silence at the bottom of their categorical hierarchy.

7. For a more detailed discussion of these Japanese values, see Nakano, 105.

8. In an unrecorded informal talk given to female therapists at the Women's Therapy Clinic in Berkeley, California, Asian American social worker Gloria Saito addressed problems of interpreting the silences and gestures of Asian American female clients in therapeutic diagnosis, emphasizing that there is "a fine line between what is culturally appropriate and maladaptive." She specifically cautioned therapists against reading the downcast eyes of Asian American clients as "evasiveness."

9. See Chodorow's *The Reproduction of Mothering*, and Gilligan's *In a Different Voice*.

10. The relative lack of studies on the culturally specific differences in the mothering experience limits psychological interpretations of the mother-daughter relationship in girls' development of self. Although I have found a few discussions on Japanese mothering practices, they are usually subordinated to the larger Western psychological perspective of the mother's role. See Willard 227, and Belenky et al. 178.

11. It should be noted that Mrs. Sugimoto is portrayed as a more assimilated Nisei.

12. See Spelman, especially chapter 4, in which she critiques the limitations of Chodorow's notions of the mother-daughter relationship.

13. Stack, among others, makes a similar assertion about the need to consider gender as a "construct shaped by the experience of race, class, culture, and consciousness" (111).

14. It should be noted that when Naomi's family is relocated to the interior in 1942, Aunt Emily, given the choice of staying with them, decides to go to Toronto, where she can better continue her activism on behalf of her community. She does not see her family again until 1954, after twelve years of separation.

15. In *Mapping the Moral Domain*, Gilligan distinguishes between two moral perspectives, which she designates as "care orientation" and "justice orientation" (119). Within this scheme, "care orientation" arises out of a sense of ongoing attachment and connection, while "justice orientation" is grounded in the more privileged, psychological notion of detachment. From her argument that both perspectives have their benefits and limitations, Gilligan points out that clear, moral conviction, which certainly informs Aunt Emily's resonant and articulate voice, does not necessarily signal better psychological health or a more developed sense of self: "If the persistent error in care reasoning is vacillation and lack of clear judgment resulting from a tendency to include all possible ways of seeing, the persistent danger in justice reasoning is moral arrogance, the irrational faith in the infallibility of judgments from principles rigidly applied to a situation" (134). Similarly, in the theoretical categories established in *Women's Ways of Knowing*, Aunt Emily might be characterized as a "received knower" for whom "there are no gradations of truth—no gray areas. Paradox is inconceivable because received knowers believe several contradictory ideas are never simultaneously in accordance with fact" (41). The authors attribute this particular position to the patriarchal constraints of education, which emphasize and privilege rational clarity. I would add that the equally important factors of history, culture, and race must also be considered in such assessments. Aunt Emily's either-or way of thinking is as much a product of the racism and injustice she suffered at the hands of her government as it is a product of her being a woman in a patriarchal society.

16. While feminist psychologists clearly acknowledge the importance of listening, they listen, in a sense, with "ears" attuned primarily to the dissonances of gender difference. Consequently, there is a tendency to subordinate listening to the imperative for women to find their "voice" as the most effective means of combating the patriarchal directives to women to keep quiet.

17. Gilligan rightly observes that "the choices that women make in order to survive or to appear good in the eyes of others (and thus sustain their protection) are often at the expense of women's relationships with one another" (*Making Connections*, 26). Aunt Emily's situation as an Asian American, however, clearly draws attention to the equally dangerous risk of making choices that threaten her connection with her culture and community.

Works Cited

Belenky, Mary Field, Blythe McVicker Clinchy, Nancy Rule Goldberger, and Jill Mattuck Tarule. *Women's Ways of Knowing: The Development of Self, Voice, and Mind*. New York: Basic Books, 1986.

Chien, Ching-Piao, and Joe Yamamoto. "Asian American and Pacific Islander Patients." [No other bibliographical information available.]

Chodorow, Nancy. *The Reproduction of Mothering*. Berkeley: U of California P, 1978.

duCille, Ann. "The Occult of True Black Womanhood: Critical Demeanor and Black Feminist Studies." *Signs* 19.31 (1994): 591–625.

Fetterley, Judith. *The Resisting Reader: A Feminist Approach to American Fiction*. Bloomington: Indiana UP, 1977.

Gilligan, Carol. *In a Different Voice*. Cambridge: Harvard UP, 1982.

———. "Teaching Shakespeare's Sister: Notes from the Underground of Female Adolescence." *Making Connections: The Relational Worlds of Adolescent Girls at Emma Willard School*. Ed. Carol Gilligan, Nona P. Lyons, and Trudy J. Hanmer. Cambridge: Harvard UP, 1960. 6–27.

Gilligan, Carol, and Grant Wiggins. "The Origins of Morality in Early Childhood Relationships." *Mapping the Moral Domain*. Ed. Carol Gilligan, Janie Victoria Ward, and Jill McLean Taylor. Cambridge: Center for the Study of Gender, Education and Human Development, 1988. 111–137.

Glenn, Evelyn Nakano. *Issei, Nisei, War Bride: Three Generations of Japanese American Women in Domestic Service*. Philadelphia: Temple UP, 1986.

Kogawa, Joy. *Obasan*. New York: Doubleday, 1981.

Nakano, Mei. *Issei, Nisei, War Bride: Three Generations of Japanese American Women in Domestic Service*. Berkeley: Mina Press Publishing, and San Francisco: National Japanese American Historical Society, 1990.

O'Brian, David, and Stephen S. Fugita. *The Japanese American Experience*. Bloomington: Indiana UP, 1991.

Saito, Gloria. "Asian American Women in Therapy." Professional Colloquium for Women's Therapy Center, Berkeley, March, 1993.

Saltzman, Judith P. "Save the World, Save Myself: Responses to Problematic Attachment." *Making Connections*. Ed. Carol Gilligan et al. Cambridge: Harvard UP, 1990. 110–146.

Schweickart, Patrocinio P. "Reading Ourselves: Toward a Feminist Theory of Reading." Ed. Patrocinio P. Schweickhart and Elizabeth A. Flynn. *Gender and Reading: Essays on Readers, Texts, and Contexts*. Baltimore: Johns Hopkins UP, 1986. 31–62.

Spelman, Elizabeth V. *The Inessential Woman: Problems of Exclusion in Feminist Thought*. Boston: Beacon Press, 1988.

Stack, Carol B. "The Culture of Gender: Women and Men of Color." *An Ethic of Care: Feminist and Interdisciplinary Perspectives*. Ed. Mary Jeanne Larrabee. New York: Routledge, 1993. 198–211.

Surrey, Janet L. "The 'Self-in-Relation': A Theory of Women's Development." *Women's Growth in Connection: Writings from the Stone Center*. Ed. Judith V. Jordan et al. New York: The Guilford Press, 1991. 51–56.

Willard, Ann. "Cultural Scripts for Mothering." *Mapping the Moral Domain.* Ed. Carol Gilligan et al. Cambridge: Center for the Study of Gender, Education and Human Development, 1988. 225–243.

Yamamoto, Traise. "Different Silences." *The Intimate Critique: Autobiographical Literary Criticism.* Ed. Diane P. Freedman, Olivia Frey, and Frances Murphey Zauhar. Durham: Duke UP, 1993. 127–134.

7

Motherlands and Foremothers: African American Women's Texts and the Concept of Relationship

Sally L. Kitch

When women construct the adult domain, the world of relationships emerges and becomes the focus of attention and concern.

Carol Gilligan

The claims of Carol Gilligan and other contemporary theorists that women develop a consciousness of themselves in relationship to, rather than in isolation from, others has intriguing implications for the work of many modern African American women writers. The two novels used to represent that work in this essay abound with references to women's sense of connection and relationship. Indeed, they are predicated on women's sense of relationship through both time and space, particularly with their racial forebears. At the same time, the relationships portrayed in these novels in some ways defy Gilligan's notion of female gender identity.

Particularly supportive of Gilligan's work is the assertion in the novels of the special importance of women's connection with other women. Like many protagonists in contemporary African American women's fiction, the major female characters in Paule Marshall's *Praisesong for the Widow* and Gloria Naylor's *Mama Day* take their strength and build their identities on the strengths and identities of their foremothers. Marshall's Avey Johnson, an affluent widow in her sixties, must come to terms with and integrate into her being the voice and demands of her dead great-aunt Cuney, whose ghost has begun to haunt her dreams. Avey's vision of Cuney recalls her childhood summers on Tatem Island

and her great-aunt's stories of slaves who walked on water back to Africa. So powerful is Aunt Cuney that, in her spectral presence, Avey's life of the previous thirty years seems to vanish down a "yawning hole" (Marshall 172). Naylor's Cocoa Day has two powerful women in both her imagination and her life. Raised by her great-aunt Miranda (Mama Day)—a conjure woman, healer, and rootworker—and her grandmother Abigail, the twenty-something Cocoa sees herself, even in her New York life, as an outgrowth of her relationship to those powerful, but loving women from the South. Like *Praisesong*, Naylor's novel makes clear, however, that a sense of relationship is not sufficient. In order to achieve their own identities, the women in both novels must actively reclaim their female ancestors and strive to comprehend the meaning of their lives.

The novels' exploration of the female self in connection to female ancestors does not, however, conform precisely to the object relations theory that underlies Gilligan's work. As articulated by Nancy Chodorow, whom Gilligan quotes, that theory attributes women's relationship-focused gender personality to the intimate mother-daughter relationship allegedly typical of Western culture, in which infants are left primarily in their mothers' care. Because of their physiological similarities to their daughters, mothers in that (our) culture tend to identify with them. As a result, the mother-daughter pair develops a gender-based psychological bond that remains loosely intact throughout the daughter's life. Early mother-daughter symbiosis is eventually translated through the daughter's development into a more generalized need and respect for relationships. "Girls . . . experience themselves . . . as . . . continuous with and related to the external object-world," writes Chodorow. Because of the difference in sex between mothers and sons, quite a different form of gender identity develops for boys. Mothers perceive sons as the "other," and, therefore, boys form identities that depend upon a sense of separation and individuation. (Because theirs is an "otherness" associated with power, however, boys eagerly embrace their difference from Mother and turn to Father for a model.) Becoming masculine in the female-dominated world of mothers and children requires an escape from the feminine identity of connection (Gilligan 7–8). Thus, according to Gilligan and Chodorow, women's sense of connectedness is rooted in the mother-daughter relationship. It forms the basis of women's feminine gender identities, and from those identities, women make the decisions and choices that shape their lives.

While the focus in the Marshall and Naylor novels on the reestablishment of characters' connections with their female roots in the search for self and the resolution of life's conflicts parallels the Chodorow/Gilligan model, the texts' indifference to the literal or biological mother-daughter relationship suggests other forces are at work. The novels also contain elements that suggest deviation from the model: Avey's, Miranda's, and Cocoa's reclamation of their heritages not only excludes their own mothers and minimizes the importance of maternal nurture; it also transcends their personal upbringings. In addition, the novels insist on the importance to the characters' identity formation of mother*lands* as well as human female heroes and role models. For example, the moment of Avey's self-recognition, represented by her reclamation of her full given name, Avatara, coincides with her performance of a ritual dance in which her feet instinctively remain in contact with the ground she has come to understand as her ancestral soil. Indeed, her shuffle step is "designed to stay the course of history" and connect her to a history that is hers, whether she knows it or not (Marshall 250). Similarly, Cocoa Day carries within her not only the voices of her great-aunt and grandmother, but the sights, sounds, smells, history, and mysteries of her Sea Island home, Willow Springs. "Home," she thinks. "You can move away from it, but you never leave it. . . . It took only a little while for her body to remember how to flow in time with the warm air and the swaying limbs of the oaks" (Naylor 50).

Furthermore, the purely personal developmental model in object-relations theory seems inadequate to explain the interconnection between Avey's and Cocoa's individual identities and their identification as members of a race whose history and values, whether experienced directly by them or not, give meaning to their lives. Indeed, in the context of these novels, the pursuit of a purely individual identity or one that focuses entirely on the natal family is inscribed as a mistake, a misdirection of energies, and an abandonment of that which makes an individual most herself.

Understanding these novels' many layers requires at the very least a revision of the Freudian "Family Romance" that underlies object-relations theory. Even though, by valorizing the mother-daughter relationship and the importance of maternal influence in the pre-Oedipal period, American feminist interpreters of Freud, like Chodorow, have debunked such aspects of the nuclear family triangle as penis envy and the Electra complex, they remain somewhat fixated on the traditional nuclear family triangle—mother, father, and child—in which the father plays the vital role of mediating between the overly intimate mother-child relationship.

That nuclear family model is problematic for African American family structures, which have historically had a more varied composition—less reliance on fathers for economic support, more collective nurture by other-mothers, and more multigenerational and female-centered households (even if males are present)—than white families.[1] The legacy of slavery has historically located the African American family less in the *union* than in the threatened or actual *separation* of mothers and children. Slavery also eliminated the possibility of a protected mother-child unit, and its legacy has rendered African American families less economically and psychologically secure than the typical white, middle-class family. Slavery also established the limits of black mothers' control of their children (clearly giving the lie to the concept of black matriarchy) and forced family units into a kind of "horizontal relatedness" with those around them, rather than the "vertical" transfer of bloodlines and names from fathers to sons that characterized free families. In contrast to the Freudian nuclear family model, the African American experience of slavery also rendered the black father, even when present, a cipher, made invisible by the "captor father's mocking presence" (Spillers, "Mama's Baby" 73–75, 79–80). Theorists of the third world, whose analysis of colonialism resonates with the African American experience, reject claims of universality for the nuclear family triangle. Gayatri Spivak, for example, criticizes developmental theories for ignoring race and class and for creating idealized and mythical "regulative type-cases" (Spivak, "French Feminism" 82). If the nuclear family is not the paradigm for African Americans, then the premise for object-relations theory and its analysis of women's sense of self in relationship must be reexamined.

Also stretching the boundaries of the Gilligan/Chodorow theory is the novels' insistence on the supernatural in their exploration of their protagonists' identities and life purposes. Both texts inscribe the importance of dreams, visions, ghosts, magic, and ritual to the deeper meaning of the characters' relationships to their forebears. Indeed, one critic has categorized *Praisesong* as a ghost story, in the tradition of both West African and slave cultures (Smith-Wright 159–64). Had that critic studied *Mama Day,* she may well have placed it in the same category. For Avey, Cocoa, and Miranda, the achievement of identity and the comprehension of self involve more than a relationship with actual people or a sense of connectedness with others. Theirs is a relationship with race history and its ghosts.

The novels' mystical layers can in part be explicated as an encoding of the folklore and folkways of Africa and the Caribbean that first infiltrate and then dominate the characters' lives. But that explanation alone is inadequate. The novels' mystical qualities can also be read in terms of the characters' deep psychic structures, which, when interpreted in light of certain French psychoanalytic theory, connect individuals to culturally mediated psychosexual processes and relationships. According to such theory, nonrational, dream, and preverbal imagery signifies the *feminine*—"that which has been 'left out,' de-emphasized, hidden, or denied articulation within Western systems of knowledge" (Jardine 36). In the context of these racially charged works, the *feminine* expands to include both sex and race, and the concept of "relationship" in the formation of female identity takes on cultural aspects, as well as strictly personal issues of psychosexual development and relationship formation. Consistent with this theoretical perspective, the novels' mystical and non-rational elements help establish a connection between individual development and "the reality and the strength of social mediations" (Spivak, "French Feminism" 148). Thus, the relationships valued by the novels' protagonists extend beyond the world of individual experience to a collective history now knowable primarily through its vestiges in the protagonists' unconscious minds. Having been erased or twisted by the dominant culture, their history now consists of mystery and whispers.

The Novels: In the Presence of the Ancestors[2]

This abstract exploration of female gender identity and relationship becomes clearer through a discussion of the two novels. Paule Marshall's *Praisesong for the Widow* (1983) opens as Avey Johnson, affluent black widow of successful accountant, Jerome Johnson, is feverishly packing her six matched suitcases with the abundance of clothing and accessories she has amassed for a sumptuous Caribbean cruise. She is leaving the cruise when it docks at Grenada because she has developed a vague feeling of unwellness, of not being herself either physically or emotionally. In fact, she has had such a severe panic attack on the ship that she has become unable to recognize herself in mirrors. She feels haunted by a feeling that "something . . . had dramatically expanded her vision, offering her a glimpse of things that were beyond her comprehension" (59).

Although Avey first wants nothing more upon leaving the ship than to return to her lovely home in White Plains, New York, she finds herself instead accompanying a large group of Granadans to their native island of Carriacou. She is swept up in the tide of their yearly excursion to Carriacou, which symbolizes "home" even for those who were not born there. Each year, the Granadans celebrate their origins, their "nations," and dance the Beg Pardon, an homage to their ancestors whose memories and spirits they might inadvertently have offended during the past year. Avey is at first mystified by the way the Grenadan/Carriacoun citizens carry around their collective pasts in their present lives, but soon she too begins to feel part of their heritage. She also comes to terms with her own memories, involving the earlier, poorer but happier years of her marriage and her childhood visits with her powerful Great Aunt Cuney, who has suddenly started to haunt her dreams.

The novel repeatedly entwines Avey's personal memories with a kind of racial memory. The early days of her marriage to the fun-loving man she knew by his nickname, Jay, are associated in her mind with a self-affirming sense of racial unity. Avey has always regretted that the couple's journey out of the poverty of Halsey Street in Brooklyn, where their marriage began, simultaneously meant their alienation from black culture. As Jay became more successful, the small rituals of their lives—impromptu dances in the living room, "spending their Sunday mornings listening to gospels and reciting fragments of old poems while eating coffee cake," jazz and blues records on the phonograph, and passionate sex with a man "who knew how to talk to a woman in bed" (95)—disappeared, and with them went "an ethos they held in common," qualities that joined "them to the vast unknown lineage that made their being possible." Avey mourns the loss of "this link, these connections" that "had both protected them and put them in possession of a kind of power," which they had allowed "to slip out of the living room, down the stairs and out of the house, where it had vanished, along with Jay [who thereafter became Jerome], in the snowy wastes of Halsey Street" (137–38). In the process, Jerome became downright racist: "If it was left up to me I'd close down every dancehall in Harlem and burn every drum! That's the only way these Negroes out here'll begin making any progress!" (132).

Avey's trip on the flimsy boat to Carriacou is marked in the novel as a journey toward her racial heritage partly by its association with her family's yearly excursions up the Hudson River from Harlem to Bear Mountain, which produced young Avey's happy identification with her people. Standing on the pier with a large crowd waiting for the boat, she "would feel what seemed to be hundreds of slender threads streaming out from her navel and from the place where her heart was to enter those around her . . . threads [that] went out not only to people she recognized . . . but to those she didn't" (190). The Carriacou journey is further marked as a rite of passage by its cleansing effect on Avey's mind and body. In her Granada hotel, the night before boarding the small boat, Avey had endured visions of Jerome's scolding ghost, an encounter that had emptied her mind "of the contents of the past thirty years" and lessened her disappointment and rage at the spiritual sacrifices they had made for the achievement of material comfort (151). The excursion over rough waters completed the expurgation by causing violent vomiting and excretion of all that had made her feel bloated and unwell, until her body became "flat, numbed, emptied out" (214).

The journey to Carriacou is also identified as a spiritual or religious ritual for Avey through its association, as a sense of sickness overtakes her, with an impassioned Easter sermon she had heard as a child. Like the turbulent waters of the Caribbean, the intensity of the sermon had rocked and nauseated her, and the chocolate Easter egg she had eaten after breakfast had begun "sloshing around like a great sour wave inside her" (203). The preacher's voice had become God's voice, judging and condemning her until Avey could no longer control her heaving stomach (203). Thus, her vomiting on the heaving *Emmanuel C,* whose Christ-like name adds to its redemptive role, both parallels and imaginatively replaces her childhood religious experience, thereby becoming a new initiation ritual appropriate to establishing a new identity.

Avey's dead Great Aunt Cuney is perhaps the novel's clearest emblem of the transformative racial heritage Avey seeks. Cuney deliberately constructs Avey's racial heritage by insisting that she visit Tatem every summer and that she answer to her full name, Avatara, a "matronymic" from Cuney's grandmother. Only through her great-aunt does Avey learn the stories and values that constitute her ethnic past. Cuney's stories of the Ibos, coupled with her own strong and rebellious spirit, represent a non-slave alternative to the racial heritage more commonly known in American culture. Cuney embraced nothing that paid homage to slavery or white rule because, like her grandmother's, her "mind was long gone with the Ibos," a group of slaves who, upon arriving at The Landing on Tatem, turned around and walked back to Africa. Blessed with second sight, the Ibos could "tell you 'bout things happened long before they was born and things to come long after they's dead." Having seen into the future, they "looked at the white folks what brought 'em here, and walked on back down to the edge of the river . . . and they didn't bother getting back into the small boat drawed up here—boats take too much time. They just kept walking on out over the river." Still shackled with wrist and ankle irons, "they just kept on walking [across the ocean] like the water was solid ground. . . . They feets was gonna take 'em wherever they was going that day" (37–39).

Parallels between Avey's childhood experience and the Carriacou journey are obvious. Cuney's storytelling, in the mode of the griot, reflects the reenactment of ancestral dances and stories on the island. Her insistence on a yearly ritual journey to The Landing, with young Avey in tow, reflects the fierce dedication of the islanders to their annual pilgrimage to their ancestral home.

Until her ill-fated third cruise on the *Bianca Pride,* whose name matched perfectly its white ethos of materialism and spirit-crushing upwardly mobile life, Avey had suppressed her childhood identification and fascination with Aunt Cuney and the Ibos.[3] But on that cruise, after her dream about Cuney, the weight of her middle-class, materially comfortable life suddenly becomes too heavy to bear. With the arrival of her aunt's spiritual presence, along with her recurrent memories of happier days in marriage, Avey gradually realizes that the white-imitation life she has lived does not represent her real identity. The novel suggests that her reclamation of that identity requires the reclamation of her gendered personal and racial past. The process is facilitated in her imagination by her spiritual vision of Aunt Cuney and the resurrection of her suppressed memories, as well as by an elderly, lame man, Lebert Joseph, whose rum shop Avey stumbles into while she is waiting on Grenada for her plane to New York. It is Joseph who diagnoses Avey's problem as an inability to "call [her] nation" (175). The accuracy of his observation, and the significance of his suggestion that Avey join him on the excursion to Carriacou, are underscored by the fact that once Avey succumbs to his persuasion, she realizes that "the strange discomfort in her stomach was gone and her head had stopped aching" (184). In stark contrast, the once-comforting memory of her elegant White Plains dining room suddenly revived "the peculiar clogged and bloated feeling in her stomach and under her heart" that had plagued her on the ship (181).

After her experience on Carriacou, Avey no longer values her life of individual success. She signifies her desire for a relational identity by deciding after the excursion to sell the elegant house in White Plains and use the proceeds to build a house in Tatem, on the land left to her by Aunt Cuney. She reveals the collective nature of her new identity by vowing to re-create the family and ethnic ties her aunt had forged through her virtual abduction of Avey to Tatem every summer. As a grandmother herself, Avey decides that she will insist that her two grandsons spend time with her on the island. She even thinks of inviting her militantly Afrocentric daughter, Marion, whose self-inflicted poverty and racial consciousness had previously irritated her, to teach some of the poor children she would bring to the island for a kind of summer camp.

In part, Avey's pursuit of a relational identity after decades of living by the mores of white-American individualism and consumerism does conform to the theories of Chodorow and Gilligan. Avey is made sick by an individuated life that has denied her heritage and alienated her from her important connections to others of her race and family, especially a symbolic mother, a powerful female figure. Indeed, Marshall provides an almost perfect metaphor for the Gilligan/Chodorow concept of interdependent, relational female gender identity in Avey's image of silken threads connecting her to others of her race. That image recurs on Carriacou, where, just before Avey joins in the dance that will bring her back to her true name, "she felt the threads streaming out from the old people around her in Lebert Joseph's yard" (249). Her sense of wholeness and well-being, so strong that it makes her feel like a girl "with her life yet to live" (249), depends on that web of connection. But we must note the difference: the mother is symbolic; the connections involve race and ethnicity, as well as gender.

Gloria Naylor's *Mama Day* (1989) also posits a world that conforms, in part, to the Gilligan/Chodorow scenario of female gender identity development. In Naylor's world, as in Marshall's, a woman protagonist determines her identity through her relationship to women ancestors. Like Avey Johnson, Naylor's protagonist is a double-named woman—Ophelia/Cocoa—whose past and present are populated by powerful women. Like Avey's, Cocoa's roots are embedded in islands off the American coast. Although much closer to the slave-culture mainland than Carriacou, like that Caribbean retreat, Cocoa's Sea Island home of Willow Springs symbolizes a separate culture. Willow Springs lies outside the jurisdiction of any state because the bridge connecting the island to the mainland lies exactly on the border between South Carolina and Georgia. Neither state claims Willow Springs and neither state controls it. Cocoa's heritage deviates only slightly from Avey's by involving not one but two important women—her great-aunt, Miranda, known to the citizens of Willow Springs as Mama Day, and her grandmother, Abigail—but neither is her biological mother. Cocoa's mother, Grace (Abigail's daughter), died shortly after Cocoa's birth, so the two sisters raised Cocoa together. Abigail gave Ophelia her "crib name," Cocoa, hoping to "put color" somewhere on the very pale child (40). The name also represents the girl's own desire to be dark-skinned, an early identification with her race.

But as in the Marshall novel, the Gilligan developmental approach does not explain the collective elements of the novel, which, as in the other text, involve physical and spiritual roots. As the novel opens, Cocoa is preparing to make her annual August pilgrimage to Willow Springs. Like the Carriacouns and the young Avey, Cocoa regards the ritual visit as sacred. In fact, she sabotages a desperately needed job opportunity in New York in order to take the trip. When told the job would begin earlier than she had expected, Cocoa tells her prospective employer, George Andrews (who would one day become her husband), that she must decline if it interfered with her responsibilities as the only living grandchild.[4]

Like *Praisesong*, then, the novel establishes immediately the primacy of roots and their importance to individual consciousness, but it deemphasizes the mother-daughter bond in which Gilligan locates the concept of connection in female identity. Yet, as in Naylor's text, the novel embeds the key to identity—which involves both race and gender—in the often quite mystical powers of women, especially of Miranda. Indeed, even more urgently than in *Praisesong*, the reclamation of a woman's female lineage becomes a key to actual survival in *Mama Day*. At the novel's end, Miranda saves Cocoa's life by discovering the name of the Day family's founding matriarch, a slave who had inherited the island from her master.

As in Marshall's *Praisesong,* Cocoa understands that the women in her family have power in part because of their connection to their ancestral lands: "I was from Willow Springs and brought up by some very shrewd old women" (103). It was the combination that created her legacy of independence, self-reliance, common sense, and respect for nature, which could be both nurturing and brutal. More than *Praisesong,* however, Naylor's text complicates the concept of heritage. Willow Springs appears paradisiacal only to outsiders, like George, who do not recognize its hidden hazards. Cocoa warns George, for example, not to think of the island as Eden—bare bottoms are bound to encounter red ants, she cautions (222). She even risks her relationship with George by objecting to a hypothetical relocation from New York to Willow Springs. On their visit to the island together after four years of marriage, George toys with the idea of abandoning his city life as an engineer and moving there to farm or fish for a living. Cocoa wants none of that: "You would not chain me down here while you played at growing tomatoes and corn." Even when it becomes clear that he is really seeking reassurance that she would follow him anywhere, Cocoa declares, "Not in Willow Springs" (220). At the same time, she loves her home. She basks in the love and attention of her grandmother and the gruff wisdom of her great-aunt. She leaves after each yearly visit laden with the two women's homemade gifts and fattened by their homegrown and lovingly prepared food. And when she's away from her two "mothers" in New York, she carries their example and lessons with her. "If Grandma had raised me alone," she thinks, "I would have been ruined for any fit company. It seemed I could do no wrong with her, while with Mama Day I could do no right . . . together they were the perfect mother" (58). Cocoa allows herself to live within a contradiction about heritage: while it cannot be denied, while it shapes and nourishes the spirit, it can also hurt and entrap.

Naylor's depiction of Willow Springs as dangerous and of Cocoa's ambivalence about her heritage prevents the romanticization of rural black life and women's communities. Such romanticization annoys critics like Gayatri Spivak, Michelle Wallace, and Hazel Carby. Wallace, for example, criticizes nostalgia and the valorization of the rural and the illiterate because it precludes "the necessity for generational conflict and critical dialectic" among the generations and ignores the lives of urban blacks (60). Hazel Carby also complains about fiction that "represents the rural folk as bearers of Afro-American history and preservers of Afro-American culture" and thereby marginalizes the "fictional urban confrontation of race, class, and sexuality" (Wallace 88). Naylor's text takes pains not to romanticize the Day clan's roots. Its heroic slave-founder murdered the master who gave her the island, possibly by means of both dagger and poison (reminiscent of Claudius' murder in Shakespeare's *Hamlet,* which may serve as a loose textual analogy for the novel) (Saunders 8). Her descendants who would rather not know the details discover they will pay for their ignorance, even of the poisoned tips of their roots. Willow Springs abounds in hazards and spells and is highly susceptible to killer hurricanes, whereas the most dangerous thing on Marshall's Carriacou is the disgruntled ghost of an Old Parent, whose nation had not been properly danced or whose pardon had not been sufficiently begged.

Naylor's text constructs danger as the underside of power, strength, independence, and freedom. The same folk wisdom and knowledge that make Mama Day a healer, midwife, and sage promote evil and death in the wrong hands. That danger is personified in two characters, Dr. Buzzard and Ruby. Buzzard is no doctor, although he promises to heal and sells remedies. As Miranda points out to George, "You know what he gives folks when they got an ache in their left side? Moonshine and honey. And for an ache in their right side? Honey and moonshine" (196). Buzzard runs a still, cheats at cards, and exploits ignorance. Mama Day finds him repulsive because he has given a bad name to the skills she has developed authentically. In contrast to Buzzard, her healing powers are based on empirical evidence, experimentation, and a deep knowledge of plants and herbs. Even Dr. Smithfield from "across the bridge" trusts and learns from Miranda's skills—"Being a good doctor, he knew another one when he saw her" (84). For example, when Mama Day diagnoses as ovarian cysts the alleged pregnancy pains of a young islander who was desperate to conceive a child, Dr. Smithfield not only believes her but he also takes notes when she prescribes chokecherry bark to ease the pain. At the same time, however, Mama Day is not above using a little magic to promote her point of view. After insisting that Cocoa write back to George about the job she threw away, Miranda added a little yellow powder to the envelope just for good measure. The powder both attracted George's attention and inspired him to help Cocoa find another job (54).

Although Miranda's contempt for Buzzard is legend—she tells him regularly that "nothing human could have put [him] on this earth" (46)—he is depicted as relatively harmless compared to Ruby, whose use of herbs and roots is motivated not by a wish to heal others but by a jealous possessiveness of her youthful and reluctant lover, Junior Lee. In contrast to Mama Day, Ruby uses her knowledge to curse and punish others, especially those, including Cocoa, to whom Junior is attracted. Everyone in Willow Springs also suspects that Ruby, a mountain of a woman at least fifteen years older than Junior, uses voodoo to keep him interested in her.

Miranda publicly discounts the effects of such potions, but the text makes clear that she knows that Ruby's magic can be very effective. For example, when Ruby's rival, Frances, asks for a counter-potion to attract Junior, Miranda tells her that "a man don't leave you unless he wants to go . . . and if he's made up his mind to go, there ain't nothing you, me, or anybody else can do about that" (90). But when Miranda discovers a bag of dill, verbena, and graveyard dust under her porch steps the day Cocoa and George are scheduled to arrive, she takes note. She recognizes that Ruby's use of verbena, the herb of grace, is a special weapon against Cocoa, the child of Grace. Miranda understands the full extent of Ruby's treachery, however, only after Cocoa suffers directly at her hands, becoming deathly ill after having her hair cornrowed by Ruby. Miranda quickly connects Cocoa's symptoms to the traces of nightshade on her niece's scalp, and with no law to resort to, she relies on the laws of nature that she understands and can manipulate so well: she calls down lightning to blow up Ruby's house.

The novel's ambivalent, double-edged treatment of Cocoa's cure and Ruby's death represents its generally complex view of relationships and ethnic values. The text constructs a world that reflects nature's own double identity as both giver and taker of life. Thus, endemic to human relationships in the novel are the seeds of both good and evil, satisfaction and despair. That George and Cocoa love and adore one another implies that they also have the power to destroy one another. The same natural forces that have given Willow Springs its independence from white society have also located the island in the path of killer hurricanes. Likewise, while the island's lack of officially sanctioned social institutions contributes to its inhabitants' freedom, it also deprives them of objective justice and makes them vulnerable to the machinations of a Dr. Buzzard or a Ruby. In a vacuum, power belongs equally to all who would seize it.

Even Miranda's beneficent powers have resulted both from her dedication and intelligence and from her life's pain. The source of her power—her ancestral home in the West Woods known mysteriously as the "other place"—partakes of nature's beauty and bounty, on the one hand, and of human tragedy (of which Grace's death is only the most recent example), on the other. The novel's metaphor for that pain is a loss of peace by the Day women over many generations. Sometimes the loss is depicted literally—the death of a girl named Peace—and sometimes figuratively—an emotional state. Miranda and Abigail's mother, the first Ophelia, was the first to lose a daughter named Peace. She drowned in the family's well. Like her Shakespearean namesake, Ophelia first grieved over her loss and then drowned herself. Her excessive grief robbed Miranda of the chance for a normal life and motherhood. "No time to be young. Little Mama. The cooking, the cleaning, the mending, the gardening for the woman who sat in the porch rocker, twisting, twisting on pieces of thread. Peace was gone," Miranda thinks, "*But I was your child, too*" (88). Miranda delivered other women's babies, kept house, took care of her mother until her suicide, and, finally, sacrificed her one chance for romance with "the boy with the carnival smile, lean as an ear of Silver Queen corn and lips just as sweet" (89).

Abigail was the second Day woman to lose Peace. Racked with guilt over her mother's grief and death, Abigail named her first baby Peace. But instead of assuaging her guilt, the name became a curse. The second Peace died as well. Abigail's second daughter, Grace, abandoned the quest for Peace, but she insisted on naming her little daughter Ophelia, a name that signified to her a woman's capacity to break a man's heart. Grace wanted to instill that ability in her daughter in order to avenge her anger at the husband who had abandoned her in the eighth month of pregnancy.

Although her other-mothers' protectiveness has kept her unaware of this mixed legacy, Ophelia/Cocoa nevertheless carries the Day female curse with her. By the novel's end, she achieves her own inner peace, but only after losing the man she loves while he tries to help save her from Ruby's nightshade poisoning. True to the Day curse, George's congenitally damaged heart is "broken" by Cocoa's illness, and he dies.

Also implicated in the novel's presentation of double-edged swords is the conflict between the folkways of Willow Springs, rooted in its mythical origins in the master-slave relationship, and the rational, technological, individualized world of New York, represented by George Andrews's occupation as an engineer and his no-frills upbringing in a boys' home. When nature and folk magic turn nasty in Willow Springs, first in Ruby's nightshade-laced hairdressing service and then in a violent hurricane that destroys the bridge and, therefore, George's only hope of getting the violently ill Cocoa off the island, George no longer finds the island idyllic. He disparages Mama Day's apparently voodoo-inspired approach to the tragedy, even when she admits to needing his help: "I can do more things with these hands than most folks dream of—no less believe," she tells George, "but this time they ain't no good alone . . . it ain't gonna be complete unless I can reach out with the other hand and take yours. You see, she done bound more than her flesh up with you. And since she's suffering from something more than the flesh, I can't do a thing without you" (294). He ridicules as "mumbo-jumbo" Miranda's instruction to reach behind the old red hen in her chicken house and bring her anything he finds. Even when he begins to understand how serious and mysterious Cocoa's illness is and gives Miranda's method a try, his engineer's mind and weak heart are not up to the task. The red hen attacks him, and the exertion of the fight kills him. In an ironic fulfillment of Mama Day's intuition about his importance to Cocoa's survival, George's death brings peace and saves Cocoa's life.

Underlying the novel's ambivalence towards heritage, however, is a consistent compulsion to know and embrace it, warts and all. This concern represents graphically the process that critics such as Marjorie Pryse have identified as characteristic of black women's fiction. "Wherever we find interest in folklore in novels by black women we also find stages in the tradition's emerging perception that women have the ability to reclaim their 'ancient power' " by reclaiming their ancestors' ancient stories (Pryse 20). Indeed, Miranda's ultimate contribution to Cocoa's cure, after her healing powers against the nightshade have been exhausted, is her tenacious insistence on discovering the name of the first Day, the slave who somehow inherited the island from Bascombe Wade, the master who loved her. Although the reader is presented with a genealogical chart for the Day family that names the founding matriarch, Sapphira, at the book's beginning, Miranda does not learn her name until the novel's end, when she secludes herself at the "other place" and searches for evidence of her identity. What she finds is inconclusive, just a faded bill of sale: "Sold *to Mister Bascombe Wade of Willow Springs, one Negress answering to the name Sa* . . . Water damage done removed the remainder of that line" (280). She must wait for a dream to discover the name Sapphira. But once she does, she feels she has "reached back to the beginning . . . to find the chains to pull" Cocoa out of her illness (294). Miranda also forces herself to relive her own childhood and its attendant tragedies in order to effect the cure. It is the knowledge of the past rather than the past itself that ultimately empowers Miranda and saves Cocoa.

Rootless George, abandoned by his prostitute mother, has learned too well the boys' home adage that "only the present has potential" (26). Perhaps it is his lack of knowledge of the past that prevents him from surviving in the historically enriched (and encumbered) world of Willow Springs. Still, the novel does not prescribe a return to the past. It valorizes its characters' relationship to the past, even in its strengths, as a springboard rather than a destination.

The Theoretical Alternative: "Inspiriting Influences"[5]

The rich and complex texts of Marshall and Naylor suggest that the concept of relationship among women of different generations is more than a legacy of nurture and care. Rather, they suggest that concept extends beyond mothers and daughters altogether to a much larger network of women and forces with female identities and connotations. Indeed, the most important relationships for Avey, Cocoa, and Miranda are not with their own mothers or even with the women who gave them primary nurturing care. It is a great-aunt, the unmaternal Miranda, rather than the nurturing grandmother Abigail, who serves as Cocoa's strongest link with life. Avey needs to reclaim not her mother but her paternal great-aunt who claims her for her own lineage: "It's my 'Gran' done sent her," Cuney says. "She's her little girl" (Marshall 42). Miranda also looks beyond her own mother, who failed her, to Sapphira (her father's ancestor) for her identity and psychological sustenance.

Mothering, per se, then, is not as important in the texts as is the process of linking a child with her female-identified ethnic past. Avey's ordinary, loving mother, concerned with everyday things, is defined as ultimately inadequate because she cannot see that Cuney "had entrusted [Avey] with a mission." In her ignorance, her only role was to complain after each summer's trip about the child's tattered stockings and burnt skin from "tearing around in the sun all day behind that old woman" (Marshall 42). In Naylor's work, biological mothers are either crazy or dead. Only the "racial mothers"—Sapphira, Miranda, the women on the boat to Carriacou, Aunt Cuney—who see significance beyond the personal or the immediate in raising "daughters," have psychological importance. Some such "mothers," like Sapphira, are simply spirits; they need have nurtured no one in order to become a primary feminine presence.

The novels also valorize the concept of relationship differently than Gilligan does. Female connection is not conceptualized as a basis for specific behaviors or values. Rather, it forms the basis for an individualized identity, for a woman's becoming herself, whatever that may be, by understanding her structural relationship to her heritage, as constructed by both race and sex. Connection with that heritage is also essential for women's physical survival. Without reconciliation and identification with important racial mothers, women's lives are, at best (as for Avey), misdirected and, at worst (as for Cocoa), endangered. Furthermore, the texts inscribe the acquisition of personal gender identity, rooted in the forces of racial heritage identified as female, as a process of reclamation rather than of recognition, thereby suggesting its previous disappearance or repression rather than, as Gilligan and Chodorow suggest, its psychological endurance and easy availability in everyday life.

Those clues, coupled with the texts' focus on land as heritage, on ethnic as well as gender identity, on the supernatural, and on other elements neither explored nor explained by object-relations theory, suggest the need for another (or additional) perspective if a deeper understanding of such novels is to be achieved. Such a perspective can be found in post-structuralist psychoanalytic theory in which concepts of gender identity are linked not only to the mother-child relationship but also to cultural forces and the structure of language and the unconscious. In contrast to the stronger focus on maternal nurturing behavior in object-relations theory, post-structuralist psychoanalytic theory configures the mother as a split subject, the "locus of the semiotic . . . present and absent, omnipotent and powerless, the body before language, unrepresentable, inexpressible, [and] unsettling." Although significant, the link of physical similarity between mothers and daughters does not fully explain gender identity. Rather, the mother—who signifies the *feminine* in both culture and discourse—encodes that which resides outside the phallic, paternal, symbolic stratum; it is an otherness that phallocentric culture strives to repress because it is an otherness that can dismantle and rupture its power (Hirsch 171–72).

The enigmatic and contradictory qualities of the feminine with which maternal nurture is associated inhabit a child's unconscious mind, or imagination, as much or more than the experiences of an actual relationship with a specific mother. Although obviously analogous to the cultural status of women, the feminine is not a simple equivalent of women's lives, behaviors, personalities, or values. Rather, the feminine embodies all qualities, images, affects, and persons who have been relegated to the margins by phallocentric culture. The feminine's locus in discourse is either silence or "noise" (Finke 25). Because of women's subordinate status in society, the qualities of silence or noise, marginalization or exclusion are often represented in discourse by women, whose symbolic identity is often mistaken for, and reinforces, historical or social reality. In the post-structuralist scenario, a black woman's role in discourse is especially powerful. She is marked by both race and sex as feminine—silenced or cacophonous, marginalized or excluded. If a white woman is the "noise" of culture, then an African American woman is the noisiest of the noise, the racial margin of the gender margins (or vice versa) of Western culture.

At the same time, however, discursive representations of noisy feminine noise, which Alice Jardine calls *gynesis,* can disrupt and redefine the very Western, white, male symbolic structures that have repressed it. Giving voice to the "mad, unconscious, improper, unclean, non-sensical, oriental, [and] profane" noises, and occupying spaces, hitherto unexplored, "unknown, terrifying, [and] monstrous," undermines the very foundations of Western culture and philosophy: Man, the Subject, History, and Meaning (Jardine 73). A change in the position of the feminine requires a textual recasting of "the discursive truth of the dominant order" (Jardine 44). Thus, the feminine is the mark not simply of victimization but also of revolution. Inscribed by the marginalized, the *feminine* becomes a powerful and disruptive voice in Western discourse.

Before re-exploring the novels in light of post-structuralist psychoanalytic perspectives, we should note that some African American critics regard those perspectives as tainted by both male and white authorship. Even those, like Hortense Spillers, who accept its concept of the feminine as a position in discourse, rather than primarily a reflection of lived female experience, warn that use of the theory must entail "what the 'feminine' can do from its own vantage point" (*Reading Black* 249). With such caveats in mind, interpretations of the feminine help unlock the depths of the novels being considered here and shed new light on the significance of relationship in the gender identities of women. Through their valorization not only of heroic female figures (who loom larger psychologically than the biological mother) but also of the nonrational imagery of dreams, the dualistic (split) power of natural/female forces, and the inescapable effects of magic and ritual, texts such as Naylor's and Marshall's seem perfect examples of gynesis, of the putting into discourse of the feminine and the disruption of hegemonic cultural assumptions and foundations. What Western culture has repressed such texts bring to the forefront of personal and cultural consciousness.

As we have already seen, post-structuralist theory enlarges the interpretation of the novels' inclusion of nonstandard dialect, ghosts, ecstatic ritual, magic potions, and powerful dreams beyond their reference to African folkways and customs. Their psychic/cultural implications challenge dominance and inscribe the "illegitimate" power of the muted language of the invisible crying out boldly in its own voice, as Avey does in Grenada when, grieving her past, she utters the "deep-throated cry" of "some Dahomey woman warrior of old" (130). Further, post-structuralist theories of the feminine give new meaning to the texts' representations of female sexual pleasure and passion, which have historically gone undepicted or silenced in Western discourse. In contrast to the "desexualized" portrait of the mother in the object-relations scenario, in which mothers are characterized primarily by their nurturing behavior (Jessica Benjamin, in Grosskurth 30), mother and motherhood in these texts are linked with sexuality and female sexual *jouissance*. The link of motherhood and sexuality is explicit, for example, in Avey's insight about her parents' sexual relationship as she watches them dance on one of her family's trips up the Hudson River. Seeing them flirt, she "understood . . . for the first time . . . that it was out of this holding and clasping, out of the cut-eyes and the private smiles that she and her brothers had come" (89–90). That realization empowers Avey and validates through cultural associations her own passionate sex with Jay. Avey celebrates her memory of the way Jay's talk "turned her into a wanton with her nightgown bunched up around her neck like an airy boa." She associates her own sexual pleasure with ancient African goddesses—"Erzulie . . . Yemoja . . . Oya," and she characterizes Jay in coitus as "surrounded by a pantheon of the most ancient deities who had made their temple the tunneled darkness of his wife's flesh" (127).

Naylor's text also valorizes female sexual pleasure and identifies it with the feminine value system of Cocoa's root culture. The novel portrays Mama Day as both sexually active, even at age 88, and at least subtly communicative about sexual matters with her grand-niece. When Cocoa complains, for example, that she already has about as much of Mama Day's homemade lavender water as she can use for life, Miranda first reminds her that it makes a good douche and then adds, "And it don't taste bad, either" (153). Although embarrassed by her great-aunt's innuendo, Cocoa learns from it that sexual pleasure is culturally sanctioned and consistent with her familial role.

The texts' inclusion of sexuality in maternal identity challenges the Western uterine social organization—"the arrangement of the world in terms of the reproduction of future generations"—that object relations emphasizes. It suggests instead what Gayatri Spivak calls a clitoral social organization—one that rebels against the symbolic (or actual) excision of female sexual pleasure in the service of regeneration ("French Feminism" 152).

Post-structuralist psychoanalytic theory also elucidates the disruptive potential of black female authorship. Since Western conventions of writing have emerged from its primary text, the Bible, white male authorship is the cultural norm. Only those who resembled the white male God could historically claim rights of authorship for any text. Black men first established their authorial authority by claiming the power of black folk magic, an oral rather than a written tradition. Black women began to share in that authority after Zora Neale Hurston recorded black folklore and folkways (Pryse 9–10).

The texts of Naylor and Marshall embody a new foundation for black women's authorial authority in the oral tradition of women, whose strength signifies the release of a repressed heritage of female spiritual and cultural power. That heritage inevitably entails the assertion of new creation stories and religious metaphors that challenge the hegemony of Judeo-Christian tradition. In *Praisesong,* spiritual importance is attached to Avey's sexual pleasure as it transports both her and Jay to the ancient temple of the goddesses of the seas, winds, and rains (127). Avey's primal scream comes not from Job or Jesus but from a Dahomey woman warrior (130). She cherishes the spiritual guidance not of her childhood preacher (whose words nauseated her) but of the "presiding mothers of Mount Olivet Baptist church"—her mother's, not her father's, church—who directed the spiritual proceedings from the front pews (194). On Avey's adult spiritual journey to Carriacou, the strength and dignity of those mothers are reincarnated in the women who nurture and soothe her through her illness on the boat. Avey's journey is further assisted by Lebert Joseph's daughter, Rosálie Parvey, who ritually cleanses and massages her body before the Big Drum. As Avey begins to reclaim her true origins, the one "nation" and dance mentioned by Lebert Joseph that she recognizes is the Juba, a women's dance named for "the once-proud, imperial seat at the heart of equatoria," the true beauty of which depends on the dancer's gestures with her skirt (178). Most significantly, the alternative story of Avey's own and her people's "creation," the story of the Ibos, is conveyed to her through female voices, those of her great-great grandmother and of her great-aunt. The Ibos' story replaces the legacy of enslavement, through which blacks have historically been dominated, disempowered, and disparaged—marginalized/feminized—with an inexplicable, fantastical—proudly feminine—story of extraordinary power, freedom, and self-respect. Once she embraces it, the Ibos' story becomes to Avey as magical and powerful as Genesis or the Gospels, to which it is textually linked: when ten-year-old Avey asks Cuney, "how come [the Ibos] didn't drown?" she gives her a withering look and answers in a "quietly dangerous" voice, "Did it say Jesus drowned when he went walking on the water in that Sunday School book your momma always sends with you?" (40). Avey's own entry into her feminine legacy of self-determination, power, and community depends on her acceptance of her true name, Avatara, which means "spirit incarnate" (Panill 72). Given to her by her great-great grandmother via her great-aunt's dream, the name establishes Avey's female gender identity apart from her own mother; it also circumvents the patrilineal implications of Cuney's identity as her father's relative. As Sojourner Truth might have said, the name Avatara came from two women; man had nothing to do with it.

The feminine creation story in *Mama Day* is even more explicit. The text clearly identifies Sapphira as the family's spiritual, as well as primary biological ancestor. Cocoa instinctively calls her "the great, great, grand, Mother—as if [she] were listing the attributes of a goddess" (218). Like Yaweh's, Sapphira's name is neither spoken nor known, except by a select few. Also like Him, she rested after producing the seventh of her most precious creations (sons, in her case), and so she named the family "Day." Her power to name the family transforms patrinominal to matrinominal powers and establishes the biblically male (because bestowed on Adam) privilege of naming as the province of woman. At the same time, it establishes matrilinearity despite Sapphira's production of only male children.

The text also identifies Sapphira as a kind of goddess in Willow Springs. Vestiges of her worship remain in the community's ritual of Candle Walk; its celebration on December 22nd has to the present day displaced the celebration of Christmas. Most islanders do not remember the real meanings behind the ritual exchange of homemade or homegrown gifts and the ritual greeting, "Lead on with light," that accompanies the lifting of lighted candles on the streets of the island (110). But Mama Day knows that Candle Walk originated with the singing of "ancient songs" and the retelling of Sapphira's story by the bluff, over which some believe she leapt to her death. She also knows that the greeting was once a prayer, "Lead on with light, Great Mother. Lead on with light." Miranda's father, John-Paul, had told her "that in his time Candle Walk was different still. Said people kinda worshipped his grandmother, a slave woman who *took* her freedom in 1823" (111).

Balancing her role as Creatrix and reflecting the double-edged identity of the feminine is Sapphira's linkage with the power of the novel's destructive hurricane. Indeed, that linkage embodies both the racial and gender qualities of the repressed feminine: the storm starts in Africa; "it splits the earth until the waters come gushing down—all to the end of birthing a void," and it is "the working of Woman. And She has no name" (250–51). As the feminine is released, Sapphira/nature embodies the powers of creation and the powers of death, like the split maternal subject of post-structuralist psychoanalytic theory. She/it portends the disruption of the symbolic system that relies upon reason alone and dares to ignore the powers of the unseen and unexpressed. Appropriate to the concept of the feminine, Sapphira's powers descend directly into Miranda's unconscious through the dream in which she discovers the matriarch's name. That dream allows the full development of Miranda's power to overcome Cocoa's illness. Devoid of proper spiritual/unconscious connections, Ruby's and Buzzard's powers are inscribed as a hollow mockery of the feminine heritage that offers redemption.

Post-structuralist psychoanalytic theory also helps to explain the importance of motherlands in the novels. Contrary to the Western tradition of denying land ownership to both blacks and women, the texts depict African American women landowners. They further identify the key feminine ancestral lands as islands, so remote from the mainland that white society has little interest in their destinies, and so firmly intertwined with black identity that what interest whites show can easily be deflected. In *Mama Day,* the island of Willow Springs represents an especially defiant landscape. Indeed, it is effectively a black female nation, since its original owner, Bascombe Wade, was a Swede whose citizenship is unknown. Day land in Willow Springs is passed from mother to daughter, a system of inheritance inscribed in the women's lifelong retention of their matrinominal surname: "You live a Day and you die a Day," married or not (218). In *Praisesong,* Tatem has remained a black enclave, where independent and Afrocentric blacks, like Aunt Cuney, can forget enslavement and construct their own history. Carriacou's identity as a semiotic or feminine repository of repressed African heritage, modified by centuries of Caribbean life, is embodied in its location as the easternmost Caribbean island and, therefore, as far from dominant white culture (and the closest to feminine Africa) as it is possible to get in the Americas. The island exists as a spiritual home for Africans of the diaspora, a free and safe place in which to practice ancient rites, a promised land (Busia 207). With its discursive and imaginative connection to Tatem, Carriacou allows Avey to integrate her conscious identity with her feminine unconscious, give names to the unnamed (repressed) feelings and longings she has experienced, and, finally, to listen to the voice of Aunt Cuney that holds the key to her identity. It is the locus of her first genuine expression of self in more than thirty years. In that way, Carriacou, like the novels' other islands, represents the feminine both as a sign of exclusion and as a sign of "noise," a site for the eruption of expression outside the boundaries of sanctioned discourse.

Carriacou also partakes of the disruptive qualities of the feminine by partaking in Avey's symbolic reversal of the Middle Passage. Her journey to the island is linked to that historical tragedy by her fleeting impression, during her sickness on the boat, "of other bodies lying crowded in with her in the hot, airless dark. A multitude it felt like lay packed around her in the filth and stench of themselves, just as she was. Their moans, rising and falling with each rise and plunge of the schooner, enlarged upon the one filling her head. Their suffering—the depth of it, the weight of it in the cramped space—made hers of no consequence" (209). Underscoring the island's discursive significance as a locus for the reiteration of Avey's feminine/African heritage is the association of Lebert Joseph with the lame African deity Legba, who, in Ewe religion, protects households and thresholds and, in Yoruba religion, presides over crossroads and serves as messenger of the gods. His name is invoked in an epigram at the start of the novel's third section, "Papa Legba, ouvri barrière pou' mwê" ("Papa Legba open the gateway for me") (Pollard 289). As a god of the crossroads, Lebert precedes Avey into the unfamiliar territory she must travel and introduces her to her feminine origins so that she may return home (Busia 204–05).

Against these highly charged feminine landscapes, the novels' dreams, magic, ritual, and natural powers become the tools of cultural revision, the eruption into discourse of the unconscious individual and collective mind, whose inexplicable contents are both repressed and feared by rational, linear, phallocentric, white, male Western culture. Those who choose to ignore that feminine space and language, like Avey, those who underrate them, like Cocoa, and those who fight them, like George, face psychological and physical danger. The novels establish the feminine connotations of such tools by inscribing their accessibility to women and their rejection by those men who cling to the dominant culture's values.[6] But those tools are not denied to men categorically; indeed, black men share at least the racial marginality that offers access to the feminine. Although the feminine is not for women only, however, women seem to have an easier time recognizing and valuing its powers. While Avey and Cocoa are eventually saved through their connection and identification with feminine forces, George and Jerome are not because they do not understand the task at hand. George's insistence on overpowering Miranda's red hen, rather than working with its power, results in his death; Jerome's acceptance of white values of achievement and material success, to the destruction of his black identity, brings on a heart attack and premature death.

All of this suggests that the key form of relationship in these novels is to the unseen and unacknowledged underpinnings of a genuine (albeit despised and misunderstood) racial and gender identity, inscribed in the texts as women's dreams, visions, myth, and magic. Establishing that relationship both threatens the "Western economics of representation" (Finke 6), and creates "new configurations within which women may act as subjects" and speak a new language signifying "other" spaces hitherto unknown and profane (Jardine 48, 73). Issues of individual identity development pale in comparison to such powerful forces.

The feminine codes of Marshall's and Naylor's works take on increased significance in light of other literary works by African American women writers. Many such works include ghosts and visions, mystical and magical events, dreams, and even ghouls in the representation of women's lives. Ghosts populate the works of Toni Morrison. Jewell Gomez writes of vampires. Octavia Butler depicts time travel from pre-slavery to modern times. Myths give power to the novels of Zora Neale Hurston and Alice Walker. Yet, none of these writers would identify her work as fantasy or science fiction. I would argue that they, like Marshall and Naylor, use such images to represent their intuition about African American women's identities as larger than a personal developmental project. Their texts inscribe those identities as inclusive of all that has been repressed and silenced and all that must be heard and expressed if both women and Western culture are to be redeemed.

Whether the similarities in fantastical and mythic imagery in the works of African American women writers is deliberate is difficult to say. Critics have long debated the existence of a black women's literary tradition. Some, such as Missy Kubitschek and Michael Awkward, believe that the folklore and folkways of Zora Neale Hurston's work are central to all writers who have followed her. Hortense Spillers has identified black women writers as a community "conscious of itself"; she notes that "books, like genetic parents, beget books" (*Conjuring* 250). Marjorie

Pryse has observed the repeated appearance in African American women's writing of root-workers and conjurers, quilting and storytelling as images that give "back power to the culturally disenfranchised" and articulate a vision that can be shared "through its heritage, roots, survival, and intimate possession" among black women alone (Pryse 5).

It would be appropriate to the post-structuralist psychoanalytic view of the feminine for the trend in African American women's works toward ghosts and dreams to be unconscious; for well beyond reflecting black history, such images signify both the repression and the recovery of a cultural rather than an individual unconscious. Indeed, an unconscious relationship among texts and authors would be a perfect metaphor for the alternative feminine sense of relationship discussed in this essay. It also would signify the process through which Naylor's and Marshall's novels can best serve their disruptive purposes—by direct communication to the repressed feminine forces lurking within the dominant culture.

Notes

1. Patricia Hill Collins discusses these and other aspects of the African American family. See *Black Feminist Thought*, 46–48, 95, and 119–23.

2. This subtitle refers to a phrase of Toni Morrison's ("Rootedness" 343).

3. According to several sources, Paule Marshall equates consumerism with white American culture. For example, in a 1991 interview she explained that she was exploring "the dangers of unbridled, unquestioning materialism" among blacks that causes them to relinquish "what has made [them] unique as a people" (Seaman 410–11).

4. Here, as elsewhere in the novel, Naylor seems to be asserting a theme of interconnection even in her own creative process by alluding to characters from another of her works. In this case, the work is *Linden Hills* (1985). In explaining her status as only grandchild, Cocoa tells George that the other remaining grandchild, her cousin Willa Needed, along with her husband and son, were killed in a Christmas fire the previous year in Linden Hills. Willa is also listed in the book's genealogy of the Day family. Readers of the earlier novel will recall that Willa's move to Linden Hills was an attempt to disconnect from her roots and will undoubtedly see Naylor's use of intertextuality as an attempt to explain further why Willa was fated to meet a tragic end.

5. This subtitle, from Michael Awkward's book of the same name, embodies the complexity of female relationship that emerges in the novels under consideration here.

6. That some men, such as Lebert Joseph, do not perish indicates Marshall's understanding of the potential in both sexes to recognize the life force of the feminine. The young Jay is depicted as having that understanding, too.

Works Cited

Andrews, Larry R. "Black Sisterhood in Gloria Naylor's Novels." *CLA Journal* 33.1 (September 1989): 1–25.

Awkward, Michael. *Inspiriting Influences: Tradition, Revision, and Afro-American Women's Novels.* New York: Columbia UP, 1989.

Busia, Abena P.A. "What Is Your Nation?: Reconnecting Africa and Her Diaspora through Paule Marshall's *Praisesong for the Widow.*" *Changing Our Own Words: Essays on Criticism, Theory, and Writing by Black Women.* Ed. Cheryl A. Wall. New Brunswick: Rutgers UP, 1989. 196–211.

Carby, Hazel V. "The Quicksands of Representation: Rethinking Black Cultural Politics." *Reading Black, Reading Feminist: A Critical Anthology.* Ed. Henry Louis Gates, Jr. New York: Meridian, 1990. 76–90.

———. *Reconstructing Womanhood: The Emergence of the Afro-American Woman Novelist.* New York: Oxford UP, 1987.

Christian, Barbara T. "Ritualistic Process and the Structure of Paule Marshall's *Praisesong for the Widow.*" *Callaloo* 6 2.18 (Spring–Summer 1983): 74–84.

Collins, Patricia Hill. *Black Feminist Thought: Knowledge, Consciousness, and the Politics of Empowerment.* Boston: Unwin Hyman, 1990.

Finke, Laurie A. *Feminist Theory, Women's Writing.* Ithaca: Cornell UP, 1992.

Gilligan, Carol. *In a Different Voice: Psychological Theory and Women's Development.* Cambridge: Harvard UP, 1982.

Grosskurth, Phyllis. "The New Psychology of Women." *New York Review of Books.* 24 October 1991: 25 +.

Hirsch, Marianne. *The Mother/Daughter Plot: Narrative, Psychoanalysis, Feminism.* Bloomington: Indiana UP, 1989.

Jardine, Alice A. *Gynesis: Configurations of Woman and Modernity.* Ithaca: Cornell UP, 1985.

Kubitschek, Missy Dehn. *Claiming the Heritage: African-American Women Novelists and History.* Jackson: Mississippi UP, 1991.

Marshall, Paule. *Praisesong for the Widow.* New York: E.P. Dutton, 1984.

Morrison, Toni. "Rootedness: The Ancestor as Foundation." *Black Women Writers, 1950–80.* Ed. Mari Evans. New York: Doubleday, 1984. 339–45.

Naylor, Gloria. *Mama Day.* New York: Vintage Books, 1989.

Pannill, Linda. "From the Wordshop: The Fiction of Paule Marshall." *Melus* 12.2 (Summer 1985): 63–73.

Pollard, Velma. "Cultural Connections in Paule Marshall's *Praisesong for the Widow.*" *World Literature Written in English* 25.2 (1985): 285–298.

Pryse, Marjorie. "Introduction: Zora Neale Hurston, Alice Walker, and the 'Ancient Power' of Black Women." *Conjuring: Black Women, Fiction, and Literary Tradition.* Ed. Marjorie Pryse and Hortense J. Spillers. Bloomington: Indiana UP, 1985. 1–24.

Sandiford, Keith A. "Paule Marshall's *Praisesong for the Widow:* The Reluctant Heiress, or Whose Life is it Anyway?" *Black American Literature Forum* 20:4 (Winter 1986): 371–92.

Saunders, James Robert. "The Ornamentation of Old Ideas: Gloria Naylor's First Three Novels." *The Hollins Critic* 27.2 (April 1990): 1–11.

Seaman, Donna. "The Booklist Interview: Paule Marshall." *Booklist* 88.4 (October 15, 1991): 410–11.

Smith-Wright. "In Spite of the Klan: Ghosts in the Fiction of Black Women Writers." *Haunting the House of Fiction: Feminist Perspectives on Ghost Stories by American Women*. Ed. Lynette Carpenter and Wendy K. Kolman. Knoxville: Tennessee UP. 142–65.

Spillers, Hortense J. "An Order of Constancy: Notes on Brooks and the Feminine." *Reading Black, Reading Feminist*. Ed. Henry Louis Gates Jr. New York: Meridian Books, 1990. 244–71.

———. "Afterword: Cross-Currents, Discontinuities: Black Women's Fiction." *Conjuring: Black Women, Fiction, and Literary Tradition*. Ed. Marjorie Pryse and Hortense J. Spillers. Bloomington: Indiana UP, 1985. 249–61.

———. "Mama's Baby, Papa's Maybe: An American Grammar Book." *Diacritics* 17.2 (Summer 1987): 65–81.

Spivak, Gayatri Chakravorty. "Feminism and Critical Theory." *In Other Worlds: Essays in Cultural Politics*. Ed. Gayatri Spivak. New York: Methuen, 1987. 77–92.

———. "French Feminism in an International Frame." *In Other Worlds*. New York: Methuen, 1987. 134–53.

Wallace, Michele. "Variations on Negation and the Heresy of Black Feminist Creativity." *Reading Black, Reading Feminist*. Ed. Henry Louis Gates, Jr. New York: Meridian, 1990. 52–67.

III

Moral Decision Making in the Different Voice

The justice tradition in moral philosophy is personified by the enlightenment thinker Immanuel Kant, whose rationalist theory of morality posits a supreme moral principle that commands all moral action (Lapsley 199). According to Kant, in order for an action to be truly moral, it must proceed from an apprehension of the supreme moral law, rather than, for example, from personal inclination or kindness or generosity. Influenced by Kant in his thinking about moral development, Lawrence Kohlberg, a twentieth-century moralist in the justice tradition, devised a series of hierarchically ordered stages. The first is called "The Stage of Punishment and Obedience" (409). It contrasts dramatically with the sixth and highest level of moral reasoning which "assumes guidance by universal ethical principles that all humanity should follow. . . . [These are] the equality of human rights and the respect for the dignity of human beings as individuals." As a rational human being, a person functioning at this highest stage recognizes the rightness of these principles and acts in accordance with them (412).

Having derived the basic principles of his theory from studying a group of males as they grew to manhood, Kohlberg observes that he has found a large number of women clustered at Stage 3, a moral position where consideration of interpersonal relationships is paramount and the moral good is embodied in service to other people. Strikingly, as Carol Gilligan has noted, women—absent from Kohlberg's original research—rarely reach the higher levels of moral development defined by his scale (*DV*, 18). Thus, according to Kohlberg's evidence, women are deficient in moral reasoning when compared with men.

Establishing that women exhibit an alternative—not inferior—trajectory of moral development, Carol Gilligan describes an "ethic of care," one in which women frequently construct moral dilemmas by envisioning them as "a network of connection, a web of relationships that is sustained by a process of communication" (*DV* 32). Gilligan's research shows that, for the most part, but not categorically, women do not make moral decisions with reference to those universal principles that characterize the justice tradition in general and Kohlberg's sixth stage in particular. Instead, moral crises are perceived by women as situations that take place within a certain context and must be responded to in terms of the individuals involved. Women's socially appointed role has been to nurture and to care, to build and maintain those close relationships on which we all depend. Thus, says Gilligan, it is not surprising that they evaluate their own and other women's goodness by measuring their capacity to care (*DV* 17). And it is on the basis of this ethic of care that women appraise moral situations.

Like Kohlberg, Gilligan constructs a schema of phases that elaborate a progression in moral development. In describing the ethic of care, she identifies a first level marked by a focus on the self, an "orientation to individual survival" ("Self and Morality" 297). Those positioned at level 2 express what Gilligan calls the "conventional women's voice," which demarcates the self's principal function as caring for others. This level is named "goodness as self-sacrifice" ("Self and Morality" 291). At level 3, "the morality of nonviolence," the imperative to care for self and other becomes a universal moral responsibility ("Self and Morality" 302).

For an analysis of the origins of an ethic of care, Gilligan takes into account Nancy Chodorow's (1978) discussion of the formation of the feminine self. Because of nearly universal child care arrangements in which most small children are raised primarily by women, girls' early identity formation is part of an ongoing, nurturing relationship with a person of the same gender. When young girls recognize that they are female, they become attached to their mothers in ways that boys do not, thus "fusing the experience of attachment with the process of identity formation" (*DV* 8). Similarly, mothers feel a sense of identity with their daughters, one which they do not share with their sons. Boys' process of identity formation consequently requires greater maternal separation leading to increased individuation. Because girls form their identities by staying close to their mothers (whereas boys tend to distance themselves), girls can acquire instead, from their formative years, a capacity for "empathy." These processes of identity formation rooted in childhood have implications for the future development of both sexes, since "masculinity is defined through separation while femininity is defined through attachment" (*DV* 7–8).

Gilligan's redefinition of human growth presumes intimate links between personal identity and morality. Recognizing the significance of a continuing sense of attachment expands moral development theory to include "for both sexes the importance throughout life of the connection between self and other, the universality of the need for compassion and care" (*DV* 98). Through Gilligan's work, it has become abundantly clear that all paths to moral maturity cannot be accommodated by male-derived theories.

This gulf reveals the need for feminist moral philosophies. If the value accorded to autonomy and objectivity is based on men's experience in the public sphere, and if women's care perspective arises from their lived experience with home and family, then we may need to evaluate women's responses to moral dilemmas according to different criteria (Kittay and Meyers 13–14). Sara Ruddick, in her theory of maternal thinking, advances this view by claiming that women's moral experience as mothers—protecting and nurturing children, training them for life in society—would benefit the public domain from which women have traditionally been excluded (241).

Nel Noddings, like Sara Ruddick and Carol Gilligan, bases her approach to ethics on the importance of caring and responsibility towards others. Calling this a "relational ethic," Noddings distinguishes her model from the traditional ethical paradigm which finds its meaning in the rights of the individual (184). Rather, she uses the "dyad" in which the "one caring or the carer . . . responds to the needs, wants and initiations of the second." The "cared for" member's responsibility in the relationship is recognition of the caring (185).

Noddings' relational ethic, which puts a premium on connectedness as a fundamental human need and moral right, informs her ideas about good and evil. Evil for Noddings has always to be associated with "pain, separation and helplessness." She identifies as morally reprehensible a deed that "induc[es] the pain of separation" or "neglect[s] relation so that the pain of separation follows" (221). In contrast, actions identified as "good" according to relational ethics would be those nurturing deeds or caring responses that contribute to maintaining connection. Noddings' philosophy, along with other feminists' thinking about moral development, gives voice to differences in moral decision making. This groundbreaking research continues to strengthen the field of moral philosophy with its inclusion of gender-based experiences previously dismissed or neglected altogether.

In this section, "Moral Decision Making in the Different Voice," Susan Currier's study, "Liberation Fables 'in a Different Voice': Virginia Woolf's *To the Lighthouse* and Margaret Drabble's *The Waterfall*," analyzes the protagonists in these two works of fiction. She notes how closely they reflect Carol Gilligan's theory that, for women, self-definition is achieved more often "through connection" than through the male ideal of separation. When contrasted with Joyce's Stephen Dedalus, Lily Briscoe and Jane Grey grow and develop in ways that have not been readily perceived by male literary critics who equate a character's maturation with the separation of self from others, a value judgment made within the justice tradition of moral development. The "different voice" and different values that Virginia Woolf's and Margaret Drabble's protagonists follow suggest that these novels by women represent "the possibility of another paradigm—a model female liberation fable."

Lily the painter and Jane the writer express their desires to produce works where all elements are integrated: when exclusion or detachment of parts occurs, they experience that disconnection as a source of artistic frustration. In art and in life, the developmental quest for both Lily and Jane is toward a "new morality" in which they can "exercise responsibility to and for themselves without abandoning others and thus severing the connections they so value." Referring to Jessica Benjamin's ideas about mutual recognition as an antidote for "Western culture's idealization of the separate self," Currier shows that in these two liberation fables, the tensions are not resolved absolutely, for to do so would be to participate in exclusion or domination by a single subjectivity. Instead, Woolf and Drabble support the life-affirming qualities of connection and inclusion as principles of moral choice that free, rather than limit, their main characters.

The life-affirming qualities of attachment are similarly seen in Mirella Servodidio's essay, "A Case of Pre-Oedipal and Narrative Fixation: *The Same Sea As Every Summer*." In this novel by Esther Tusquets, the narrator's adult development is viewed as having been sabotaged by a mother who, in refusing to offer the approval and symbiosis her young daughter needs, obstructs and dooms the girl's journey toward individuation. The only two possible, early relationships of "positive mirroring" for the narrator—one with Sofia, her caretaker, and the other with the narrator's grandmother—fail to "displace a negativism created by failed maternal bonding." Perpetually longing for the mother who has betrayed her, the narrator is unable to reproduce anything but disconnection in her adult relationships with daughter, husband, lover, and self. Analyzing the significance of pre-Oedipal bonding, Servodidio portrays the pain and dysfunction in the narrator's emotional life as having been rooted in her detached mother's unwillingness to nurture, clearly portrayed in Tusquet's novel as an act of moral negligence.

Making an extended analogy in the novel between "mother-daughter bonding and textual bonding," Servodidio widens her discussion of female bonding: as the narrator returns to the books of her childhood, "literature exercises the formative influence imputed to the mother and acts as the reliable presence that cushions the child's painful solitude." Ever-caught in her fixation, the narrator hopelessly experiences moral defeat as she seeks consolation for her mother's rejection. In this state of desperation, she can participate only in a relentless, circular journey, comparable to the motion of the sea each summer.

In her essay, "The Bonds of Love and the Boundaries of Self in Toni Morrison's *Beloved*," Barbara Schapiro analyzes a very different mother, one who sees in her enslavement no choice but to deny her child maternal recognition. Morrison's character's moral principles and social reality contrast starkly with that of the narrator's mother in Tusquets' novel. Sethe in *Beloved* kills her daughter "to save her from psychic death," which, as Schapiro defines it, "involves the denial of one's being as a human subject." Sethe's murderous act is presented as paradoxical in that the slave woman's decision to cut her baby's throat seems a moral response to racist society—by definition, immoral—in which the subjugated mother had been deprived of the experience of nurturing her own child. Not only mother but also child experience this loss of recognition so deeply that Beloved, the murdered infant, returns years later as a ghost, seeking the maternal affirmation she was denied. In Beloved's reincarnation, we sympathize with her arrested rage, linked as it is "directly . . . to the power of Sethe's love."

Schapiro finds Benjamin's ideas about the yearning for mutual recognition helpful in illuminating the way in which Morrison's novel captures the "intrapsychic effects of growing up as a black person in such a system, one in which intersubjectivity is impossible." All of the main characters hunger for recognition that Schapiro locates within Benjamin's view of desire: the pursuit of affirmation of one's being that can be satisfied only under the gaze of the beloved. This wish and drive to see oneself reflected lovingly in another's eyes appears overwhelming and often threatens interpersonal boundaries. Schapiro points out that this fluid "love-hunger," which Carol Gilligan and Nancy Chodorow have asserted is more typically female than male in expression, stems from the pre-Oedipal bond of essential identity forged between the same sex mother and child. In her novel, Morrison dramatizes this basic human need for nourishment in the form of recognition, showing that the autonomous self is deeply "rooted in relationship." However, where a culture institutionalizes relationships of domination, those whose lives are enslaved will suffer moral defeat and psychological loss that "take on destructive proportions in the inner world." These losses of selfhood and human dignity affect generation after generation when mothers, deprived of autonomy, cannot give to their children the recognition they will need to provide maternal affirmation to posterity.

Also responding to analytic emphasis on the mother's "crucial, determining role in the development and continuing welfare of the child," Susan Suleiman probes the fantasy of maternal omnipotence in writing about Mary Gordon's novel, *Men and Angels*. What interests Suleiman in Gordon's work is the novelist's portrait of the moral dilemma mothers in the real world face when they have to attend to creative work as well as take responsibility for the engulfing occupation of child-rearing. When Gordon's protagonist, Anne, who is an art curator, discovers in her research that Caroline, the respected painter, had denied warmth and affirmation to her son who died young, Anne cannot help but accuse the distinguished artist of having contributed, in her maternal negligence, to poor Stephen's death. Suleiman identifies several mother-"doubles" in this novel who illustrate the split sense of self that many mothers have: Caroline is a "bad" mother to son Stephen, but a "good" mother to his wife, Jane; Laura, the au pair, "mothers" Anne's children well in Anne's absence, but becomes for the protagonist the "bad, other mother" when Laura's premature, accidental death—a result of "maternal" carelessness—almost causes Anne's children's deaths as well. Psychologically, Laura's demise allows Anne to safeguard and even exaggerate her own self-image as passionately and wholly devoted to her children. Morally, Laura's death raises painful questions for Anne of whether she, as acting "good" mother to Laura, should have "mothered" her better by not ignoring the young woman who desperately sought her attention. Mothers, Suleiman contends, often construct a split self-image: they are either the "murderous" or the "nurturing" mother.

In "Maternal Splitting: 'Good' and 'Bad' Mothers and Reality," Suleiman's literary analysis calls to mind Nel Noddings' work in which goodness is equated with nurturing behaviors that neither harm nor threaten another person. If women are, as Noddings says, predisposed to "relational ethics," then Suleiman's essay reveals one reason why many mothers agonize when they work away from their children: women hold themselves consistently responsible for reducing, not increasing, "the pain of separation" in children's lives (Noddings 221). Thus, occupation that takes a mother away from her children challenges a woman's concept of self as "moral." This suggests a heightened sense of self-importance that many women have developed in perceiving their maternal role. Suleiman wonders why "even the most enlightened among us . . . often discover in ourselves the stubborn belief that mother is the only one who really counts." Her response, which derives from her reading of *Men and Angels*, is that our society today still punishes women's "attempt to pursue full and integrated personal lives and remain mothers," leaving a mother's "ideologically and psychologically regressive" claim to her children as perhaps the last stronghold of self-protection for women. Suleiman suggests the need for social policy reform if it is hoped that women—and men—who parent will stop falling prey to harmful fantasies of their own omnipotence as caretakers.

Finally in this section, we have another mother's story analyzed through the lens of feminist moral development theory: "Be True: Moral Dilemma in *The Scarlet Letter*." In this essay, Donna Simms applies Gilligan's distinction between the moral perspectives of "justice" and "care" to Arthur Dimmesdale and Hester Prynne in their different ways of deliberating their shared predicament. Devoted to a system of rules, "constricted by his ethical orientation," Arthur can only interpret his union with Hester as evil. Hester, however, "literally defines herself in relationship" symbolized by her badge of adultery and the child their union has conceived. Hester's moral judgment is concerned not with laws but with betrayal.

Both Roger Chillingsworth and little Pearl represent what Simms calls "blended perspectives" in that each embodies salient characteristics of the justice and care orientations. Simms reveals Hawthorne's dramatization of two "conflicting definitions of the self and the moralities that correspond to these definitions." She discusses the symbol of the scarlet letter as that which both unites and divides these two moral perspectives. In Simms' work, as in the other essays in this section, feminist psychological theory illuminates literary representations of moral issues and conflicts in intimacy that shape fictional portraits of the self-in-relation across the life span.

Works Cited

Chodorow, Nancy. *The Reproduction of Mothering: Psychoanalysis and the Sociology of Gender.* Berkeley: U of California Press, 1978.

Gilligan, Carol. *In a Different Voice: Psychological Theory and Women's Development.* Cambridge: Harvard UP, 1982.

———. "In a Different Voice: Women's Conceptions of Self and of Morality." *The Future of Difference.* Ed. Hester Eisenstein and Alice Jardine. New Brunswick: Rutgers UP, 1985. 274–317.

Kittay, Eva Feder, and Diana T. Meyers, eds. "Introduction." *Women and Moral Theory.* Savage: Rowman and Littlefield, 1987. 3–16.

Kohlberg, Lawrence. *The Philosophy of Moral Development.* Vol. 1. San Francisco: Harper and Row, 1981.

Lapsley, Daniel K. *Moral Psychology.* Boulder: Westview Press, 1996.

Noddings, Nel. *Women and Evil.* Berkeley: U of California Press, 1989.

Ruddick, Sara. "Remarks on the Sexual Politics of Reason." *Women and Moral Theory.* 237–260.

8

Liberation Fables "in a Different Voice": Virginia Woolf's *To the Lighthouse* and Margaret Drabble's *The Waterfall*

Susan Currier

Contrasting patterns of development for males and females in her controversial *In a Different Voice*, feminist psychologist Carol Gilligan describes the male paradigm as self-definition "through separation" and the female counterpart as self-delineation "through connection" (35). Within these paradigms, she asserts that male success is measured against some "abstract ideal perfection," while female success is "assessed through particular activities of care" (35). Gilligan documents and deplores the dominance of the male model in our culture, and she selects Joyce's Stephen Dedalus to represent its liabilities: "The concept of the separate self and of moral principles uncompromised by the constraints of reality is . . . the elaborately wrought philosophy of a Stephen Dedalus, whose flight we know to be in jeopardy" (98). In her more recent work of feminist psychoanalytic theory, *The Bonds of Love*, Jessica Benjamin continues Gilligan's assault on Western culture's idealization of the separate self. She posits alienation, mitigated only by interpersonal relations of dominance and submission, as its inevitable consequence. To represent the hopeless dynamics of such relations, she selects Pauline Réage's *Story of O*, in which a capable woman narrates her own surrender to erotic violation and psychosexual bondage. Like Gilligan, Benjamin proposes a re-evaluation of the importance of connection in our lives, but she delineates in more depth crucial distinctions between connection's life-affirming and life-denying variations.

Gilligan's multiple references to *Portrait of the Artist* and Benjamin's analysis of *The Story of O*, contextualized as they are within broader explications of male and female development, invite us to counterpoise female fictional figures against Stephen and O, and to ask again, this time from the perspective of Gilligan's and Benjamin's theories, one of the most profound questions in women's studies: Where are the female (and male) alternatives to the traditional *bildungsroman*, on the one hand, and to traditional narratives (whether romantic, comic, erotic, and/or pornographic) of female submission to male domination, on the other?

This essay examines two such alternatives and discovers in them the possibility of another paradigm—a model female liberation fable distinguished by the female protagonist's voice and maturation process, the author's narrative strategy, and the form of the work. The alternatives from which this model is derived are two twentieth-century texts by British women writers—Virginia Woolf's *To the Lighthouse* and Margaret Drabble's *The Waterfall*. Both works map routes out of alienation and domination, but these maps are not readily visible to many male critics. In particular, *To the Lighthouse* still elicits responses such as Alex Zwerdling's reading of the novel in his 1986 *Virginia Woolf and the Real World*. There he argues that Woolf's own ambivalence toward her family and the Victorian world of her youth compromises the resolution of this autobiographical novel precisely because it fails to resolve into domination/submission, on the one hand, or into alienation, on the other. In support of his judgment, he cites Avrom Fleishman's conclusion from his 1976 *Virginia Woolf: A Critical Reading* that *To the Lighthouse* almost qualifies as a traditional comedy in which a new order displaces an old one, but finally "lacks the revolutionary movement that overthrows the established, usually elder generation and reorders the world" (qtd. in Zwerdling 200). Thus, Zwerdling concludes Woolf has rejected the "nineteenth-century marriage plot" (207). But clearly, Zwerdling is more troubled by Lily's failure to abandon her relationships altogether than he is by her failure to marry. Unlike Stephen, whose developing independence from family and friends informs the structure of Joyce's text, Lily remains apparently enmeshed with and dependent upon the Ramsays even in middle age. For Zwerdling, the male paradigm for development as described by Gilligan defines the "modern liberation plot," which succeeds the "nineteenth-century marriage plot" (207). *Portrait of the Artist* qualifies under the new rubric, but *To the Lighthouse* doesn't: "Everything about *To the Lighthouse* is invented to do away with the necessity of exclusive choice, from the individual sentence to the book's overarching structure" (205). The "continuous presence in Part III of such compromised rebellious gestures makes it impossible to see Woolf's novel as a liberation fable" (200).

Of course, *To the Lighthouse* isn't a "liberation fable" as long as that genre is construed almost entirely in psychosocial terms of separation and exclusion. Nor does the novel qualify clearly under the rubric of any other established literary form, including the novel of development. On this latter point, Zwerdling is quite specific as he discounts any reading of *To the Lighthouse* as "a kind of *Bildungsroman* with Lily as the central character and the growth of her independent vision as its teleological design" (198). However, if, as Gilligan argues, female development occurs within the context of connection, and if, as Benjamin advances, women (and men) can discover a lost paradise in a kind of connection or "mutual recognition" she describes as intersubjective (78), then *To the Lighthouse* is a liberation fable according to criteria different from, but as profound as, Zwerdling's.

If we are prepared to hear it, Gilligan's distinction between the relative values of separation and connection for men and women is just as evident in *To the Lighthouse* and *The Waterfall* as it is in Gilligan's interviews with her research subjects. We have only to listen to the voices with which Lily Briscoe and Jane Gray interpret experience and contrast them with that of Stephen Dedalus. While Stephen ultimately reduces connections of all sorts to "nets" that impede the solo flight of his soul (203), Lily and Jane crave intimacy. So important is it to Lily that early in *To the Lighthouse*, as she ponders how she might merge with Mrs. Ramsay, she equates intimacy with knowledge more valuable than "inscriptions on tablets" or anything "written in any language known to men" (51). Imbued with similar values, Jane confesses directly the depth of her desire for connection: "God, how I have always desired and envied intimacy, with what jealousy have I heard its language and listened to its exclusive laughter" (136).

The same distinctions continue in the language with which each of these artist-protagonists considers his or her work. The aesthetic issue that consumes Stephen, if one takes seriously his "applied Aquinas" (209), is the separation or distillation from everything else in the world of the essential aesthetic object. But for Lily, the problem that abides in her painting is "how to connect this mass on the right with that on the left" (53). For Jane, the most profound challenge in her book is how to integrate its alternating first- and third-person voices: "I can't make the connections: I can't join it up . . . I must make some effort to comprehend. I am tired of exclusion" (99).

Perhaps the most compelling contrast between male and female voices in these works becomes audible in Stephen's and Lily's separate fantasies of themselves as artists. Stephen's image of himself as a smith who forges in his soul "the uncreated conscience" of the Irish (253) epitomizes his inclination toward emotional distance as well as moral judgment. His association of the people who are his subject matter with a malleable

metal quite separate from himself suggests the relation between alienation and domination that Benjamin finds prevalent in Western culture.
On the other hand, Lily's metaphors for the artist she would like to become replace detachment with feeling and judgment with care:

> There might be lovers whose gift it was to choose out the elements of things
> and place them together and so, giving them a wholeness not theirs in life,
> make of some scene or meeting of people (all now gone and separate) one
> of those globed compacted things over which thought lingers and love plays.
> (192)

Lily's artist connects her disparate subjects, viewers, and self through
love. Her art stimulates the commingling of thought and love in its audience, undoing the same dissociation upon which Stephen's depends.

Given the differences that inhere between Lily's and Jane's voices, on
one hand, and Stephen's, on the other, it is no surprise that the processes
by which these two female protagonists grow also contrast with that by
which Stephen develops. By the end of *Portrait*, but at an age younger
than those at which we meet Lily and Jane, Stephen seeks the exile he
believes he requires to produce the abstract and ideal perfection he will
project as the missing conscience of his race. Very little ambivalence accompanies his exclusion of what he perceives as false claims of all sorts:
family, friends, love, religion, Irish independence, and socialism. Christian and classical patrimonies merge: Stephen's "I will not serve" (239)
unpinions him for Dedalian flight. If he succeeds, his surely counts as a
"liberation fable." If, like Icarus, he fails, he drowns gloriously redeemed
in his own tragedy.

However, given their commitment to connection, neither Lily nor Jane
can save herself or her art by opting for separation or alienation to escape
domination by false claims that threaten each of them as well. Instead,
Lily and Jane develop in the context of relationships, which they transform rather than abandon. Gilligan's model for female development describes a progression from (1) a selfish orientation requiring the sacrifice
of other to self to (2) a selfless orientation requiring the sacrifice of self
to other to (3) a dual orientation in which affirmation of self and other
replaces sacrifice of self or other. From the perspective of Gilligan's
model, the challenge for both Lily and Jane is to exercise responsibility
to and for themselves without abandoning others and thus severing the
connections they so value. Their quests are for alternatives that indeed
defy Zwerdling's "necessity of exclusive choice"—quests uncharted by
maps from either Christian or classical myth.

Lily's progress in this quest is aptly demonstrated by the contrast between her resolutions to conflict in two of the most frequently discussed

scenes in the novel.[1] In the first of these, at the dinner party that climaxes Part I, Lily sacrifices her self to Charles Tansley and Mrs. Ramsay in order to preserve connection. In spite of Tansley's insistence that "Women can't paint, women can't write," Lily petitions him to take her to the lighthouse (48). Before she does so, she reconsiders the old "code of behavior" that requires women to reflect men at twice their size and that requires men to rescue women in physical peril. But telepathic pleas she hears emanating from Mrs. Ramsay thwart her resistance. Imagining that Mrs. Ramsay will drown in "seas of fire" and that "life will run upon the rocks" unless she obeys the code (92), Lily surrenders. She secures harmonious connection among the guests and between Mrs. Ramsay and herself, but at a price.

In the second scene, Lily and Mr. Ramsay confront each other on the lawn ten years later. Asked this time to solace Mr. Ramsay's grief, as she had once soothed Tansley's inflamed ego, Lily resists an impulse to emulate "the glow, the rhapsody, the self-surrender, she had seen on so many women's faces" (150), and she remains silent. During this dreadful pause, Lily imagines herself as a "dried-up old maid" (151) and a "miserable sinner" (152). But then she compliments Mr. Ramsay on his boots, and, together, they are transported to an Edenic new world—"a sunny island, where peace dwelt, sanity reigned and the sun forever shone" (154)— quite different from the Ramsay household with its storms and sulks, and from World War I Europe with its exploding shells, its death-colored ships, and its blood-polluted seas. Lily discovers she can care for Mr. Ramsay and herself in a way that injures neither.

Like Lily's, Jane's quest for integrity in relationships also leads her out of Gilligan's second stage (sacrificing self to other) into the third (extending care to self and other). If the early Lily can't risk fracturing her bond with Mrs. Ramsay to protect herself, neither can young Jane afford to test the affections of her mother. Unlike her younger sister, who "remained a whole person because she managed to accommodate protest in her manner" toward their parents, Jane recalls, "I split myself, I went underground" (136). But guilty of harboring the fugitive self she sacrificed, Jane comes to believe that she is "a dangerous woman" (29). Therefore, she marries another misogynous Charles Tansley—in the form of a musician named Malcolm—to enforce the imprisonment of that self.

However, by the time we meet Jane in the early chapters of *The Waterfall*, she also has begun to question the traditional code of female self-sacrifice that she, like Lily, absorbed from her mother (or mother surrogate) and which Gilligan identifies as conventional feminine goodness. Like Lily facing Mr. Ramsay on the lawn and seeking a new code by which to care for the self she once sacrificed to Charles Tansley, Jane is also searching for a new morality that will approve her severed self. For

Lily, the inspiration for the quest is fueled by those tragic tributes to the old code: World War I and the deaths of Andrew and Prue. For Jane, the motivation derives from a more local, but equally futile war—her marriage to Malcolm. In the course of her quest, Jane, like Lily, feels herself sinful. More important, though, Jane, like Lily, also endures voluntary isolation. If Lily turns herself into a "lifeless old maid," Jane becomes a self-exiled agoraphobe. Both brave loss of connection long enough to loosen the ties that require sacrifice of self to other. If Gilligan's observation that female gender identity is as threatened by separation as male gender identity is by intimacy is accurate (8), both demonstrate profound courage in so doing. By way of reward, each succeeds in her quest for a code that will admit her self as well as other, and each discovers it in the context of an encounter or relationship with a man she will never marry. For Lily's chaste interlude with Mr. Ramsay, Jane substitutes an enduring love affair with her cousin's husband, an affair in which she will ultimately exercise care for an entire cast of characters, including her self. In spite of the immoral (according to the old code) dimensions of this relationship, Jane finds in it a new world comparable to Lily's sunny isle: "an undiscovered country" with "miles of verdure, rivers, fishes, colored birds" (252). Lily and Jane both find their new codes are keys to unlock Eden.

In order to appreciate the experience of Eden, itself, as it is adumbrated in these two novels, we have only to turn to Benjamin's theory. Her emphasis on intersubjectivity at all levels of psychological development derives from her observation that an individual's ability to "recognize" an other is just as essential as is his or her ability to separate from an other. Recognition means many things: "to affirm, validate, acknowledge, know, accept, understand, empathize, take in, tolerate, appreciate, see, identify with, find familiar love" (15–16). It always entails the apprehension of an other as simultaneously similar to and different from the self and, consequently, as a subject rather than an object. According to Benjamin, mutual recognition is a rare and blessed occurrence in which two or more individuals achieve such attunement that they can share one another's mental states without risking the domination or absorption of one personality by the other.

This is the Eden, the lost innocence or paradise to which Lily and Jane are both admitted after each braves isolation. It is quite different from either the exile toward which Stephen flies in the final pages of *Portrait* or that den of sadomasochism, Castle Roissy, to which O is brought in Réage's novel. Lily's trip to her sunny isle and Stephen's walk on the Strand are both ecstatic episodes, but for her the revelation is intersubjective connection and for him it is intrapsychic autonomy. Rejecting the old code that polarizes gender roles, Lily apprehends Mr. Ramsay as similar to as well as different from herself. Having acknowledged her self as an object of care, she experiences his need as less threatening and more analogous to her own. She recognizes Mr. Ramsay, and he does her. Apparently pleased because she appreciates his boots, Mr. Ramsay is also delighted that she survives his attempt to absorb or destroy her. Now he has received recognition from a subject instead of empty empathy from an object. Lily is similar—appreciative of good boots, but different— unavailable for immolation on demand. Overwhelmed himself by this unexpected pre-lapsarian encounter, Mr. Ramsay also cares for Lily—he ties her shoelaces into superior knots.

Another foray to paradise, this time with Mrs. Ramsay, reveals the same dynamics. When, early in the novel, Lily yearns for closer connection to Mrs. Ramsay, she ponders how to become "one with the *object* one adored" (51; emphasis mine). But once she finds she can care for her self even as she cares for an other, and so becomes her own mother, she can approach Mrs. Ramsay as a subject—similar to herself in her orientation toward care, but different in her inclination toward self-immolation. Lily's recognition of Mrs. Ramsay is so powerful that it resurrects her, and Lily's transmutation of the "ordinary" into "a miracle . . . an ecstasy" (202) proves as potent as that which Stephen Dedalus fantasizes for himself as a "priest of eternal imagination, transmuting the daily bread of experience into the radiant body of everliving life" (224). The difference is that Lily includes her self in the miracle she creates, while Stephen, in his identification with Lucifer and Icarus, excludes himself from any hope of heaven. The moral error for Stephen and his mythic ancestors may be pride, but it derives from a more profound psychological error of defining relationships only in terms of domination/submission, on the one hand, or separation to the point of alienation (in the case of Icarus, literal self-destruction), on the other. Stephen translates "I will not serve" into self-exile at the end of *Portrait*, only to reappear in *Ulysses* questing for connection.

If Benjamin's notions of intersubjectivity and recognition help illuminate Lily's liberation, they are just as useful in the case of Jane's. Indeed, Jane seems to allude directly to those notions by defining her relationship with James as a "sequence of discovery and recognition that I would call love" (52) and by crediting James' powers of recognition with the reclamation of her severed self: "He redeemed me by knowing me" (58).

Like the joy discovered by Lily and Mr. Ramsay in *To the Lighthouse*, that which flows between Jane and James in *The Waterfall* depends on mutual affirmation of similarity as well as difference. But in the case of Jane and James, we see the same process of mutual affirmation worked out in more explicit detail. In their verbal exchanges, James and Jane invoke repetition to affirm their likeness:

James: You were gone so long. I missed you, you've never been out so long.
Jane: Oh it was long. It was too long. I'm sorry it was so long.
James: What did he say?
Jane: He said I was all right. He said I was all right.
James: I knew you would be all right. Of course you would be all right. (48)

This ritual, in which Jane mirrors James by echoing his language and James mirrors Jane by echoing hers, affirms the presence of two subjects. However, just as important, so does their mutual acknowledgment of difference in other portions of the text—James learns to talk of nursery schools and Jane of garages—until his utterances become more to her than "representations of speech and symbols uttered in another language," until she begins "to acquaint herself with his daily anxieties, as *he with hers*" (171, emphasis mine).

The sexual dialogues between Jane and James also evolve toward intersubjectivity. When Jane wakes from their first night together in the same bed, she is startled by James' nearness and "alarmed, as ever, by the physical manifestations of otherness, of man" (39). However, Jane grows to trust James, and eventually they achieve a sexual epiphany in the description of which Jane interweaves the language of male creation from *Genesis* and of female creation from childbirth until they are inextricable and the similarities between male and female are at least as evident as the differences:

> He had done it: he had made her, in his own image. The throes, the cries, the pains, were his; and he could no more dissociate himself from them than from his own flesh. She was his, but by having her he had made himself hers . . . a woman delivered. She was his offspring, as he lying there between her legs, had been hers. (181)

As in the verbal exchange above, each leads and each follows, but now each does both simultaneously rather than sequentially.

If intersubjective connection is the goal toward which Lily in *To the Lighthouse* and Jane in *The Waterfall* develop, it is also the ideal that governs narrative strategy in both novels. Realignment of relationships away from domination/submission and alienation is so essential to Woolf and Drabble that it becomes the structural as well as thematic nexus of these liberation fables, reverberating in multiple contexts simultaneously.

Salient similarities between the preoccupations of Lily as she works on her painting in *To the Lighthouse* and those of Woolf as she records her progress on the novel in her diary attest to the importance of intersubjectivity in the narrative strategy of this work. While Lily ponders how to join masses in her art without breaking the unity of the whole, Woolf worries how to connect Parts I and III of her novel with "Time Passes," given its "consequent break of unity" in her design (79). The break of unity is occasioned by the shift in perspective from a close-up of a single day in the life of the Ramsays to a distant view of a decade of largely nonhuman events interspersed with occasional references to World War I and parenthetical notice of three deaths in the Ramsay family.

Corollary to the shift in perspective is the substitution of nature for humans as center-stage *subject* in this middle section of the novel. Within it, conventional roles are reversed: humans slumber and nature wakes; humans are passive and nature is active. Part of the description of Mrs. Ramsay's dinner party, which climaxes Part I, reveals the imperative for this shift. When, at her command, the candles are lit, a glow permeates the gathering and the night is shut out beyond "panes of glass, which, far from giving any accurate view of the outside world, rippled it so strangely that . . . inside the room seemed to be order and dry land," but "outside, a reflection in which things wavered and vanished, waterlily" (97). The decade encompassed in "Time Passes" shatters this mirror-window and belies the illusion. Early in "Time Passes," the mirror-window reappears as mirror-tidepools in which pre-war beach walkers find reflected their fondest fantasies—"that good triumphs, happiness prevails, order rules" (132). But after the intrusion of the ashen ship and the purple stain, it grows difficult "to marvel how beauty outside mirrored beauty within." Indeed, "to pace the beach was impossible; contemplation was unendurable; the mirror was broken" (134).

The significance of the shattered mirror in *To the Lighthouse* can hardly be overstated, and Benjamin can help us understand why. When she reviews the workings of alienation and domination in our culture, Benjamin traces their roots to the reduction of mother to mirroring object vis-à-vis her children in both our psychological theory and our generalized consciousness. From that early error, sons, in particular, derive an inclination to regard others, particularly women, as extensions of themselves, as objects that exist only in relation to their own needs, as objects they may consume in the satisfaction of those needs. Daughters, in contrast, seek to please, by mirroring male subjects in order to gain vicarious recognition, to escape their own fates as female objects, but in so doing they surrender any potential claims to subjectivities of their own. This is the story of O opposite her male masters, René and Sir Stephen. However sexist this association of masculinity with subjectivity and femininity with objectification, Benjamin insists that, on some level, the misery is finally mutual. For an important paradox eludes the men of Roissy as well as Stephen Dedalus: "Establishing myself (Hegel's "being for itself") means winning the recognition of the other, and this, in turn, means I must finally acknowledge the other as existing for himself and not just [as mirror] for me" (Benjamin 36). As women surrender their own subjectivities in ill-conceived efforts to achieve and sustain connection with men who enjoy the status of subjects, they lose their power to recognize or validate that status. If the women are then discarded as useless objects, as is O, the men end up alone and alienated, and thus invisible as subjects. Not surprisingly, this deathly cycle also reaches beyond relationships between men and women to others, such as that between humans and nature, at least as it is detailed in the above passage from *To the Lighthouse*. The mirror the beach walkers project onto nature is very similar to that men project onto women. The beach walkers expect to use nature much as Mr. Ramsay expects to use Lily before their unexpected induction into Eden.

Human recognition of nature in this novel results from the same kind of tension between similarity and difference that characterized Lily's resolution of conflict with both Mr. and Mrs. Ramsay. Signs of spring approaching in "Time Passes" are interpreted by the beach walkers as a sympathy or similarity between humans and nature. Indeed, nature appears "to have taken upon her a knowledge of the sorrows of mankind" (132). However, just as Lily refuses immolation on demand, reduction of her self to mere mirror opposite Mr. Ramsay, so does nature assert its difference from the fantasies humans project upon it. Rather than corroborating the false visions of the mirror-window or the mirror-tidepools, it defies its own objectification at the hands of humans. As Mrs. Ramsay and the beach walkers negate nature, nature negates Mrs. Ramsay in an untimely death and the beach walkers with storms and chaos.

Woolf's narrative strategy in *To the Lighthouse* thus bifurcates a story of human beings to accommodate another of nature. Nevertheless, the point is not to alienate humans and nature but rather to guide humans beyond the illusion of their status as sole subjects in an apparent universe of objects and then into intersubjective connection with nature. Thus, Lily and Woolf must reconcile short- and long-range perspectives in Part III. Before she can complete her painting, Lily alternates between a close-up focus on Mrs. Ramsay and a distant focus on Mr. Ramsay. Having just recognized Mr. Ramsay, Lily is filled with a new appreciation for the latter, more distant view: "Distance had an extraordinary power; they had been swallowed up in it, she felt, they were gone for ever, they had become part of the nature of things" (188). However, as she also recalls and recognizes Mrs. Ramsay, simultaneously appreciating her more immediate focus on human affairs, Lily integrates the two perspectives, completes her vision, and connects the heretofore unrelated masses in her painting.

Meanwhile, among the generalized society represented by the beach walkers, the war inspires a popular interest in Mr. Carmichael's poetry—about the desert, the camel, the palm tree, and the sunset—about the elemental nature on the other side of the mirror. That vision communicated, its author joins Lily at the novel's close—in the guise of a Neptune complete with trident and weeds in his hair, with the power to calm as well as to create storms. Unlike the "spring," which only seemed "to take upon her the sufferings of mankind," this nature god spreads his hands "over all the weakness and suffering of mankind," and surveys "tolerantly and compassionately, their final destiny" (208). Nature recognizes humans, just as humans recognize nature.

Narrative strategy in *The Waterfall* operates similarly. Jane's equivalent to Lily's problem of the unconnected masses in her painting is the unconnected (until the end) first- and third-person threads of her novel. As Woolf intersects revelatory recognition between Lily and the Ramsays with revelatory recognition between humans and nature, Drabble intersects revelatory recognition between Jane and James with revelatory recognition between the dissociated sides of Jane's divided self.

The "sequence of discovery and recognition" that Jane calls love is confined to Jane's third-person narrative for most of the novel. But Jane transposes it into her first-person voice near the end of the work, simultaneously reversing roles assigned to James and herself in her third-person account. While Jane (with some justification as already noted) chooses to describe the third-person narrative as a "dialogue," Gayle Greene describes it as a traditional romance, the old "story of she," characterized by passivity and surrender on the part of the woman and by efficacious activity on the part of the man (52). Despite all the recognition that James bestows on Jane's unawakened, underground self in this narrative, the orchestration of their relationship falls almost exclusively to him. However, after their automobile accident, James lies unconscious in a hospital bed for weeks. He adopts the role of "sleeping partner" (161), and Jane adopts that of active rescuer. She handles the police, the relatives, her children (mimicking James by constructing a motorized model Ferrari for her son) and, it might be argued, reclaims James through her vigils by his bed.

The internal realignment in Jane that facilitates this role reversal requires that she build a new relationship between the dissociated sides of her self—one based on mutual recognition rather than on domination of one side by another or on alienation of one side from the other. The realignment unfolds through a series of dialogues between the split halves of her personality, as they are embodied in her third-person narrative and her first-person analysis. These dialogues are the narrative strategies she devises for their unification. They have as analogues those other dialogues between Jane and James within the narrative, but these internal dialogues require Jane to resolve a rift in the structure of her art as well as in her psyche.

At the beginning of *The Waterfall,* Jane's familiar above-ground self permits her buried self four chapters of third-person dialogue with James before she intrudes to criticize and, temporarily, stop the story. She is alarmed by the resurrection of her underground self (other), just as she is disturbed by the re-entry of masculinity (other) into her bed. She is also disquieted by the third-person voice that approves the disinterring of her alien self and that delights in its recognition by James. So, after reflecting on the selfishness of salvaging her "dangerous" self, Jane rejects the third-person narrative out of hand: "It won't, of course, do: as an account, I mean, of what took place" (51). But neither can Jane's self-censorious "I" satisfy the buried "she" that is awakening to James. Her "she" understands her "I" only as the enemy that interred her. Therefore, Jane resorts to a "broken medium" (51), a strategy of alternating voices to give each its due.

However, by the middle of the novel, distinctions between the first- and third-person passages blur as each of her selves begins to recognize the other. First, Jane introduces her "I" to her "she." Heretofore mute within the context of the narrative and alienated from her "she," it initially sounds to her "she" as if it were "another woman's voice" (160). But it also sounds "reasonable" to her "she," particularly as it protests the exclusion of ordinary life, what Jane calls "quotidian reality" and of other voices (including its own) from the romance narrative (99). In contrast to Malcolm, who, like Charles Tansley and the men of Roissy, connects to women only to negate their subjectivities, James also recognizes this other half of Jane, skillfully engaging it in dialogue as soon as it enters the narrative.

The old boundaries separating Jane's selves also shift in the opposite direction. As Jane prepares to leave for Norway, her "I" anticipates welcoming her "she" into ordinary life by transposing the discourse of the romance into that of economics: "I had been so reluctant to try to exchange any of the promises that we pledged one another into the currency of real life; but now . . . no more toy money, but chips, worth five-pound notes: those dialogues in bed were going to be coined" (203). James is not the only rescuer of her sleeping "she." Her "I" also recognizes and so saves her "she" by acknowledging the dialogues and so authenticating their existence in the practical world outside the romance.

From this point on, Jane moves more easily and more frequently between her selves and her voices, as if the distance between them had decreased. Then, just before the accident, she switches into a first-person mode, in which she remains for the rest of the novel, except for a brief passage of third-person narrative in the penultimate chapter. This modified "I" is the persona in which Jane plays rescuer to James. The most important difference between it and Jane's earlier "I" is that it requires no second interment of her once buried "she," no victory of "I" over "she" or alienation of "I" from "she." Jane, herself, is careful to distinguish this "I" from that of her skeptical analysis: "At the beginning I identified myself with distrust, and now I cannot articulate my suspicions, I have relegated them to that removed, third-person. I identify myself with love, and I repudiate my nightmare doubts" (250). Neither does her "she" really vanquish her early "I," for while Jane discards her doubts, she not only maintains her hold on "quotidian reality," but she revels in it.

Thus, the "broken medium" to which Jane resorts in the early stages of her story resolves into an integrated first-person narrative, the natural product of recognition between the alienated voices of Jane's split self. When James comes to consciousness, wakening to Jane as she had once wakened to him, the novel comes full circle. The occasion is marked by his recognition of her new "I," her completed subjectivity: "After a while he turned to me and what I saw in his face . . . was recognition. 'Jane,' he said. 'Jane.' As though he had not known who I was until that moment, as though he had just worked out who I was" (265).

Since the focus of the structural resolution in *The Waterfall* is internal to Jane (between her alienated selves), unlike that in *To the Lighthouse* which extends outside Lily (between society and nature), it can seem less important to those who privilege what is public over what is private. But such a judgment reflects still another hierarchical duality nurtured by our culture's idealization of the separate self, a pattern of thought abjured by Gilligan and Benjamin. Both emphasize continuities rather than divisions between the arenas of the public and private, and so does Drabble in addition to Woolf. Even before Jane reaffirms her existence in the larger world beyond James (while remaining connected to him), she acknowledges the reverberations of her internal process of recognition outwards: "I know, too, that by the end I could see my parents-in-law as people, as real people, not merely as symbols, or as pawns in some game of my own playing" (111).

If we accept intersubjectivity as the controlling nexus—governing theme and narrative strategy—in *To the Lighthouse* and *The Waterfall,* the question of form for both novels appears in a new light. Rather than measuring these novels against traditional forms premised on male models of development and finding them wanting (as do Avrom Fleishman and Alex Zwerdling in their analyses of *To the Lighthouse),* we do better to adopt an approach befitting the radical visions of the works. A fictional reader and critic, as well as poet and autobiographer, Jane can guide us in the effort. She, herself, rejects the forms of traditional romance and tragedy in her intermittent dialogues with literature from the past—folklore, Elizabethan love lyrics, and nineteenth-century novels by women writers. She also observes of her own work that "there isn't any conclusion" (220) and "it's odd there should be no ending" (282). She even attempts to explain its absence: "Perhaps the pattern is not completed: the machine, which throws up every month some new juxtaposition and some new reflection, is striving for an effect too huge to conceive" (282). Since intersubjectivity admits the possibility of an infinite number of subjects, there are no necessary limits to its "pattern" of inclusion and connection. Indeed, in the Edenic worlds associated with intersubjectivity in these novels, any traditional authorial compulsion toward closure probably ought to be suspect.

However, either/or propositions (including assertions that this novel does or doesn't have an ending) violate the visions of these works. So Jane complicates her exploration of the absence of conclusion in *The Waterfall* by hazarding the possibility of its presence. She does this by considering both a "feminine ending" (280) and a traditional generic classification for her work: "[O]ur adventures resolved into comedy, not tragedy" (283). Jane's notion of a "feminine ending" seems appropriate to both *The Waterfall* and *To the Lighthouse* because they resolve into patterns of connection rather than simple trajectories into isolation. Jane's designation of comedy is also appropriate if one distinguishes Jane's usage of the term from Fleishman's. His understanding of comedy as a displacement of an old order by a new one through some "revolutionary movement" refers to works in which members of one order dominate or absorb members of another. Whether lightly romantic or darkly ironic, such works contain within them the prototype for Réage's novel, the fundamentally Pyrrhic victory of a dominant subjectivity. An obvious example is Jane Austen's *Emma*. Jane Grey expresses a particular distaste for the marriage between Emma Woodhouse and George Knightley which resolves this novel. Sandra Gilbert and Susan Gubar underscore the erasure of Emma's voice and subjectivity in her acceptance of Knightley's proposal: "What did she say? Just what she ought, of course. A lady always does" (396). In contrast, *To the Lighthouse* and *The Waterfall* represent comedies in which members of new and old orders save themselves and one another, where "revolutionary movement" is replaced by the more radical dynamic of "mutual recognition."

In these, perhaps most promising of all liberation fables, tensions aren't entirely resolved, but what that means is open to question. Zwerdling finds ambivalence, even paralysis, in Woolf's apparent inability to resolve *To the Lighthouse* into the old "nineteenth-century marriage plot," as represented by *Emma* and caricatured by the *Story of O,* or the "modern liberation fable," as represented by *Portrait of the Artist.* However, ambivalence and paralysis aren't what many readers experience as the spirit of these novels. Benjamin's theory provides the basis for another interpretation. For Benjamin, intersubjective relations depend on tensions between sameness and difference to produce a "continual exchange of influence" (49). The absolute resolution of tensions would entail the elimination through exclusion (as in *Portrait*) or domination (as in *Emma* and the *Story of O*) of all but a single subjectivity and, thus obviate any liberation as envisioned by Woolf or Drabble. In these novels of development by Woolf and Drabble, tensions are not so much resolved as realigned to support life-affirming connection among multiple subjects and the transposition of the ordinary into the Edenic.

Notes

1. Two of the earliest analyses of Lily's development between these scenes appear in Carolyn Heilbrun's *Toward a Recognition of Androgyny* (New York: Harper and Row, 1974) and Sally Alexander Brett's "No, Mrs. Ramsay: Feminist Dilemma in *To the Lighthouse*" (*Ball State University Forum* 19 [1978]: 48–56).

Works Cited

Austen, Jane. *Emma*. New York: Bantam, 1981.

Brett, Sally Alexander. "No, Mrs. Ramsay: Feminist Dilemma in *To the Lighthouse*." *Ball State University Forum* 19 (1978): 48–56.

Drabble, Margaret. *The Waterfall*. New York: Plume-NAL, 1969.

Fleishman, Avrom. *Virginia Woolf: A Critical Reading*. Baltimore: Johns Hopkins UP, 1975.

Gilbert, Sandra, and Susan Gubar. *The Madwoman in the Attic*. New Haven: Yale UP, 1979.

Gilligan, Carol. *In a Different Voice: Psychological Theory and Women's Development*. Cambridge: Harvard UP, 1982.

Greene, Gayle. "Margaret Drabble's *The Waterfall*: New System, New Morality." *Novel* 22.1 (1988): 45–65.

Heilbrun, Carolyn. *Toward a Recognition of Androgyny*. New York: Harper and Row, 1974.

Joyce, James. *A Portrait of the Artist as a Young Man*. 1916. New York: Penguin, 1976.

Réage, Pauline. *Story of O*. 1954. New York: Grove Press, 1965.

Woolf, Virginia. *A Writer's Diary*. New York: Harvest-HBJ, 1954.

———. *To the Lighthouse*. 1927. New York: Harvest-HBJ, 1981.

Zwerdling, Alex. *Virginia Woolf and the Real World*. Berkeley: U of California Press, 1986.

9

A Case of Pre-Oedipal and Narrative Fixation:
The Same Sea As Every Summer

Mirella Servodidio

The story outline of Esther Tusquets' *The Same Sea As Every Summer* evinces the characteristic markings of the traditional novel of rebirth and transformation. The mature heroine, a professor of literature, detaches herself from her familiar surroundings and withdraws to the two focal sites of her childhood: the vacant city apartment of her parents, where she ponders her husband's newest infidelity and the callous indifference of her estranged mother and daughter; her grandmother's seaside house, to which she returns for an extended period (some twenty-seven days) in the company of Clara, her student-lover. Here, with Clara acting as herald and initiatory guide, and in apparent response to the "Call to Adventure," the heroine passes through the first portal of transformation calling for severance from the outside world. As she recounts her life story to her lover, she initiates an inward journey to the causal zones of the psyche, where childhood attitudes and attachments are reviewed and made available for transfiguration. The framing myths and fairy tales that guide the heroine's narration and which give symbolic expression to consecrated *rites de passage* heighten the reader's expectation of the forward movement associated with novels of regeneration. The heroine's ultimate return and reintegration with society seal the work's apparent conformity to the monomythic archetypes as described by Joseph Campbell.

However, this *prima facie* evidence is sabotaged early in the novel by violations of the archetypal paradigms encoded in the rituals of male rebirth novels. In *The Same Sea,* enlightenment is not transformative or

191

redemptive. The dismal denouement, whereby reintegration into society signifies a derailed development, conforms more closely to the contrasting patterns of women's fiction as described by Annis Pratt. The promise of progression and fluidity held out by the traditional *bildungsroman* aborts and is displaced by the static patterns and frozen frames of spatial form which, instead, presents the reader with a *bild* or portrait of a heroine who is incapable of change.

A useful optic for viewing the psychological and narrative stasis of *The Same Sea* is provided by feminist psychoanalytic theory which highlights the mother-daughter relationship as the dominant formative influence on female development. As already noted by Elizabeth J. Ordóñez, "The theme of separation between mother and daughter, and the quest for reconciliation and union between mother and daughter through the discovery of matrilineal roots, are central" (37). In this essay, I venture the hypothesis that the originating difficulties of this relationship are grounded in a pre-Oedipal phase bereft of the symbiotic bonding and the unclouded mirroring that psychoanalytic theoreticians view as the determinants of female identity.

The importance of a girl's pre-Oedipal attachment to her mother was belatedly conceded even by Freud, who likened this discovery to that of the Minoan-Mycenean civilization behind the civilization of Greece (54). Jung, too, stressed the pervasive continuity of the mother-daughter bond and expressed the belief that "every mother contains her daughter within herself and every daughter her mother" (162). In turn, object-relations psychology has pointed to the internalization of interpersonal relationships between the infant and the primary caretaker as the determinant of adult personality. D. W. Winnicott has emphasized the mirror role of the mother in child development. Using Lacan's "Le Stade du Miroir" as a point of departure, he posits the mother's face as the child's mirror: "The mother is looking at the baby and what she looks like is what she sees there" (112). Winnicott also discusses the mother's status as permanent inner object throughout a child's life.

In addition to accentuating the primary identification with the mother in pre-Oedipal development, Nancy Chodorow eschews an Oedipal theory that posits the rejection of the mother. Rather, in Chodorow's view, the mother-daughter dyad is transformed into a triangular relationship that first includes the father and then devolves to other males. A woman's heterosexual relationships retain this third term either through a child or through her mother. Chodorow concludes that "Separation from the mother, the breaking of dependence and the establishment and maintenance of a consistently individuated sense of self remain difficult psychological issues" (58).

Jane Flax describes the bond in mother-daughter relationships as one providing grounding, the sense of "ontological security" on which the infant can rely as it moves from a symbiotic orbit into the outside world. If symbiosis is not adequate, differentiation will either be delayed or premature. Dorothy Dinnerstein also celebrates the role of the mother as witness in whose awareness the child's experience is first mirrored. Child and mother are bound in the same primitive, animal-poetic level that foreshadows adult sexuality. With the mother as the original prototypic erotic image, the homoerotic side carries more weight for the girl than for the boy. Yet, longing for the mother's body is painful, as it is associated with the powerlessness of infancy and also because it must be renounced. For Juliet Mitchell, too, pride of place as love-object is taken by the mother; the father, as well as the men following him, are only secondary objects. Writers such as Cixous, Irigaray, and Kristeva have examined the preverbal character of the pre-Oedipal mother-daughter relationship and have attempted to define the specificity of a mother tongue that is distinctive from patriarchal language.

The Same Sea offers almost a textbook illustration of the compelling force of these psychological theories. The mother-daughter dyad represents a fixed point in both the psychological and moral topography of the novel. More specifically, the failure of the mother-daughter mirroring bond is the driving force—both emotionally and scripturally—of the first-person narration of the heroine's life. It is also the catalytic agent for the other specular (i.e., mirroring) relations embedded in the work: those of the narrator and Guiomar, her daughter; Clara, her lover; her grandmother; and Sofia, her nanny. Moreover, narrative levels and conventions of time and space, of reading and telling, and of referentiality and self-reflexivity are also refracted in a game of shifting mirrors.

The novel's first sequence, in which the narrator returns to her childhood home on the heels of her husband's new deceit, creates the illusion of a journey backward in time. However, as the deeper causal factors of this visit surface, linearity is displaced by a frozen spatiality. The narrator, who at age fifty wears the air of "a prematurely aged child" (18), is psychologically anchored in the pre-Oedipal space of her first home, destined to the circular reenactment of a drama of nonreciprocal bonding. Without the resolution of the deep regressive need for fusion with her mother, her journey toward individuation has, in fact, never begun: "What we longed for in our childhood is exactly what we have been searching for our whole life and the only thing that perhaps could satisfy us" (29).

Located in a mythic space outside of linear time, the narrator's home ("my first burrow" [9]; "my only house" [10]) is a symbolic throwback to her childhood self. Barred from symbiosis by a mother who does not accede to possession, the child is consigned to the sidelines of her mother's universe, the rapt spectator of maternal departures and triumphant arrivals and of a motherly presence that encodes absence and rejection. The lingering evocations of this dazzling being, awash with sensual, lush detail, celebrate the primary magnetism of the mother as object of desire. Yet, they are counterposed with painful recollections of "distant lips that kissed so seldom" (57), of "hands . . . always dry and cold" (57), of the indifference and remoteness of a mother in name alone: "The name *mother* is merely the name with which I connect her to me in a very phantasmagoric, tentative way, since motherhood doesn't define her at all" (4). Absorbed and held by her mother's beauty, the child never sees her own reflection mirrored lovingly in her eyes. Self-enthralled, the mother confirms her own "Aryan" supremacy in a "magic mirror" (5), which shows her to be "the most beautiful and the most intelligent of all the women in the kingdom" (15). She cannot mask her displeasure with her daughter's discrepancy from the norms of beauty she upholds (she is small, dark, and thin). The child feels the sting of censorious glances ("the terrible glances of the blue eyes," 52) which leave her naked and disarmed, certifying her as inalterably "other." What concern her mother has for her is mainly as a disappointed narcissistic extension of herself. The disapproval of her daughter's inadequacies is specifically correlated to her active dislike of the house. Both are subjected to endless reforms imposed by an implacable maternal zeal that nonetheless fail to paper-over the flaws that ooze through as an ineradicable pentimento, the permanent reminder of a disharmony resistant to maternal notions of order, luminosity, and beauty:

> And while the apartment was filled with cabinet-makers, painters, decorators, plasterers, and antique dealers, the dark, long-legged runt, too thin, too dark, with an indefinable quality that invariably ruined the harmony of her movements and appearance, something always too little or too much, was dragged to dressmakers who specialized in children's clothing, French hairdressers, deluxe shoe stores, to tennis and dance classes. (15)

The need, lack, and absence that are ingrained in the pre-Oedipal years are the true source of the narrator's return to a space from which she has never departed. For, despite the semblance of successful integration into an adult, heterosexual order, her identity is locked within this house that has been "closed," "sealed-off" by her mother, its interior furnishings homogenized and hidden by the white sheets that enshroud defining contours and boundaries. The covers she snatches from each piece of furniture are the signifiers of the trappings of her adult reality. With this action, the narrator ransoms both the furniture and her childhood self from the parenthesis of shadows and silence to which they have been consigned by maternal indifference. Newly (fetally) crouched in this womb-like lair ("huddling wounded," 20), her need for nurturance and symbiosis nonetheless remains unfulfilled, for her itinerant ("absent") mother brushes off the urgency of her daughter's appeal, substituting her person with impersonal postcards dashed off from distant places: "How could I have imagined a reaction from her, if not maternal, at least human, that would make her return from the other side of the world, so I wouldn't feel so alone in my old burrow?" (13).

Nor does the heroine experience any consolatory bonding with Guiomar, her daughter, who is a professor of mathematics. In a perverse reading of the Jungian proposition that every woman extends forward into her daughter as well as backward into her mother, she feels de-realized and negated by her mother and daughter alike, "two women who are strangers to me, one at the beginning and the other at the end of my time" (70), "neither one really thinks of me; I don't really exist for either one of them" (20). Guiomar is, in fact, the perfect mirror image of her grandmother, a genetic clone, redressing the indignities visited upon the family by maternal deviance and mutation. The "pitiless" blue-eyed gaze she fixes on her mother is a chilling reproduction of her grandmother's reprobatory mirroring, another shattered reflection sending back fragmented images of the self. Equally complacent, apollonian and aloof, Guiomar is as unmoved by her mother's current plight as her grandmother and also fails to join her in her childhood home.

Two remembered interludes of positive mirroring briefly deflect the relentless negativity of the narrator's childhood. There is the positive cleaving to Sofía, her nanny, who acts as surrogate mother. A reliable, loving presence, Sofía soothes the blows to the child's self-esteem and creates a universe of shared intimacy. Laying "maternal" hands on the child's brow during bouts of illness, she tells her endless stories in which what matters is not the story but to see Sofía and to hear her voice. Loved and left by the child's tepid father, Sofía departs abruptly from the child's universe, creating a painful void.

Like Sofía, the narrator's grandmother holds up a mirror of love, a reflection in which the child discerns the unmistakable traces of a recognized self. Her grandmother is not "other" but the "same," with a physiognomy akin to her own, "very different from the imposing, ever-distant, and startling beauty of my mother or of Guiomar, much more like me . . . although . . . I was never so beautiful" (114). This specularity is later repeated on other levels of the heroine's life: like her grandmother, she is delivered into matrimonial bondage and similarly seeks compensatory satisfaction through the world of the creative imagination. The heroine's self-absorbed "readings" and "tellings" that constitute the central core of the text parallel those of a grandmother who "told me romantic stories about the old days and invented others—she was always the center, always the protagonist" (117).

These two interludes of positive mirroring do not, however, carry sufficient force to displace a negativism created by failed maternal bonding. Because the self-confidence essential to the assertion of autonomy is plainly lacking, the heroine's developmental trajectory is hampered and she is unequipped to make the smooth progression to subsequent phases of growth. Her father, a supercilious and peripheral figure, never emerges as an object of desire. Coldly manipulative of both his wife and Sofía, and the undisputed wielder of the word in the script of marriage, he is not a serious rival for his daughter's affection and never dislodges the preeminence of a matrilineal universe in which, appearances notwithstanding, men assume a secondary role: "It seems to me that as much as men have moved around us and even have wielded the power, a masculine presence seems never to have existed in my family" (110).

The narrator's father is later mirrored by Julio, her husband, who embodies a patriarchal order that is, at best, irrelevant and to which she has been exiled through a maternal mediation that rejects her "ex-centricity" and upholds the orthodoxy of conventional social codes: "Julio doesn't really exist either, except as an institution . . . as a matrimonial institution—on a more social than private level" (163).

Equidistant between these negative male figures is the positive portrayal of Jorge, who arrives upon the scene during the heroine's adolescence, the herald of an initiatory rite involving passage away from the dyadic relationship with her mother. Jorge briefly holds out the prospect of freedom at a time when the young heroine is caught between the neurotic desire for her mother ("the forbidden, incestuous love," 55) on the one hand, and the impulse to loosen her mother's hold ("her Olympian, omnipresent influence," 56) on the other. Jorge, the brash outsider and iconoclast, is valued as much for his mockery of a world that has invalidated and rejected her as for himself. In choosing to run off with him, the heroine is primarily invested in striking a blow against her mother and in vindicating her own worthiness as an object of desire. Hers is a choice against her mother more than one in favor of Jorge, as the following obsessive passage illustrates: "If my mother knew about Jorge—that I had met Jorge . . . if my mother knew that the man I was waiting for had finally come into my life . . . if my mother had known all that" (55). Jorge's unexplained suicide on the eve of their flight is a double betrayal. By excluding her from the causes of his (unsuspected) torment, he not only denies her reality as trusted partner and equal but her very status as existent. The absence and need that his death reactivates offer a mirror image of maternal rejection, propelling the heroine regressively to the fixed, unbendable point of emotional infancy and unfulfilled yearning.

Despite the narrator's trance-like acquiescence to marriage and her apparent compliance with cultural codes, she nurses the latent desire, in the words of Irigaray, for "identification with the mother, for copulation with mother or sister, for parthogenetic impregnation, for reproduction of her image as self-same" (96).

Early on in the text, the narrator's lesbian affair with Clara, who has been hoisted on her consciousness by the machinations of Maite (a decadent friend), offers compelling evidence that her childhood condition has not been cured. She is drawn to Clara precisely because of the self-recognition that the young girl stirs. In her waif-like plainness and frailty, in her forlorn air of "motherless princess" forever unloved, Clara is a startling mirror image of the narrator herself. Conversely, as reflected in Clara's gaze, the narrator takes on the desirability and centrality associated with her mother: "In her eyes I am the only one who fills this world" (127) . . . "the most beautiful and youngest one, even if I am almost fifty" (89).

In what she labels a secret, initiatory rite, the heroine instinctively pulls Clara back with her (psychologically and chronologically) to the green world of her grandmother's house, which, like her mother's apartment, is a symbolic throwback to a pre-Oedipal orbit:[1]

> My grandmother's house . . . and my parents'—my mother's—old apartment . . . two vegetal and aquatic houses, dark and whispering . . . where some part of me, a tenacious, malignant, deeply rooted, underground plant, continued mysteriously to grow. (67)

Here, as she reviews the events of her past for Clara, the numerous masks of the narrator's adult reality (mother, wife, professor) are peeled off, revealing her unchanged status of "desolate girl" (71). Time is again spatialized as "the house, Clara, my childhood, are suddenly a single, tremulous, warm thing, so intimately mine" (120). In a simulacrum of the rituals of childhood, she carries Clara ("My thin doll," 68) to her former nursery, still inhabited by the stuffed toys and books that are the icons of her past. Crooning, cradling, and rocking Clara with infinite tenderness and transport, the heroine arrives at a state approximating symbiosis as she becomes mother-lover to herself. The impossibility of language to encompass this union is further certification of a regression to what Kristeva defines as a preverbal semiotic space prior to entry into a symbolic order. Preceding the mirror stage with its distinction between "same" and "other," "subject" and "object," it is the space of privileged contact with the mother's (female) body. In this episode, the rejection of socio-symbolic codes is conveyed in an intonational, alternate language in which the narrator "writes her body." Calling upon "strange," hidden words, inscribed in her anatomy and never uttered to "any man" (107), she communicates in a vocabulary of love that stands outside male discourse:

> Incredible, strange words . . . not even uttered, but chanted, sung, spilled out thickly . . . hidden for so many years in the most intimate and secret center, to gush forth at last in this bloodred darkness, in this den (108). I begin to whisper strange words, words which don't have meaning and belong to an unlearned language. Here I am . . . dissolving in words, flowing completely from myself in a torrent of words . . . this language doesn't originate first in thought . . . it is born from deep inside and is already a voice . . . I am melting, dissolving, bleeding in words. (123–24)

In this central love episode, the narrator's severance from the world, her plunge into the unconscious and the reconciliation with "self" that her union with Clara implies, all suggest the successful completion of a midlife rebirth journey. But the last portal of transformation is never crossed. Because she has, in fact, chosen her immutable self in the guise of another (Clara), the heroine cannot join her lover in positing a prospective, evolving reality. She is permanently installed in a matrix space, recognizing herself primarily in a modality of time that is spatialized and regressive: "[Clara] is building an impossible future for both of us, an improbable future that opposes . . . my implausible, perpetually reinvented past" (145).

The heroine's fixation to the past and the precariousness of her new self-esteem are demonstrated in an encounter with her mother and Guiomar that overlaps with the Clara affair. In contrast to the composed elegance of the two women, the narrator perceives herself as malodorous, febrile, uncontrolled, "damp and dirty from head to toe" (113). Maternal rejection, transposed and reinscribed as self-rejection, undermines the narcissistic gratification of her lesbian affair. By reactivating her self-loathing, this episode lays the groundwork for her separation from Clara (mirroring her mother's betrayal) and her spineless reconciliation with Julio. The heroine's "return"—bereft of transformation—is semantically linked to the sea of the novel's title, "the same sea as every summer."

In this novel, the failure of female bonding impinges directly on the acts of reading and telling. The heroine's reliability both as reader and narrator is seriously weakened by evidence that literature functions exclusively under a sign of substitution.

Through an early modal shift that focuses attention on the narrator as reader, the analogy between mother-daughter bonding and textual bonding is clearly established. Barred from unity with her mother, the child ("that sad girl who had no other company but her phantoms," 20) seeks a compensatory closeness to the fairy tales, myths, and legends that are the traditional repertoire of childhood reading. In this game of substitution, literature exercises the formative influence imputed to the mother and acts as the reliable presence that cushions the child's painful solitude.[2]

In her quest for identity, the child comes to see herself primarily in relationship to storytelling codes: "The magical storybook world where I learned to choose words and fall in love with dreams" (52); . . . "I learned to live the wrong way, choosing words, never realities" (49). So powerful is this bonding, that the tales and myths of her childhood become the permanent framing texts of the narrator's life, a habitual observation post from which to view reality. They alone have the unfailing capacity to strike an emotional chord within her. "The only things that always make me cry are . . . silly children's stories" (104–5). Even more, alternate creative modalities are subjected to a revisionary language to bring them into conformity with the vocabulary of stories and myths (e.g., an opera is "rewritten" as a fairy tale).

The childhood reliance on literary imagination and convention serves as an effective buffer in subsequent adult relationships. Thus, when Julio is newly unfaithful, she seeks solace through a renewed bonding with the books of her childhood: "There isn't . . . anything more important, more urgent than . . . to reread so many books . . . telling myself again for the thousandth time the interminable, the inexhaustible old stories" (19). By emphasizing her primary identity as "reader," the heroine's status as wronged wife is rendered auxiliary and, therefore, more bearable.

The Same Sea abounds in evidence of the continuous transformation of social codes into narrative codes and of the close alignment of topographic and textual spaces. The narrator's childhood home, for example, is valued primarily as a border crossing to a world of childhood reading and invention: "I think that we—the old house and the dark girl—sealed a pact in the darkness. We invented strange Orphic myths, secret subterranean rites" (17). Her grandmother's house also represents a return to a familiar landscape of "old books . . . my childhood books" (118). Equally, the ice-cream parlor with its Alice-in-Wonderland-like mirror, visited by the narrator with Clara, or the university classroom where, as a professor of literature, she interprets classic texts, are the sites of migration to a universe shaped by literary imagination.

However, the protagonist proves to be an unreliable reader. As suggested by Nichols, "Excessive readings improperly decoded have exacerbated innate peculiarities" (380). Wishing to see her reflection in the stories she reads, the child redesigns them to mirror her own existential dilemmas and lacks. Not recognizing herself in "Wonderland and Never Never Land" (17), this traditional domain of fiction is displaced by a

dark, subterranean realm that is more akin to the alien space of her childhood home. The signifier of the child's mental state, it is a universe
marked by "disorder, anguish, what was ambiguous and mutilated" (17).

Psychologists have demonstrated that fairy tales provide a coping
mechanism for the anxieties and apprehensions of childhood. Working
through analogy, they offer ways to solve problems and hold out the
promise that a happy end will be found. In *The Same Sea,* the salutory
function imputed to fairy tales is offset by the narrator's misreadings: "I
understood stories . . . backward . . . I infallibly took the side of the losers
and the persecuted, and I might well cry inconsolably at the supposedly
happiest endings" (151). The clear dichotomies and positive choices that
fairy tales allow ("good and evil—absolute truths, closed realities," 64)
are supplanted by revisionary distortions and negative inversions.
Locked in the labyrinth of her own disordered psyche, the child is unable
to do battle with the nursery demons, ogres, and minotaurs that are the
signifiers of concupiscent energies and unadmitted longings for the
mother. Fixated within the limited horizon of her own reflections, her
readings offer the relentless replay of a single story from which the proverbial "And they lived happily ever after" has been banished: "This
story . . . constantly repeated without possible variants—written once
and for all with its unhappy ending" (104).

The protagonist's narration is also an exemplum of the correlation of
writing and the failure of bonding. The author's lack of autonomy and
selfhood impinges on textual production: the result is the biography of a
subject painfully unable to constitute itself. Fiction, rather than mimetic
reality, is the primary referent of the narration. The literary allusions that
saturate the text and that range from Homer to Shakespeare to Kafka in
part reflect the cultural sophistication one would expect of a professor of
literature. Calling effortlessly on the literary references stored away in a
lifetime of reading, she affixes literary labels on reality with affected self-
indulgence. In this process, people and places become a dimension of
fictional discourse. A movie theater is an "enchanted castle"; a climb
downstairs at the theater is a "descent into Hades"; the betrayal of Sofía
is a "third-act finale" scripted by a "father-author" complete with "epi-
logue" and "footnotes"; her failed marriage is a "cheap farce," a "sordid
story," a "third-rate film" with a "weak script," and so on.

Nonetheless, the transfiguration of life into literature, with the critical
detachment it allows, is more than a stylistic quirk. It is rooted in the
childhood practice of reading life rather than living it. The narrator's
autobiography is, in fact, a sign signaling the absence rather than the
presence of reality.

In this first-person account, the traditional distinctions between the act
of reading, the act of narrating, and the narrated product fade. The hero-

ine is both narrator and narratee, both the sender and receiver of discourse, both storyteller and story told.[3]

The author-narrator has a fixed repertoire of two stories ("stories that I renew, revive, and repeat," 140). They are the story of her childhood (the "Mother-Daughter Story") and that of her adolescence (the "Jorge Story"). Clara (her alter ego) not only triggers the creative process by acting as addressee, but also assumes the author's role in subsequent versions of the same two tales. The issue of authorial control over textual production is of critical importance. Whose stories are they really? The author's narrative authority is seriously discredited by the evidence that the literary models of her childhood are the palimpsest of her own text. The text-writer is mirrored by the text-reader, and her narrative bears the same distortions of childhood readings, further undermining authorial credibility: "(the stories) may never have been the way I recall and tell them" (141).

The intertext of both stories is provided by mythology: both share the pessimism and tragic endings common to myths. In each, the mythical labyrinth and the minotaur figure largely as the site and embodiment, respectively, of an occult, pre-Oedipal sexuality of which the narrator is ashamed.

The mother, varyingly described as "goddess" or "queen," is rewritten as a supreme being of absolute power. Inhabiting a realm inaccessible to ordinary mortals and embodying demands too rigorous to be met, she is the mimetic reflection of the Olympian gods of mythology. Even more, in a curious reworking of several myths, she is a Demeter in reverse, who banishes Kore to the mythical labyrinth with only the fearsome Minotaur as her companion.

The "Jorge Story" is at first a censored text resistant to the imposition of authorial order or control. It is dredged up in segments in a painful working-out process reminiscent of therapy. The narrator casts herself as the Ariadne to Jorge's Theseus and, again, misreads the original myth. In this retelling, although Ariadne helps Theseus gain his freedom, the proverbial Minotaur is never slayed. Rather, it is Ariadne who—betrayed by Theseus—is entrapped in the lethal labyrinth where the bull-demon roams.

Because the narrator and Clara are interchangeable sign systems, the "Clara Story" is but another instance of literary borrowing and mimesis. It begins as a pastiche of familiar tales and appropriates the lexicon and style associated with this traditional genre. Clara as "character" is varyingly cast as "Snow White," the pubertal "Rapunzel," or "Beauty," whose unselfish love can redeem The Beast to human form. Mostly, however, Clara is a rewrite of the narrator as Ariadne who, after Theseus' abandonment, is permanently grounded in the labyrinth "in the hidden chamber of innocent, perverse, forbidden rites" (65). Here, in the only script with which the author is truly comfortable, Ariadne yields once more to an anterior love relationship with the Minotaur rooted in a pre-Oedipal sexuality: "In a certain way Theseus was always superfluous in this story" (69).

In these stories that constitute the narrator's permanent repertoire, what strayings from the intertext occur are designed to ensure the inevitability of unhappy or deviant endings. The foregrounding of reading as a central function of the creative process seriously impugns the narrator's artistic credibility. The correlation between failed bonding and the inhibition of normal separation and individuation carries over to the level of narrative discourse. Unable to break with the mother-text, the daughter-reader it produces cannot script her own story. Her identity in this auto-biography proves to be an imaginary construct, a response of literature to literature.

If the narrator's lack of ontological security produces a writing that is really a reading, it is also the cause of her conversion into a "character" who is fabricated by other "authors." Although she is the presumed "creator" of the text, the heroine does not move freely through narrative space but rather is enclosed, smothered, and stifled by the discourse of others who, in narrating her, divest her of her control over enunciation. Assigned to an auxiliary rhetorical status, she is merely a signifier that cannot signify itself.

In her mother's originating script, the protagonist is objectified by a discourse that defines her as lack, void, as "other." As her mother revises and rewrites her daughter in expurgated versions that deny her deviation and despair, the relationship between maternal and textual (re)production is made clear. The heroine's brief attempt to free herself from her mother's appropriating discourse during the Jorge episode is completely derailed. By his arrogation of the word and his unilateral scripting of his suicide, Jorge denies her the opportunity to posit herself as a speaking subject. Here again, she is but the signifier for Jorge's signified, her identity subsumed by his authorial control: "Jorge died before giving me the opportunity to express myself, to take some small action, to play a part, even though it might be to spit out my disappointment . . . to argue with him" (177).

The subsequent story of her marriage to Julio is one invented by the narrative complicity of her mother and Jorge ("this revenge that Mama and Jorge planned for me," 167). Permanently exiled from narrative discourse, she simply allows the writing and telling to happen as her mother, Julio and Guiomar co-author the current edition of her life, which depicts her as a fulfilled person of privileged status and rank.

Even the "Clara Story" is not her own. It is at first scripted by Maite, who "manipulates" her erotic imagination with her seductive descriptions of the young girl. Though she is at first offended by Maite's lack of style in this "cloying soap opera" (45), the heroine appears ready to respond to the creative challenge the adventure allows and to finally effect a *prise de la parole*: "(Maite's) delicious description . . . was going to launch me . . . into making up stories, pursuing images" (45). Emerging briefly from the narrative layers that encircle her, she comes to find her voice outside of masculine discourse and she assumes the prerogatives and privileges of narrative authority. Ultimately, she is unable to escape the pattern of narrative and ontological dependence, and the final product is no more than the mirror image of the matrix text that stands transparently as its primary referent: "My story and Clara's . . . a mere pretext for me to tell and relive old stories" (82).[4]

Later she is the passive text-reader of Clara's own script. Clara appropriates narrative discourse becoming the subject rather than the object of the active verb ("Clara has broken into speech, breaking her stubborn, hostile little-girl silence," 146) and thereby parts with the relentless circularity of the heroine's text, reinstating the forward movement of diachronicity: "She is meanwhile constructing a different reality: a reality based on words, situated in an unknown place in time and space" (145). Unlike Jorge, Clara invites the protagonist's creative participation in the narrated product. When Julio, as an errant Odysseus, returns to reclaim her (and the word), Clara challenges her to co-author the last chapter ("the last silk thread," 159) of their common story. Positioned like Penelope at the loom, the heroine is unable to do more than reweave the incessant tapestry of a single text. Rejoining her husband, she replaces herself in the situation of being objectified in the discourse of others ("My mother and Julio and Guiomar will meet happily and conspiratorially," 180). Again absolved of authorial responsibility, she sinks "with enormous relief" into the accustomed abyss of solipsistic reverie, the enclosure of a narrative structure that blocks her progression from reader to writer of herself.

The psychological fixity that spatializes time also gives the narrative of *The Same Sea* its spatial form. Moving along a vertical axis, it emphasizes perception (the mental time and space of one individual) and setting (two childhood homes) over action or story. Taking place within strictly limited temporal bounds (some twenty-seven days), the narrated events are not seen primarily in their dramatic or causal character, but as part of the total, static pattern of a permanent destiny. The novel's central section—which has been described by Nichols as "a 170 page parenthesis within the syntagma of the text with its scant 28 pages of introduction, 27 of conclusion" (365)—is entirely cyclical and overpowers the linear inscription of time. The shift from "story" to "portrait" is accompanied by the self-conscious awareness of the novel as artifact, which creates the aesthetic distance of spatial form. The violations of the traditional boundaries separating narration, reading, and narrated product and the foregrounding of literary codes and conventions bring the text-act reader continuously against the presence of the work as a fictive entity. Aesthetic distance is also reinforced by the frequent use of ironic allegory, satire, and parody.

The author effectively applies and develops narrative techniques that spatialize the text. The manipulation of the narrative to approximate a static present is already evident in the novel's initial sequence, which jolts the reader back forty years, creating a jumbled realm of no-change. Throughout the book, transitions are perfunctory or ignored, implying the lack of a developmental principle. The absence of chapters or clear demarcations of time oblige the reader to resort to reflexive reference not so much to project forward as backward or sideways. The reader's main task is to create a synchronic context from which to make sense of the segments of the narrative that are fragmented and juxtaposed without regard for sequence. The "Jorge Story" is a case in point. While it is of critical importance to the reader in unravelling the narrator's mental state, it is mentioned obliquely on page 54, picked up in bits and pieces at subsequent intervals, reinstated with fanfare on page 149 ("I begin The Story of Jorge for Clara"), but never fully narrated until the novel's near conclusion. The "Story of the Life" is thus interrupted by the "Story of the Telling of the Life." This creates a suspension that forces the reader to engage in his/her own sequential ordering.

The attenuation of chronology is also aided by other elements of style. Although the frequent use of apostrophe suggests some dialogic consciousness, the narrator's oppressive, solipsistic monologues banish the give and take of interlocution. The one exception to this is Clara's utterance "And Wendy (Clara) grew up," drawn from Barrie's masterpiece which, by implication, contrasts with the heroine's arrested development. Yet, because it comprises the novel's final sentence, the prospect of any dialogic movement is effectively foreclosed. Moreover, its verbatim repetition of the novel's epigraph is a further inscription of sameness and circularity.

A stationary, anti-narrative quality, mirroring the narrator's psychological state, is also produced by the slow, close-up attention to detail and the enlargement of each minute, inner event. The web of images, leitmotifs, and literary references that are woven and rewoven with fanatic insistence also arrest all forward flow. Some segments are repeated in their entirety, like the story of the narrator's childhood that surfaces again at the novel's end ("Once upon a time there was a King and Queen," 149). The conflation of language, style, and theme is everywhere apparent. In the novel's final sequence, for example, the heroine's abdication and moral defeat are mirrored in repetitive patterns that sever momentum on the level of discourse: "letting me rest, letting me sleep, letting me die . . . leave me free . . . drained . . . leave me in peace once and for all" (181).

Syntactic complications, verbal complexity, and density of style, characterized by the abundant uses of figures of speech, heighten the effect of retardation, slowing the reader's progress. There appears to be a desire to infinitize the writing process with endless run-on sentences, some taking several pages. Clauses are elongated or held in suspension by digressions, disjunctions, parenthetical insertions, and interpolations, and by persistent use of locutions such as "perhaps," "maybe," "if," which introduce exhaustive explorations of all the permutations of the narrator's tortured thought-processes, creating a linguistic embodiment of "a well within a well that is within another well" (61). This type of sentencing and the refusal to paragraph serve an important function of rhythm and sequence that reduce the reader's speed of reception and fortify the work's thematic concerns.

Thus, the compulsive ruminations that rotate eternally in the narrator's mind come to rest in the immutable patterns set by narrative structure, language, and style. *The Same Sea As Every Summer* is a saga of desperate fixation in which mothering, mirroring, and textual production are inextricably entwined.

Notes

1. Annis Pratt identifies a "Green World" archetype that reflects the identification of young women with nature providing solace and retreat from the real world (139–40).

2. Winnicott stresses the importance of the baby's experience of maternal "reliability" over a period of time as a key factor in producing the child's self-confidence (109). In *The Same Sea*, books offer a substitute reliable presence.

3. A useful distillation and classification of literary terms are offered by Robert C. Spires in *Beyond the Metafictional Mode: Directions in the Modern Spanish Novel*.

4. Like Scheherazade, Penelope, and Wendy Darling, all alluded to in the text, the narrator's energy is primarily invested in the repetitious spinning of tales, which help keep reality at bay.

Works Cited

Bettelheim, Bruno. *The Uses of Enchantment: The Meaning and Importance of Fairy Tales.* New York: Vintage Books, 1977.

Campbell, Joseph. *The Hero with a Thousand Faces*. New York: Bollingen Series XVII, 1953.

Chodorow, Nancy. "Family Structure and Feminine Personality." *Woman, Culture and Society*. Eds. Michelle Zimbalist Rosaldo, and Louise Lamphere. Stanford: Stanford UP, 1974.

Cixous, Hélène. *La Jeune Neé*. Paris: Union Générale d'Editions, 1975.

Dinnerstein, Dorothy. *The Mermaid and the Minotaur: Sexual Arrangements and Human Malaise*. New York: Harper and Row, 1976.

Flax, Jane. "The Conflict Between Nurturance and Autonomy in Mother-Daughter Relationships and Within Feminism." *Feminist Studies* 4, 1 (1978).

Freud, Sigmund. "Female Sexuality." *Women and Analysis*. Ed. Jean Strouse. New York: Dell, 1974.

Irigaray, Luce. *Ce Sexe qui n'en est pas un*. Paris: Minuit, 1977.

Jung, Carl G. "The Psychological Aspects of the Kore." *Essays on a Science of Mythology*. C.G. Jung and C. Kerenyi. New York: Bollingen, 1963.

Kristeva, Julia. *Desire in Language*. Ed. Leon S. Roudiez. New York: Columbia UP, 1980.

Mitchell, Juliet. *Psychoanalysis and Feminism*. New York: Vintage Books, 1975.

Nichols, Geraldine C. "The Prison-House (And Beyond): *El mismo mar de todos los veranos*." *Romanic Review* 75 (1984): 366–45.

Ordóñez, Elizabeth J. "A Quest for Matrilineal Roots and Mythopoesis: Esther Tusquets' *El mismo mar de todos los veranos*." *Crítica Hispánica* 6 (1984): 37–46.

Pratt, Annis. *Archetypal Patterns in Women's Fiction*. Bloomington: Indiana UP, 1981.

Spires, Robert C. *Beyond the Metafictional Mode: Directions in the Modern Spanish Novel*. Lexington: The UP of Kansas, 1984.

Tusquets, Esther. *The Same Sea As Every Summer*. Trans. Margaret E. W. Jones. Lincoln: The U of Nebraska P, 1990.

Winnicott, D.W. "Mirror-Role of Mother and Family in Child Development." *Playing and Reality*. New York: Basic Books, 1971.

10

The Bonds of Love and the Boundaries of Self in Toni Morrison's *Beloved*

Barbara Schapiro

Toni Morrisons's *Beloved* penetrates, perhaps more deeply than any historical or psychological study could, the unconscious emotional and psychic consequences of slavery. The novel reveals how the condition of enslavement in the external world, particularly the denial of one's status as a human subject, has deep repercussions in the individual's internal world. These internal resonances are so profound that even if one is eventually freed from external bondage, the self will still be trapped in an inner world that prevents a genuine experience of freedom. As Sethe succinctly puts it, "Freeing yourself was one thing; claiming ownership of that freed self was another" (95). The novel wrestles with this central problem of recognizing and claiming one's own subjectivity, and it shows how this cannot be achieved independently of the social environment.

A free, autonomous self, as Jessica Benjamin argues in *The Bonds of Love*, is still an essentially relational self and is dependent on the recognizing response of an other. *Beloved* powerfully dramatizes the fact that, in Benjamin's words, "In order to exist for oneself, one has to exist for an other" (53); in so doing, it enacts the complex interrelationship of social and intrapsychic reality. For Morrison's characters, African Americans in a racist, slave society, there is no reliable other to recognize and affirm their existence. The mother, the child's first vital other, is made unreliable or unavailable by a slave system that either separates her from her child or so enervates and depletes her that she has no self with which to confer recognition. The consequences on the inner life of the child—

the emotional hunger, the obsessive and terrifying narcissistic fantasies—constitute the underlying psychological drama of the novel.

"124 was spiteful. Full of a baby's venom." The opening lines of the novel establish its psychic source: infantile rage. A wounded, enraged baby is the central figure of the book, both literally, in the character of Beloved, and symbolically, as it struggles beneath the surface of the other major characters. Even the elderly grandmother is significantly named "Baby," and the ferocity of a baby's frustrated needs colors the novel's overt mother-child relationships, as well as the love relationship between Sethe and Paul D and that between Beloved and her sister Denver. A baby's frustrated needs refer here not to physical needs but to psychic and emotional ones. The worst atrocity of slavery, the real horror the novel exposes, is not physical death but psychic death. The pivotal event, or crisis, of the novel is Sethe's murder of her baby daughter Beloved. The reader is allowed to feel, however, the paradoxical nature of the murder. Sethe, having run away from the sadistic slave-master School-teacher, is on the verge of being recaptured. Her humanity had been so violated by this man, and by her entire experience as a slave woman, that she kills her daughter to save her from a similar fate; she kills her to save her from psychic death: "if I hadn't killed her she would have died and that is something I could not bear to happen to her" (200).

Psychic death, as the novel makes clear, involves the denial of one's being as a human subject. The infant self has an essential, primary need to be recognized and affirmed as a whole being, as an active agent of its own legitimate desires and impulses, and the fulfillment of this need is dependent on the human environment, on other selves. The premise of object-relations theory, as Jessica Benjamin notes, is that "we are fundamentally social beings" (17). Human beings are not innately sexual or aggressive, they are innately responsive and relational.[1] As Harry Guntrip explains, the "need of a love-relationship is the fundamental thing" in life, and "the love-hunger and anger set up by frustration of this basic need must constitute the two primary problems of personality on the emotional level" (45). The experience of one's cohesiveness and reality as a self is dependent on this primary relationship, on the loving response and recognition from an other. This issue is repeatedly illustrated and explored in Morrison's novels. Sula, for instance, speaks of the two most formative experiences of her life: the first concerns her overhearing her mother state matter-of-factly that she simply didn't "like" her (Sula), and the second involves her having thrown a child, seemingly by accident, into the river to drown. "The first experience taught her there was no other that you could count on; the second that there was no self to count on either. She had no center, no speck around which to grow" (118–19). These experiences are intimately related: the lack of an affirming, reliable other leads to an unconscious, murderous rage and the lack of a coherent, reliable self.

In *The Bonds of Love*, a feminist psychoanalytic study of the problem of domination in Western culture, Benjamin modifies object-relations theory to form what she calls "intersubjective theory." She maintains the primacy of relationship in self development, but argues that the self grows through relationship with another *subject* rather than through relations with its object. The child has a need to see the mother, or his or her most significant other, "as an independent subject, not simply as the 'external world' or an adjunct of his ego" (23). The intersubjective view, which Benjamin sees as complementary to intrapsychic theory, conceives of self and other "as distinct but interrelated beings" (20) who are involved in an intricate dance of assertion and recognition. The essential need is for *mutual* recognition—"the necessity of recognizing as well as being recognized by the other" (23). Benjamin also emphasizes the concept of attunement, a "combination of resonance and difference" (26) in which self and other are empathically in tune while maintaining their distinct boundaries and separateness. When the boundaries break down and the necessary tension between self and other dissolves, domination takes root. The search for recognition then becomes a struggle for power and control, and assertion turns into aggression.

Beloved does not delve into the roots of white domination, but there is a suggestion of fear and inadequate selfhood underlying the problem. The white farmer Mr. Garner, while still sharing in the cultural objectification of blacks, nevertheless boasts that his " 'niggers is men every one of 'em.'" When another farmer argues that there " 'Ain't no nigger men,'" Garner replies, " 'Not if you scared, they ain't . . . But if you a man yourself, you'll want your niggers to be men too'" (10). A self wants the recognition of another self; this form of mutuality is more desirable, Garner implies, than mastery of an object. Garner, however, dies—his perspective cannot prevail in a world in which domination and the denial of recognition are built into the social system.

Beloved explores the interpersonal and intrapsychic effects of growing up as a black person in such a system, one in which intersubjectivity is impossible. How can a child see self or mother as subjects when the society denies them that status? The mother is made incapable of recognizing the child, and the child cannot recognize the mother. As a young girl, Sethe had to have her mother "pointed out" to her by another child. When she becomes a mother herself, she is so deprived and depleted that she cannot satisfy the hunger for recognition, the longed for "look" that both her daughters crave. The major characters in the novel are all working out of a deep loss to the self, a profound narcissistic wound that results from a breakdown and distortion of the earliest relations between self and other. In the case of Beloved, the intense desire for recognition evolves into enraged narcissistic omnipotence and a terrifying, tyrannical domination.

The infantile rage in the novel is a form of frustrated, murderous love. The baby ghost of Beloved wreaks havoc in Sethe's home, prompting Denver to comment, " 'For a baby she throws a powerful spell,' " to which Sethe replies, " 'No more powerful than the way I loved her' " (4). The power of Beloved's rage is directly linked to the power of Sethe's love. The intimacy of destructive rage and love is asserted in various ways throughout the book—Sethe's love for Beloved is indeed a murderous love. The violation or murder of children by their parents is a theme that runs throughout much of Morrison's work, from Cholly raping his daughter in *The Bluest Eye* to Eva setting fire to her son in *Sula*, and in these cases too the acts are incited by feelings of love.[2] If the infant is traumatically frustrated in its first love relationship, if it fails to receive the affirmation and recognition it craves, the intense neediness of the infant's own love becomes dangerous and threatening. The fear, as Guntrip (27) and others have discussed, is that one's love will destroy. The baby's enraged, destructive love is also projected outward onto the parent, which suggests one perspective on the strain of destructive parental love in Morrison's novels.

Because the first physical mode of relationship to the mother is oral, the earliest emotional needs in relation to mother are also figured in oral terms in the child's inner world. Frustration in this first oral stage of relationship leads to what object-relations theorists call "love made hungry," a terrifying greediness in which the baby fears it will devour and thus destroy mother, and conversely, that mother (due to projection) will devour and destroy the self (Guntrip 35). A preponderance of oral imagery characterizes Morrison's novel. Beloved, in her fantasies, repeatedly states that Sethe " 'chews and swallows me' " (213), while the metaphor of Beloved chewing and swallowing Sethe is almost literal: "Beloved ate up her life, took it, swelled up with it, grew taller on it" (250). Denver's problems of identity and self-cohesion, too, are often imaged in oral terms: leaving the house means being prepared to "be swallowed up in the world beyond the edge of the porch" (243). When Denver temporarily loses sight of Beloved in the shed, she experiences a dissolution of self—"she does not know where her body stops, which part of her is an arm, a foot or a knee"—and feels she is being "eaten alive by the dark" (123). Beloved, in the second part of the novel, is said to have two dreams: "exploding, and being swallowed" (133). Everywhere in the novel, the fantasy of annihilation is figured orally; the love-hunger, the boundless greed, that so determines the life of the characters also threatens to destroy them.

Sethe repeatedly asserts that the worst aspect of her rape was that the white boys " 'took my milk!' " (17). She feels robbed of her essence, of her most precious substance, which is her maternal milk. We learn that as a child, Sethe was deprived of her own mother's milk: "The little whitebabies got it first and I got what was left. Or none. There was no nursing milk to call my own" (200). Sethe was not physically starved as a baby—she did receive milk from another nursing slave woman—but she was emotionally starved of a significant nurturing relationship, of which the nursing milk is symbolic. That relationship is associated with one's core being or essence; if she has no nursing milk to call her own, she feels without a self to call her own either. Thus, before she was even raped by the white farm boys, Sethe was ravaged as an infant, robbed of her milk/essence by the white social structure.

Beloved's first appearance in her incarnated form is marked by her excessive drinking, by her downing "cup after cup of water" (51), while Sethe, suddenly feeling her "bladder filled to capacity," lifts her skirts and "the water she voided was endless" (51). The dynamic suggests a mother being drained by the child's greedy, excessive need. Sethe's voiding is also associated with her own child-self in relation to her mother: "Not since she was a baby girl, being cared for by the eight-year-old girl who pointed out her mother to her, had she had an emergency that unmanageable" (51). One might rather expect Sethe to experience thirst upon seeing her mother, but perhaps that thirst is so extreme, so potentially violent and destructive, that the more urgent need is to void, to empty oneself completely of this unmanageable hunger and rage. Sethe must drain herself in order to avoid draining, and therefore destroying, her mother. This is the fearful fantasy so central to the book; it is precisely what Beloved almost succeeds in doing to Sethe. The nursing dynamic also characterizes Denver and Beloved's relationship: "so intent was Denver's nursing" of Beloved, "she forgot to eat" (54), and she hides Beloved's incontinence. Paul D, as I will discuss more fully later, also plays a maternal, nurturing role in relation to Sethe. When he arrives, Sethe feels "that the responsibility for her breasts, at last, was in somebody else's hands" (18).

The primal nursing relationship is so fraught with ambivalence that frequently in the novel, satiation leads to disaster. The most obvious example is the grand feast Baby Suggs prepares for ninety people—"Ninety people who ate so well, and laughed so much, it made them angry" (136). The feast is the prelude to the abandonment of the community, the return of Schoolteacher, and Sethe's consequent murder of her baby. Melanie Klein has discussed the baby's extreme "envy" of the withholding breast (183), and this projected envy may underlie the anger of the neighbors at the maternal bounty of Baby Suggs—she had "given too much, offended

them by excess" (138). Similarly, the overture to Beloved's appearance in
the flesh and the ensuing disruption of Sethe's relationship with Paul D
is the festive plentitude of the carnival at which Paul D plies both Sethe
and Denver with candy and sweets. Paul D's abandonment of Sethe, too,
is preceded by a special dinner that Sethe, feeling confident that "she had
milk enough for all" (100), prepares for him.

The rage and ambivalence surrounding the love-hunger in the novel is
illustrated again in the scene in which Sethe, while sitting in the Clearing
associated with Baby Suggs and her sermons on love, experiences fingers
touching her throat. The fingers are first soothing and comforting, but
then begin to choke and strangle her, and the hands are associated with
those of both Baby Suggs and Beloved, of both mother and child. When
Denver accuses Beloved of choking Sethe, Beloved insists that she "fixed"
Sethe's neck—" 'I kissed her neck. I didn't choke it' " (101). The incident,
of course, parallels Sethe's murder of Beloved by sawing through her
neck, the oral associations once more enforced by mention of the "teeth"
of the saw (251) having chewed through the skin. After denying that she
choked Sethe's neck, Beloved adds, " 'The circle of iron choked it' "
(101), and the image recalls the collars locked around the necks of the
black slaves. Her statement is thus true in that the slave system has
choked off the vital circulation between mother and child so crucial to
the development of the self. Some of the most vivid, disturbing passages
in the novel describe the experience of having a horse's bit forced in one's
mouth; the sense of deep, searing injury to one's humanity that these
descriptions evoke is perhaps compounded by unconscious resonances of
violation at the earliest oral roots of our human identity.

The oral imagery in the novel is also closely associated with ocular
imagery, with images of eyes and seeing. Sethe is described as being
"licked, tasted, eaten by Beloved's eyes" (57); when Sethe lies hidden in
the field, anticipating the approach of one of the white boys, she "was
eager for his eyes, to bite into them; . . . 'I was hungry,' she told Denver,
'just as hungry as I could be for his eyes' " (31). For Denver, "looking"
at Beloved "was food enough to last. But to be looked at in turn was
beyond appetite; it was breaking through her own skin to a place where
hunger hadn't been discovered" (118). In the logic of the unconscious
world, the desire to get and "drink in" with the eyes is akin to the oral
wish to consume. Psychoanalyst Heinz Kohut has written about the oral-
visual relationship. If the mother is physically and emotionally distant
from the child, if she withholds her body, he says, the visual will become
"hypercathectic" for the child (116). One can also understand the connection from Benjamin's perspective in that the real hunger in this first
relationship between self and other is the hunger for recognition—the
desire to be, in Denver's words, "pulled into view by the interested, un-

critical eyes of the other" (118). The gaze of the beloved other recognizes and affirms the wholeness and intrinsic value of one's being. Denver describes the quality of being looked at by Beloved: "Having her hair examined as a part of her self, not as material or a style. Having her lips, nose, chin caressed as they might be if she were a moss rose a gardener paused to admire" (118). The look takes Denver to a "place beyond appetite," to where she is "Needing nothing. Being what there was" (118). To be recognized by the beloved is all the nourishment one needs; it brings one into coherence, into meaningful existence. Before Beloved's arrival, Denver craved this look from Sethe: none of the losses in her life mattered, she felt, "as long as her mother did not look away" (12).

Sethe's eyes, however, are described as "empty"; Paul D thinks of Sethe's face as "a mask with mercifully punched-out eyes. . . . Even punched out they needed to be covered, lidded, marked with some sign to warn folks of what that emptiness held" (9). Her eyes reflect the psychic loss and denial of self she has experienced on all levels in her life. The face of Sethe's mother was also masklike, distorted into a permanent false smile from too many times with the bit. Sethe comments that she never saw her mother's own smile (203). Sethe's mother, deprived of her authentic selfhood, her status as a human subject, cannot provide the recognition and affirmation that her child craves. The cycle is vicious, and thus Sethe's children, Beloved and Denver, will suffer the same loss. Beloved's eyes too are remarkable for their emptiness: "deep down in those big black eyes there was no expression at all" (55).

The craving for mutual recognition—for simultaneously "seeing" the beloved other and being "seen" by her—propels the central characters in the novel. Beloved says she has returned in order to "see" Sethe's face, and she wants "to be there in the place where her face is and to be looking at it too" (210). When, as a child, Sethe is shown the brand burnt into her mother's skin and is told that she will be able to "know" her by this mark, Sethe anxiously responds, " 'But how will you know me? How will you know me? Mark me, too . . . Mark the mark on me too'" (61). Love is a form of knowing and being known. Beloved repeatedly commands Paul D, " 'I want you to touch me on the inside part and call me my name'" (116). The hunger is to be touched, recognized, known, in one's inner being or essential self. This yearning is poignantly captured in the image of two turtles mating. Denver and Beloved observe the turtles on the bank of the river: "The embracing necks—hers stretching up toward his bending down, the pat pat pat of their touching heads. No height was beyond her yearning neck, stretched like a finger toward his, risking everything outside the bowl just to touch his face. The gravity of their shields, clashing, countered and mocked the floating heads touching" (105).

The yearning of Beloved, Sethe, and Denver to touch faces with the beloved other, to know and be known, is, like that of the turtles, obstructed and mocked by the shields or shells each has constructed. The shell, however, is a necessary defense; it attempts to preserve the self from a culture that seeks to deny it. As Joseph Wessling argues in an article on narcissism in *Sula*, narcissistic defenses, such as "self-division" and an inability to empathize or experience human sympathy, may be "the price of survival" (286) in an oppressive, unjust society. The shell also serves to protect the self and its boundaries from the intensity of its own frustrated desire. The hunger for recognition, as discussed, may be so overwhelming that it threatens to swallow up the other and the self, destroying all boundaries in one total annihilation.

The novel as a whole is characterized by a fluidity of boundaries, by a continuously altering narrative perspective that slides in and out of characters' minds, by a mutable, nonsequential time structure, and by an absence of the conventional lines between fantasy and reality. Such fluidity, as Nancy Chodorow and Carol Gilligan have argued, is characteristic of female, as opposed to male, modes of perception and expression. It derives from the preservation of an original identity and pre-Oedipal bondedness between self and mother. The series of monologues by Beloved, Sethe, and Denver in Part 2 of Morrison's novel, however, suggest something more extreme and dangerous than mere fluidity of boundaries: the monologues reveal an utter breakdown of the borders between self and other, a collapse that is bound up with incorporative fantasies. Sethe's section begins, "Beloved, she my daughter. She mine" (200). Denver's opens, "Beloved is my sister. I swallowed her blood right along with my mother's milk" (205), and Beloved's with the line, "I am Beloved and she is mine" (210). After that sentence, Beloved's monologue is marked by a total absence of punctuation, highlighting the fantasy of merging and oneness—"I am not separate from her there is no place where I stop her face is my own"—as the essence of her plaintive ramblings. Her words reveal the psychic loss—the denial of recognition—at the core of the fantasy:

> there is no one to want me to say me my name . . . she chews and swallows me I am gone now I am her face my own face has left me . . . Sethe sees me see her and I see the smile her smiling face is the place for me it is the face I lost she is my face smiling at me doing it at last a hot thing now we can join a hot thing (212–213)

A similar merging fantasy also figures prominently in *Sula*, in the relationship between Sula and Nel. The two characters are described as so close that "they themselves had difficulty distinguishing one's thoughts from the other's" (83); for Nel, "talking to Sula had always been a conversation with herself" (95); and Sula eventually realizes that neither Nel nor anyone else "would ever be that version of herself which she sought to reach out to and touch with an ungloved hand" (121). Each is compelled continually to seek the self through an other, and such blurring of boundaries can lead to one of the forms of domination and submission Benjamin describes: the self can surrender totally to the will and agency of the other, or the self can consume and appropriate the other as part of itself, as an object of its possession.

The repetition of the word "mine" in the monologues of Sethe, Denver, and Beloved suggests exactly this sort of possession and incorporation of the other as an object. "Mine" is the haunting word that Stamp Paid hears surrounding Sethe's house in ghostly whispers and is stressed again in a lyrical section following Beloved's unpunctuated monologue. In this section the voices of Beloved, Sethe, and Denver are joined (the identity of the speaker in each line is sometimes unclear) while at the same time each voice remains essentially isolated (the voices speak to but not *with* each other):

Beloved
You are my sister
You are my daughter
You are my face; you are me
I have found you again; you have come back to me
You are my Beloved
You are mine
You are mine
You are mine (216)

This form of possessing and objectifying the other, however, cannot satisfy—it imprisons the self within its own devouring omnipotence, its own narcissism. True satisfaction or joy, as Benjamin explains, can only be achieved through "mutual recognition" between self and other, between two subjects or selves.

Both sides of the power dynamic, both surrender to and incorporation of the other, are apparent in the relationship between Sethe and Beloved. Toward the end of the novel, Sethe relinquishes herself completely to the will and desire of Beloved. She neglects to feed or care for herself and becomes physically drained and emotionally depleted. Sethe literally shrinks while Beloved literally expands and swells; both are caught up in a mutually destructive, frighteningly boundless narcissism. The prelude to Sethe's decline is an incident that again stresses lack of recognition at the source of this narcissistic condition. Sethe has been abandoned once again, this time by Paul D (her previous abandonments include those of her mother, her husband Halle, Baby Suggs, and her two sons), and to cheer herself, she takes Denver and Beloved ice skating on the frozen creek. The three are unable to keep their balance, and as they fall on the ice, they shriek with both pain and laughter. The scene is redolent of childhood and of childlike helplessness. "Making a circle or a line, the three of them could not stay upright for one whole minute, but nobody saw them falling" (174). The phrase "nobody saw them falling" becomes the dominant motif of the scene; the line is repeated four times in the two-page description. Sethe's laughter turns into uncontrollable tears, and her weeping in the context of the scene's refrain suggests a child's aching sense of loss or absence, specifically the absence of the confirming, legitimizing gaze of the other.

Once it is asserted that "nobody saw" her falling, that there is no "other" to confer the reality of her own existence on her, Sethe falls prey to a consuming narcissism. Suddenly she consciously recognizes Beloved as the incarnation of her dead child and surrenders herself totally to her. Sethe now feels that "there is no world outside" her door (184), and that since her daughter has come back, "she can sleep like the drowned" (204). In psychological terms, she retreats from external reality and succumbs to her destructive, narcissistic fantasies, to her murderously enraged child-self as well as her insatiable need to make reparation for her murderous love. Paul D recognizes, and fears, the narcissistic nature of Sethe's love: "This here new Sethe didn't know where the world stopped and she began . . . more important than what Sethe had done was what she claimed. It scared him" (164).

Paul D is the one character in the novel who has the power to resist and disrupt the destructive, narcissistic mother-child dyad. Sethe recalls, "There was no room for any other thing or body until Paul D arrived and broke up the place, making room, shifting it, moving it over to someplace else, then standing in the place he had made" (39). Sethe also tells Beloved that she would have recognized her "right off, except for Paul D" (203). Paul D is the external "other" who triangulates the dyad, as the image of the "three shadows" of Sethe, Denver, and Paul D "holding hands" as they walk to the carnival (47) emphasizes. The excursion to the carnival is Sethe's first venture into the community since the murder; Paul D has the capacity to lead Sethe out of her narcissistic isolation and into relationship with the external world. The claims of the angry baby Beloved, however, are still too powerful to allow for these other attachments: she makes her first appearance in the flesh immediately following the excursion.

While Paul D plays the role of the saving other in contradistinction to Beloved and the narcissistic dyad, he does not represent the typical world

of the father. He is not, for instance, a token of male rationality countering the irrationality of the female world. He too is deeply affected by
Beloved's irrational power—she literally "moves" him, making him
physically restless and forcing him to sleep with her in the shed outside
the house. His power lies precisely in his maternal, nurturing quality; he
is that "other" with the power to recognize and affirm the inner or essential self. He is described as "the kind of man who could walk into a house
and make the women cry. Because with him, in his presence, they could"
(17). The women see him and not only want to weep, they also want to
confess their deepest secrets, to expose all the pain and rage bound up
with their true selves. Sethe thinks of how he "cradled her before the
cooking stove" and is deeply comforted by "The mind of him that knew
her own" (99).

Paul D has the power to satisfy the craving that fuels the novel, the
craving to be "known," to have one's existence sanctioned by the empathic recognition of the other. That Morrison bestows this quality on
an African American male character is an interesting, and unusual, point.
A common criticism of black women novelists is that their portrayals of
black males are often flat, stereotypic, or unempathic. For Morrison, the
maternal nurturing quality is a form of love that is not restricted by gender; this view expands the possibilities, and is a liberating factor, for her
characters. Yet Paul D, too, is not a totally reliable other: He temporarily
retreats when learning of Sethe's murder of her child. Like all of the other
black characters in the novel, he must work out of a condition of psychic
fragmentation—his selfhood has been severely impaired, his status as a
human subject denied by the slave culture. He feels that even the old
rooster Mister was allowed an essential integrity of being denied him:
" 'Mister was allowed to be and stay what he was. But I wasn't allowed
to be and stay what I was. Even if you cooked him you'd be cooking a
rooster named Mister. But wasn't no way I'd ever be Paul D again, living
or dead' " (72).

Only Denver does not see Paul D as the other women do; for her, he
does not play the same nurturing role. She sees him only as a threat, as
an intruder into her intense, and deeply ambivalent, relationship with her
mother. Denver is terrified of Sethe's murderous love: she has "monstrous and unmanageable dreams about Sethe" (103) and is afraid to fall
asleep while Sethe braids her hair at night. In her fantasies, "She cut my
head off every night" (206). For Denver, the idealized, saving other is her
father Halle, whom she calls "Angel Man." Yet the father is significantly
incapable of playing the savior role. The "other"—whether represented
by mother or father—is always untrustworthy in Morrison's world, rendered thus by the social environment. As a result, the self remains trapped
within its own destructive narcissism.

Sethe regards Halle as the ultimate betrayer: he witnessed her rape, she learns, but did not protest or try to protect her. His absent presence is worse than mere absence for it confirms an essential hollowness and undependability of the other and of love. Yet Halle is not simply a "bad guy"; Morrison extends her compassion equally to her male characters. The reader is allowed to see Halle too as a deeply wounded child. Traumatized by the rape of Sethe and the maternal violation that it also represents, Halle literally loses his mind—his selfhood shatters. Paul D observes him later squatting by a churn, "He had butter all over his face" (69). He smeared that butter all over his face, Sethe thinks, "because the milk they took is on his mind" (70). The image of Halle here recalls Beloved and the image at the psychological base of the book: it is the picture of a lost, greedy child whose ravenous hunger/love is out of control.

Ultimately Denver is able to escape the narcissistic vacuum, and she is helped not, as she had fantasized, by Halle, but by another maternal figure in the novel, Mrs. Jones. Denver is first propelled out of the house by literal hunger, for Sethe, locked in her obsession with Beloved, has become oblivious to food and to all external or physical considerations. Denver realizes that "it was she who had to step off the edge of the world and die because if she didn't, they all would" (239). Excluded from the Beloved-Sethe dyad, Denver is forced into the role of the outside other, and assuming that role is her salvation. She goes first to her former teacher, Lady Jones, an old woman of mixed race who has long struggled with the contempt of the black community and, equally, with her own self-contempt. Lady Jones thus has a special "affection for the unpicked children" (247), an empathy with those, like Denver, who have never been recognized or "picked," who have never had their existence validated or confirmed. After Denver asks her for food, Mrs. Jones compassionately croons, "Oh, baby," and that empathic recognition of the hungry baby within finally frees Denver from the trap of her infantile needs: "Denver looked up at her. She did not know it then, but it was the word 'baby,' said softly and with such kindness, that inaugurated her life in the world as a woman" (248).

With this recognition, Denver for the first time begins to experience the contours of her own separate self. When Nelson Lord, an old school acquaintance, affectionately says, " 'Take care of yourself, Denver,' " Denver "heard it as though it were what language was made for," and she realizes that "It was a new thought, having a self to look out for and preserve" (252). Self-recognition is inextricably tied up with self-love, and this is precisely the message of the sermons that Baby Suggs preaches to her people in the Clearing. In a white society that does not recognize or love you, she tells them, you must fight to recognize and love yourself:

"Here," she said, "in this here place, we flesh; flesh that weeps, laughs; flesh that dances on bare feet in grass. Love it. Love it hard. Yonder they do not love your flesh. They despise it. They don't love your eyes; they'd just as soon pick em out. . . . Love your hands! Love them. Raise them up and kiss them. Touch other with them, pat them together, stroke them on your face 'cause they don't love that either. *You* got to love it, *you!*" (88)

Baby Suggs continues to enjoin her people to love every appendage, every organ in their bodies, and especially to "love your heart" (89). This is the crucial lesson, but it cannot be learned in isolation; self-love needs a relational foundation and a social context. Thus even Baby Suggs is unable to sustain her convictions and heed her own teachings. After Sethe's murder, Baby Suggs retreats and ceases to care about herself or others, showing interest in nothing except "colors."

Morrison's novel, however, is not hopelessly bleak or despairing. Her characters are wounded, but not all of them are ruined. Denver and Paul D, by courageously facing their inner terrors—Denver leaves the house even though she expects to be "swallowed up," and Paul D returns to Sethe and her fearful, murderous love—are able to salvage out of the wreckage a bolstering faith in both self and other. Paul D tries to pass this faith on to Sethe at the end. He assumes again a maternal, nurturing role. He holds Sethe, calls her "baby," and gently tells her not to cry. Beloved is gone and Sethe feels bereft and lost: " 'She was my best thing' " (272), she tells Paul D. He "leans over and takes her hand. With the other he touches her face. 'You your best thing, Sethe. You are.' His holding fingers are holding hers" (273).[3] While the word "thing" still suggests a sense of self as object (an objectification of self that perhaps no black person in the slave culture could ever totally escape), the scene between Sethe and Paul D at the end comes closest to that state of mutual recognition and attunement that Benjamin describes. Paul D's gently touching Sethe's face recalls the touching faces of the mating turtles; the relationship here is not one of merging or of domination but of resonating "likeness" and empathic understanding. Paul D recalls Sixo's description of his mistress, the "Thirty-Mile Woman": " 'She is a friend of my mind. She gather me, man. The pieces I am, she gather them and give them back to me in all the right order. It's good, you know, when you got a woman who is a friend of your mind' " (272–3). The beloved other has the power to give to the self its own essential wholeness. The role of the other here is neither as an object to possess nor even as a mirror for the self; as a "friend of [the] mind" (273), the other is a subject in its own right, with an inner life that corresponds with that of the self. In such correspondence, in that mutuality of inner experience and suffering, lies the self-confirming and consoling power of the relationship.

Paul D tells Sethe in this final scene that "He wants to put his story next to hers" (273). Throughout the novel, stories and storytelling are associated with the self and with the primary oral relationship at its root.[4] Beloved is tireless in her demand, in "her thirst for hearing" Sethe's stories: "It became a way to feed her . . . Sethe learned the profound satisfaction Beloved got from storytelling" (58). Denver too feeds Beloved's craving for stories about Sethe, "nursing Beloved's interest like a lover whose pleasure was to overfeed the loved" (78). Denver's storytelling, because of the empathic identification it involves, also allows her to feel a closer bond and oneness with her mother. As she narrates the tale of Sethe's escape to Beloved, "Denver was seeing it now and feeling it—through Beloved. Feeling how it must have felt to her mother" (78). Paul D does not want to merge or incorporate Sethe's story into his own at the end; rather, he wants to "put his story next to hers." This suggests again an essential maintenance of boundaries, a balance of two like but separate selves, an attunement.

The novel does not end, however, with the scene between Sethe and Paul D, but with one last lyrical section on Beloved. The refrain of the last two pages is the line, repeated three times, "It was not a story to pass on." The final section arouses a deep sense of pathos for that unrecognized, ravenously needy infant-self that is Beloved:

> Everybody knew what she was called, but nobody anywhere knew her name. Disremembered and unaccounted for, she cannot be lost because no one is looking for her, and even if they were, how can they call her if they don't know her name? Although she has claim, she is not claimed. In the place where long grass opens, the girl who waited to be loved and cry shame erupts into her separate parts, to make it easy for the chewing laughter to swallow her all away.
>
> It was not a story to pass on. (274)

The poignancy of Beloved's story/self is that it is *not* a story/self. She has been denied the narrative of her being, the subjectivity and continuity of inner experience that should be everyone's birthright. Beloved's desolation, her sorrow, is a more extreme version of the same sorrow that all of the black characters in the novel experience. Thus Baby Suggs, finally freed from slavery, expresses not the elation of freedom, but the deep sadness of not knowing her self, of not being able to read her own story: "the sadness was at her center, the desolated center where the self made its home. Sad as it was that she did not know where her children were buried or what they looked like if alive, fact was she knew more about them than she knew about herself, having never had the map to discover what she was like" (140). In the end, the novel is more about Beloved than Sethe. Beloved's character frames the book, and it is her story—or her desperate struggle to know and experience her own story—that is the pumping heart of the novel. Beloved's struggle is Sethe's struggle; it is also Denver's, Paul D's, and Baby Suggs'. It is the struggle of all black people in a racist society, Morrison suggests, to claim themselves as subjects in their own narrative.

Beloved demonstrates, finally, the interconnection of social and intrapsychic reality. The novel plays out the deep psychic reverberations of living in a culture in which domination and objectification of the self have been institutionalized. If from the earliest years on, one's fundamental need to be recognized and affirmed as a human subject is denied, that need can take on fantastic and destructive proportions in the inner world: the intense hunger, the fantasized fear of either being swallowed or exploding, can tyrannize one's life even when one is freed from the external bonds of oppression. The self cannot experience freedom without first experiencing its own agency or, in Sethe's words, "claiming ownership" of itself. The free, autonomous self, *Beloved* teaches, is an inherently social self, rooted in relationship and dependent at its core on the vital bond of mutual recognition.

Notes

1. Object-relations theory began with Melanie Klein's pioneering work on the earliest, pre-Oedipal dynamics of the mother-child relationship. For a good explication and overview of her work, see Segal. For other influential perspectives in British object-relations theory, see Fairbairn, Guntrip, and Winnicott.

2. Madonne Miner sees Cholly's rape of Pecola as arising out of his desperate desire for recognition, for "confirmation of his presence" (179). This reading again supports Benjamin's thesis about the intertwining of love, recognition, and domination. Miner also discusses identity issues in *The Bluest Eye* in terms of a "constantly shifting balance between seeing and being seen" and the "distortion of this visual balance" (184) that sexism and racism create.

3. The emphasis here on Paul D's "holding" quality call to mind Donald Winnicott's argument about the need for the mother to provide a reliable and protective "holding environment" for the infant. Such "holding" forms the basis for trust in both self and world. See Winnicott 43–44.

4. Stories and storytelling figure prominently in the fiction of many black women writers, and their significance is rooted historically in the slave narrative and in the rich folk tradition of black culture. See Willis for a historically informed rhetorical analysis of how the black oral tradition shapes narrative form in black women's fiction; see Skerrett for a discussion of storytelling in *Song of Solomon*. My analysis of the function of stories in *Beloved* (from the standpoint of depth psychology) is compatible with and can complement historical, sociological, and rhetorical perspectives.

Works Cited

Benjamin, Jessica. *The Bonds of Love: Psychoanalysis, Feminism, and the Problem of Domination.* New York: Pantheon, 1988.

Chodorow, Nancy. *The Reproduction of Mothering: Psychoanalysis and the Sociology of Gender*. Berkeley: U of California P, 1978.

Fairbairn, Ronald. *Psychoanalytic Studies of the Personality*. London: Routledge, 1952.

Gilligan, Carol. *In a Different Voice: Psychological Theory and Women's Development*. Cambridge: Harvard UP, 1982.

Guntrip, Harry. *Schizoid Phenomena, Object Relations, and the Self*. New York: International UP, 1969.

Klein, Melanie. *Envy and Gratitude and Other Works, 1946–1963*. New York: Dell, 1975.

Kohut, Heinz. *The Analysis of the Self*. New York: International UP, 1971.

Miner, Madonne M. "Lady No Longer Sings the Blues: Rape, Madness, and Silence in *The Bluest Eye*." *Conjuring: Black Women, Fiction, and Literary Tradition*. Eds. Marjorie Pryse and Hortense J. Spillars. Bloomington: Indiana UP, 1985. 176–91.

Morrison, Toni. *Beloved*. New York: Plume, 1987.

———. *The Bluest Eye*. New York: Plume, 1970.

———. *Sula*. New York: Plume, 1973.

Segal, Hanna. *Introduction to the Works of Melanie Klein*, 2nd ed. New York: Basic, 1974.

Skerrett, Joseph T. "Recitation to the Griot: Storytelling and Learning in Toni Morrison's *Song of Solomon*. *Conjuring: Black Women, Fiction, and Literary Tradition*. Eds. Marjorie Pryse and Hortense J. Spillars. Bloomington: Indiana UP, 1985. 192–202.

Wessling, Joseph. "Narcissism in Toni Morrison's *Sula*." *College Language Association Journal* 31 (1988): 281–98.

Willis, Susan. *Specifying: Black Women Writing the American Experience*. Madison: U of Wisconsin P, 1987.

Winnicott, D.W. *Maturational Processes and the Facilitating Environment*. New York: International Universities Press, 1965.

11

Maternal Splitting:
"Good" and "Bad" Mothers and Reality

Susan Rubin Suleiman

When I first thought about writing this essay (from the beginning, it was linked in my mind to Mary Gordon's *Men and Angels*—a novel that aroused strong feelings in me even before I read it, on the basis of the reviews), I thought I would continue my exploration of the mother's subjectivity begun in an earlier work, "Writing and Motherhood." This time, however, I planned to focus not on the triangle of mother, work, and child, but on that of mother, mother-surrogate, and child. The first triangle involved a struggle between the mother's creative needs and the child's needs, the issue being work. The second triangle appeared as a logical and chronological sequel: No longer pitted against her child, the mother felt herself threatened by the intrusion of a third person, an "other mother" or maternal figure who might displace her in the child's affections while she was away pursuing her nonmaternal activities.

I knew from my own experience and from discussions with women friends engaged in self-absorptive creative careers that this anxiety does in fact exist, whatever its basis may be in reality. (Witness the box-office success of *The Hand That Rocks the Cradle*—a Hollywood nightmare version of the fantasy.) Two popular books, Nancy Friday's *Jealousy* and Phyllis Chesler's *Mothers on Trial*, reinforced my conviction. Friday shows, at great length, that jealousy, or the fear of the loss of love by the intrusion of a third party, is a well-nigh universal feeling. Chesler, in turn, documents with terrifying (and terrified) relentlessness a number of custody cases in which mothers have been legally deprived of their children by fathers who are often aided and abetted by what she calls "mother-competitors," women bent on replacing the child's biological mother both in the father's bed and in the child's affections. Even if such cases are statistically rarer than Chesler suggests, they still indicate that in contemporary America the mother's anxiety is not always a matter of fantasy but may be founded on a perception of real danger.

My beginning intention was to explore the question of the "other mother" not as a political issue but as a powerful maternal fantasy, especially as it is manifested in fiction by writing mothers. I soon realized, however, that where motherhood is concerned, personal fantasy, fictional representation, and social and cultural reality are so interconnected that it is impossible to talk about one without the others. My two triangles, too, turned out to be closely related. The notion of maternal splitting links maternal fantasies about the "other mother" with fantasies about the child and work, and in addition provides one perspective on the important question of the relations between maternal fantasy and the realities of mothering in our culture today.

Splitting the Mother: Some Psychoanalytic Views

As the fairy tales about wicked stepmothers and fairy godmothers tell us, the impulse to split the maternal figure into "good" and "bad" personae is very old indeed. Bruno Bettelheim has remarked that "far from being a device used only by fairy tales, such a splitting up of one person into two to keep the good image uncontaminated occurs to many children as a solution to a relationship too difficult to manage or comprehend. . . . The fantasy of the wicked stepmother not only preserves the good mother intact, it also prevents having to feel guilty about one's angry thoughts or wishes about her" (67, 69). Bettelheim is restating here what has long been recognized as a psychoanalytic truism: The child's feelings toward the mother are ambivalent, a conflicting mixture of tenderness, gratitude, and destructive rage. According to Melanie Klein, these feelings are already present in the very young infant, who experiences the mother's breast alternately as gratifying and pleasure giving, and (when it is delayed or withheld) as hateful and frustrating. "The baby reacts to unpleasant stimuli, and to the frustration of his pleasure, with feelings of hatred and aggression. These feelings of hatred are directed toward the same objects as are the pleasurable ones, namely, the breasts of the mother" (290). Later on, the child sees the mother as a whole person, but the coexistence of opposing feelings persists: "Feelings both of a destructive and of a loving nature are experienced toward one and the same person and this gives rise to deep and disturbing conflicts in the child's mind" (293).

In Klein's theory, these conflicts will, if all goes well, produce guilt in the child for her or his destructive fantasies, which in turn will lead to a desire for reparation. Or, Bettelheim suggests, these conflicts may produce fantasies such as that of the wicked stepmother, which deflect the child's destructive feelings away from the good mother. Or yet again, as Margaret Mahler has observed in the behavior of toddlers, ambivalence toward the mother may produce a splitting of the real object world around the child into "good" and "bad." One of the child's caretakers then becomes the "bad" mother, "protecting the good mother image from [the child's] destructive anger" (Mahler, Pine, and Bergman 99). Splitting thus functions as a defense mechanism, enabling the child to preserve the image of a protective and nurturant mother—an image that must be preserved (so the theory goes), given the child's sense of total dependence on her. Ultimately, according to Mahler, if the child is to develop a stable and harmonious sense of self, splitting must give way to the "unifying of 'good' and 'bad' objects into one whole representation" (110). This unifying might correspond to Klein's notion of repairing the mother's body or to Bettelheim's idea that, once a child grows older and more secure, no longer quite so dependent on her mother, she "can re-work the double picture into one" (68).

If in these versions of splitting what is at stake is maternal nurturance, there exists another version, first analyzed by Freud, in which splitting refers specifically to the erotic realm: what is at stake is maternal asexuality. In his essay "The Most Prevalent Form of Degradation in Erotic Life," Freud diagnosed the "mother/whore" syndrome so common in men as the result of a disassociation of sensual and tender feelings, aiming to maintain the mother's asexual "purity" by deflecting all sensual feelings onto an other, degraded object. Recently, Jim Swan has analyzed Freud's own discovery of the Oedipus complex as resulting from a similar splitting: the splitting between Freud's Catholic Nannie, who initiated him into sex (he called her his "first seductress and shamer"), and his mother, who remained the "pure object of desire."[1] It is perhaps explicable in historical terms, as a Victorian phenomenon, that the kind of splitting in which Freud himself was most interested and personally implicated was the splitting of the mother in the erotic realm. Object-relations theorists, on the other hand, seem less concerned with the child's view of the mother as asexual or sexual than with the child's view of the mother as benevolent or destructive.[2]

Whether of the strictly Freudian or the object-relations variety, all of the theories I have mentioned assume that the "unique love-object" (Mahler, Pine, and Bergman 110), as well as the single most powerful and important figure in the life of the infant and small child—and consequently, according to these theories, in the life of the adult the child will become—is her or his mother. They also assume, by and large, that this is the natural and necessary way things should be. This is not the place to survey the various critiques and modifications that have been proposed with regard to this psychoanalytic model, whether one considers it as a model of child development (positing that the individual personality is fully formed in the first few years of life) or as a model of mothering (positing that the mother-child dyad is the determining one). Such critiques have come both from male psychoanalysts such as Erik Erikson, who proposes a less infant-centered as well as a more socially oriented model of child development, and from feminist theorists such as Nancy Chodorow and Dorothy Dinnerstein, who propose a less biologically based model of mothering, or Jessica Benjamin, who emphasizes mutual recognition rather than dependence and domination in the infant-mother relationship.[3] However, the dominant analytic and cultural discourse about mothers and their children—what Ann Kaplan has called the "Master Mother Discourse"—continues to emphasize the mother's crucial, determining role in the development and continuing welfare of the child (113–137). This discourse fosters what Chodorow and Susan Contratto have called the "myth of maternal omnipotence"—the belief that whatever happens to the child on the way to becoming an adult is ultimately attributable to its "good" or "bad" mother (71).

Chodorow and Contratto make an impassioned plea for an alternative to our "cultural ideology" of "blame and idealization of mothers," which has been internalized by so many women (65). They mount an impressive critique of some of the more influential feminist writings by mothers about their experience of motherhood, showing that even feminists have not succeeded in freeing themselves from the myth of maternal omnipotence.[4] Although the feminist mothers "blame patriarchy" instead of "blaming Mom," they do not question the dominant assumption that Mom is all-important. Chodorow and Contratto claim that this assumption is itself based on fantasies about the omnipotent mother originating in infancy, but that such fantasies exist precisely because children in our culture are being "mothered exclusively by one woman." It seems that we are trapped in a vicious circle. The way out of the circle, Contratto and Chodorow suggest, is for feminists to be wary and self-critical about their own assumptions concerning motherhood and child development. They should seek models of development that "recognize collaboration and compromise as well as conflict" and that "look at times other than infancy in the developmental life span and relationships over time to people other than the mother to get a more accurate picture of what growing up is about" (71).

Intellectually, I find myself very attracted to this conclusion, as well as to the analysis that precedes it. The idea that even feminists writing about motherhood are expressing infantile fantasies about the omnipotent mother, for example, could explain the phenomenon of maternal splitting *by* the mother, in which it is not the child who through fantasy splits the mother into "good" and "bad," but the mother herself who does so. Consider the guilt fantasy about work versus child, for example, which I formulated in "Writing and Motherhood": "With every word I write, with every act of genuine creation, I hurt my child." This fear on the part of the mother that each moment of creative self-absorption is destructive to her child is widespread and potent and has found some forceful expressions in fiction. According to Chodorow and Contratto, this fantasy "repeats" both the infant's own fantasy and the cultural ideology of maternal omnipotence. If the mother did not somehow imagine herself omnipotent in relation to her child, she would not need to feel so guilty and murderous every time she turned away from the child to pursue other self-absorptive goals.

Carol Gilligan has noted that women with an absorbing career generally feel strong conflict "between achievement and care," even if they are not mothers. In her study of women pursuing advanced degrees, she found that "these highly successful and achieving women do not mention their academic and professional distinction in the context of describing themselves, and the conflict they encounter between achievement and care leaves them either divided in judgment or feeling betrayed" (159). If, as Gilligan suggests, the phenomenon of splitting is experienced by women in general, it is all the more strong when the care involved is that of a mother for her child. In both cases, however, cultural ideology plays at least as important a role as the feminine specificity one might wish to attribute to women or to mothers.

Sara Ruddick has suggested to me that the term "maternal omnipotence" does not accurately name what is involved both in the cultural ideology and in the maternal fantasy I have been describing. Ruddick proposes, instead, the term "maternal responsibility," which suggests not so much a feeling of power (mothers often feel powerless, even in relation to their infants) as the feeling that what happens to the child is ultimately attributable to the mother—hence the cultural "blame Mom" syndrome, but also the mother's own potential sense of guilt or self-blame. I find Ruddick's argument convincing, but I would propose the term "absolute responsibility" or "ultimate responsibility" to suggest the hyperbolic nature of what is involved. One could then say, refining Chodorow and Contratto's terminology, that what the young child perceives as maternal omnipotence, the mother perceives as absolute or ultimate maternal responsibility. The two perceptions are symmetrical and both are fantasies, for in reality the mother is neither all-powerful in relation to the child nor absolutely (exclusively) responsible for the child's fate.

Questions of terminology aside, I agree with Chodorow and Contratto's suggestion that a more reality-oriented attitude—an attitude reinforced or made possible by new theories of mothering and child development, a new cultural discourse—would be healthy for mothers. At the same time, when I think of my own experience as a woman with a commitment to intellectual creativity and to motherhood, as well as that of other women whom I have read or with whom I have spoken about this subject, I become painfully aware of the difficulties, both personal and social, that the realization of such a "program for mothers" entails. Can we choose or discard at will our most deep-seated fantasies and self-representations? Do we dare, in a time of increasing social conservatism and disintegrating family life, give up our sense of an absolutely privileged relationship with our children?

I am not going to try to answer these questions directly—at least not yet. Rather, I want to reinscribe them in my reading of *Men and Angels*, a novel that I think poses them in an extremely compelling and disturbing way.

Maternal Splitting: *Men and Angels*

About a month before the publication of *Men and Angels*, Mary Gordon published some excerpts from her diary in *The New York Times Book Review*, under the punning title "Mothership and Authorhood." The diary entries covered the period from December 1983 to the fall of 1984. During this time, Mary Gordon gave birth to her second child, a boy, and also finished her novel and delivered it to the publisher. In the first entry, Gordon is in a New York apartment waiting for the birth of her son, who is late in coming; she has with her the unfinished manuscript and her other child, a three-year-old girl, who is sick. Sitting at her sick daughter's bedside, she thinks of the fact that she has not even looked at the manuscript: "I have not even looked at it, partly because any action is physically difficult for me; I could excuse myself this way. But the truth is, it is impossible for me to believe that anything I write could have a fraction of the importance of the child growing inside me, or of the child who lies now, her head on my belly, with the sweet yet offhand stoicism of a sick child" (*Times Book Review* 1).

When I read that, my first reaction was, "Here we go again—not mothership and authorhood, but writing versus motherhood! The same old conflict, resolved here by a somewhat sentimental renunciation of the writing self. Will we writing mothers never get beyond this split, always having to choose the work or the child, always convinced that choosing one means sacrificing the other?" The rest of the diary entries show, however, that in reality Mary Gordon was able to choose both. After a few months of total immersion in/with her baby, she went back to writing and finished her novel. And when the novel was reviewed by Margaret Drabble (another famous writing mother) on the front page of *The New York Times Book Review*, a short boxed interview by Herbert Mitgang with Mary Gordon on an inside page showed a reassuringly unconflicted and practical author talking about her life. "I probably have it a lot easier than most writers with children. When the babysitter takes over after breakfast, I leave the house, get into my car and drive for 15 minutes to a little cabin on the Hudson River. There, I light the fire and gain the physical separation that I need to work. Between 9:30 and 1:30, I turn into a writer. "In *Men and Angels*," noted Mitgang, "Miss Gordon's heroine is happily married and has two children and a babysitter. So does Miss Gordon, whose husband teaches English at the University of New York at New Paltz, where they live" (30).

In Margaret Drabble's review of *Men and Angels*, however, I read the following: "The bloody dénouement is both predictable and plausible. Presented with a stark choice . . . Anne, in effect saves her children and sacrifices Laura" (30). Anne is the writing mother, Laura is the live-in babysitter; Anne writes, and Laura is sacrificed. It occurred to me then that "Miss Gordon's heroine" may lead a more complicated life, and be related to Miss Gordon in more complicated ways, than Mr. Mitgang realized.

A few weeks later, I went to hear Mary Gordon talk about the book and read excerpts from it at the Boston Public Library. "Who has written seriously about the inner world of mothers?" she asked, uncannily echoing a question by Julia Kristeva that I had used as an epigraph for "Writing and Motherhood": *"Que savons-nous du discours que (se) fait une mère?"* "What do we know about the [inner] discourse of a mother?"

In the first passage from *Men and Angels* that Mary Gordon read that afternoon, Anne Foster, the heroine, has just finished her day's work up in her study. She has recently accepted an important assignment: to curate and write the catalog essay for the first major retrospective exhibition of an American expatriate painter, Caroline Watson, who lived and worked in Paris and died there in 1939. (Caroline Watson is an invented figure.) Anne has been poring over Caroline's letters and feels that she is beginning to know this woman "in the bone." Now, however, it is time for her to join her children in the familiar kitchen downstairs. Walking down the stairs, "hearing her heels on the wooden floor as if they were somebody else's," Anne feels the difference within herself: "In the room with Caroline she was weightless. Sometimes it frightened her, the speed of her blood, the giddy sense of being somewhere else, in some high territory, inaccessible. With the children, there was never any flying off, flying up. A mother was encumbered and held down. Anne felt that she was fortunate in that she loved the weighing down" (*Angels* 45). When she reaches the kitchen, the children are not there. They are out in the woods with Laura, the au pair girl Anne has hired to make her writing possible while her husband is away on a year's sabbatical in France. Anne feels disappointed, then happy when the children appear. But Laura is with them, diffident, watching her—an intrusive presence. Anne, intuitively understanding how starved Laura is for affection ("She was a girl who had not, it was clear, been held enough, been treasured"), tries to convince herself that her discomfort is only momentary: "She was sure that when she got more used to living with a stranger, her unpleasant feelings would just disappear. She brought the cups to the sink, ashamed of herself for wishing Laura were not there" (*Angels* 48).

The second passage Mary Gordon read occurs in the novel's time a few weeks later. Once again, Anne is reading Caroline's letters, and this time the text of one letter is quoted in full; it is from Caroline in Paris to her son Stephen and his wife Jane, who are in Cambridge, Massachusetts. It is a warm, witty, loving letter, but all the warmth is addressed to Jane, not to Stephen. Caroline did not love Stephen; she had barely ever lived with him, had left him in the care of others in the States while she chose to work in Paris, the only place where she could paint. Stephen died young, miserable. Jane is still alive, an old and vigorous woman, childless, flourishing, with a distinguished academic career behind her.

> Whenever Anne thought of Caroline's treatment of Stephen she came upon a barrier between them that was as profound as one of language. . . . She couldn't imagine Peter or Sarah [her children] marrying anyone she would prefer to them, as Caroline had preferred Jane to Stephen. You have done wrong, she always wanted to tell Caroline. Caroline, the ghost who had taken over her life, hovering, accepting worship. . . . And even as she wanted to tell Caroline, "You have done wrong," an anger rose up in her as if the accusation had come from someone else. No one would have pored through a male artist's letters to his children as she had through Caroline's to Stephen. It was that Caroline was a woman and had a child and had created art; because the three could be connected in some grammar, it was as though the pressure to do so were one of logic. Then she wanted to defend Caroline from the accusation she herself had laid against her. What did it matter, she wanted to say to the shivering ghost whom she had left unsheltered. You were a great painter. You did what you had to do. Yet even as she shielded the ghost, she could not still the accusation: "You should not have let your child die young." For as a mother, she felt it was the most important thing in the world. You did not hurt your children. You kept your children safe. (68–69)

Hearing these two passages read by the author, I realized that *Men and Angels* was a book I had to read and write about. It is an extraordinarily powerful novel, and a veritable gold mine for anyone interested in the phenomenon of maternal splitting. That is a rather crude way of putting it, for I don't mean that Mary Gordon gives us a guided tour or a handy little catalog of maternal fantasies relating to children, creativity, and "other mothers." I mean, rather, that to those who share my current preoccupations, this novel reveals a marvelously rich and complex terrain, offering multiple paths for exploration. I want to explore here the direction of maternal splitting, to see how this notion makes possible both a detailed (albeit necessarily partial) reading of the novel[5] and a renewed consideration of the conflicts and dilemmas that real-life mothers face.

As the passages mentioned above suggest, the three principal characters in the novel variously mirror and read each other. More exactly, Anne is the central figure "doubled" on two sides by Caroline and Laura. Like Caroline, whose life and work she pores over, Anne is a creative woman and a mother. Unlike Caroline, however, Anne has a passionate commitment to motherhood. Whereas Caroline was a bad mother to her son, "allowing" him to die young (shades of the maternal omnipotence fantasy), Anne is a totally good mother to her children and has their safety uppermost in her mind. Caroline, on the other hand, was a good "other mother" to Jane, whose feelings toward her own biological mother were no warmer than (as she puts it) feelings toward "a rather distant cousin" (167). Caroline is therefore split into a murderous and a nurturing mother, depending on whether one looks at Stephen or Jane as her child. But she can also be seen as the "bad" version or double of Anne, for she was a mother who chose to sacrifice her child to her work.

Structurally, Laura occupies the most interesting position, for she functions as a negative double both for Anne *and* for Anne's children: as the bad "other mother," she allows Peter and Sarah to walk on the thin ice of a pond while she herself sits engrossed in a book (as it happens, the Bible—it's the only book she reads); it is Anne herself who, rushing down to the pond, saves the children and then turns in a fury on Laura: "As strong as her love for her children, for her husband, stronger than the things that made the center of her life was her desire to inflict damage on the smiling face of this girl who might have let her children die" (203). We can read Anne's destructive rage here as directed against the bad, murderous mother, who sits reading while the children are in danger; but the text emphasizes in various ways that this bad mother is a mirror image—what I call a negative double, and what in psychoanalytic terms might be called a split-off projection—of Anne herself. This is made most clear at the moment when, after Laura's suicide, Anne painfully drags the young woman's body to her own bed and proceeds to dress the body in her own bathrobe. It is also significant that the novel is divided into alternating sections with now Anne, now Laura as the center of consciousness. The narration thus mirrors in its language and point of view the psychological doubling between Anne and Laura.

If Laura is the negative double who must be destroyed in order to preserve the "good" Anne, the good mother, she is also the negative double of Anne's children. The novel emphasizes the adoring love that Laura feels for Anne. Having been rejected by her own mother, Laura is seeking a substitute; Anne knows this, but is unable to respond. Caroline, we recall, had one unloved child (her biological son) who died young, and another, chosen child (Jane) whom she loved. In Anne's case, the position of the unloved child is occupied by Laura, and it is this child who, like Caroline's son Stephen, is sacrificed by Anne to her work: "Each time now that [Anne] thought of her work on Caroline, she would have to wonder if Laura had been its sacrifice. Her death would touch even that. Had she not met me, she would not have died, Anne thought, listening to the priest. Had I not ignored her distress trying to finish my work" (233). In destroying Laura, Anne destroys the bad mother, but paradoxically she also destroys a child, thus reintroducing the bad mother into herself. The young woman commits suicide like a child who has suddenly discovered, to her horror, that she does not possess any "good" mother, only a murderously punitive one.

Although the complicated mirrorings among Anne, Caroline, and Laura dominate the novel, there are at least two more mothers who figure secondarily but significantly in the story. Anne's mother has two daughters; she has been a good, loving mother to Anne's sister, but a rejecting mother to Anne herself. In relation to Anne, the good mother slot may be considered occupied by her father, and possibly also by the older woman, Jane (who enters her life quite late, however, through her work on Caroline). Laura's mother also has two daughters, of whom Laura is the unloved one. By their similar position in relation to their biological mothers, Anne and Laura again turn out to be structural twins—with the crucial difference that, whereas Anne finds one, or perhaps two, good "other mothers," Laura does not. Laura's pathological attachment to Anne is an attempt to find in her a loving mother with whom she can identify. This attempt fails, however, because Anne cannot love Laura— Laura, like Stephen, is not lovable.

This may seem a highly problematic statement. Is there such a thing as an "essentially unlovable" child? Or are people like Laura and Stephen, who appear so unlovable, already the "products"—and victims—of a lack of maternal love? The very asking of this question entangles one in the fantasy of ultimate maternal responsibility, for if the child turns out unlovable because of the mother's *care-lessness,* then the mother must be blamed for the child's fate. If this view appears unduly harsh, what shall we say about the alternative explanation that some people are "born unlovable"? Could the fantasy of ultimate maternal responsibility be one way to deflect the perhaps more horrifying notion (horrifying to a mother and to a child) that some human beings are unlovable by nature? At this point, the religious and theological dimensions of Gordon's novel, introduced by the character of Laura, take on a new resonance: Is grace given or withheld at birth, or is it acquired (or lost) through the course of one's life? And if the latter, who is the agent responsible for that process?

The web of connections between the characters in the novel suggests several observations. First, the structural similarity between Caroline and Anne is evident, but so is Anne's greater complexity (and more complicated splitting), which rightly confers on her the title of protagonist, if not necessarily of heroine. Caroline is divided internally into a good and a bad mother, with her work as a crucial element in both cases (it "kills" Stephen, but it creates an emotional and intellectual bond between her and Jane). Anne, too, is divided internally, but her work functions only in a negative way: it destroys Laura (as Anne herself thinks in a passage I quoted earlier), and it also, indirectly, harms Anne's own children. After Laura's death, nothing can ever be the same for them: "they would grow up knowing life was terrible and they were never safe" (237).

In addition to this internal split, Anne is split in a quasipathological way: the "bad" mother in her is externalized in a separate figure, Laura, on whom she vents her murderous rage. One wonders whether this rage is only that of the good mother, whether it is not also, in some sense, the rage of a small child at her bad mother. Anne, Margaret Mahler might say, has never successfully integrated her own childish images of the good and bad mother. Or we could say that, if she experiences a kind of maternal schizophrenia, that is because she occupies, at one and the same time, the position both of the small child and of the mother. This would be a confirmation of Chodorow and Contratto's thesis that the maternal fantasy of omnipotence is a repetition of an infantile fantasy; only I would qualify that thesis by saying that the infantile fantasy of maternal omnipotence reinforces the maternal fantasy of ultimate responsibility, without being its only source. The other source is in the mother herself as mother—perhaps because she has internalized the cultural discourse about mothering, but also perhaps because the very fact of being a mother places her in a position symmetrical to the child. The psychoanalyst Alice Balint suggested in an essay published almost fifty years ago that "maternal love is the almost perfect counterpart to the love for the mother," both of them being archaic, instinctual, and absolute (101). If there is even a slight bit of truth in this, then it may be too simple to declare that mothers should give up their "infantile" fantasies and become more "realistic." For the mother may always reply, "Yes, I know, but still." "Yes, I know I'm not the only one ultimately responsible for my child's life," says the mother, "I know it's only a fantasy, and a terrifying one at that—but I still need to pretend it's true." Some fantasies are simply felt to be too necessary to give up.

The second observation my reading suggests is a truism, but significant: in order to survive, a child needs at least one good mother, whether it is the biological mother or an "other" one. Stephen and Laura, who find no nurturing mother, die.

Finally, in this novel no child (except perhaps Anne) has more than one "good" mother. And that raises once again the question of maternal fantasy and its relation to social reality.

If Not Fantasy, What? American Motherhood in the 1980s and Beyond

Reading *Men and Angels* as a multiple fantasy of maternal splitting, whose ultimate source or author is not so much the individual Mary Gordon as a collective contemporary American consciousness, one is led to ask: Why do mothers—even enlightened, creative, feminist mothers—in the United States today find it so difficult to acknowledge, in their deepest fantasies about their children, the possibility that they are not the only ones on whom the child's welfare, the child's whole life and self, depend? In reality, most mothers will readily admit that the father, grandparents, teachers, friends, aunts, uncles, and other adult figures can and often do play a significant mothering role. Many feminist mothers are ardent exponents of Dinnerstein's and Chodorow's thesis that fathers in particular must share that role. And yet, when we really dig down, when we really try to understand how we feel about our children, even the most enlightened among us will often discover in ourselves the stubborn belief that mother is the one who really counts. Why?

Whatever psychological explanations one can offer (regression, identification with the child, internalization of the "Master Mother Discourse," and so on), I think that there is a specifically contemporary sociopolitical explanation as well. Erik Erikson has noted that, in order to benefit both mother and child, "biological motherhood needs at least three links with social experience: the mother's past experience of being mothered; a conception of motherhood shared with trustworthy contemporary surroundings; and an all-enveloping world-image tying past, present, and future into a convincing pattern of providence" (116). The third condition, which has religious overtones, is probably not specific to mothering: In order to do anything worthwhile, one has to have a certain sense of continuity and faith in the future. The first condition, we all more or less fulfill—which is not to belittle its importance, for we know that a mother's past history is crucial to her mothering. But it seems to me that as a social problem, the first condition merges with the second; and it is precisely Erikson's second condition that has become most problematic in American society today.

In order to relinquish her fantasy of ultimate responsibility, a mother needs a "conception of motherhood shared with trustworthy contemporary surroundings"; but we live in a society where divorce is rampant, where the old presumptions no longer hold (witness the conundrum of surrogate motherhood, as well as those posed by various reproductive technologies), where women who are mothers feel increasingly threatened financially, emotionally, and legally. Even if Phyllis Chesler's *Mothers on Trial* exaggerates in viewing all fathers as potential sadists and mother haters, and all mothers as potential victims, the fact that this view exists at all has both symbolic and social significance. (It is a similar perception of mothers as victims and its attendant fear that may account for the extraordinary popular success of Sue Miller's novel, *The Good Mother*). Lenore Weitzman has shown that in divorce negotiations fathers often blackmail their wives into accepting disadvantageous financial terms by threatening to sue for custody of the children, and that in any case mothers end up much more impoverished than fathers after divorce (ch. 9, 10). But, if that is the case, if mothers really cannot feel secure in their attempt to pursue full and integrated personal lives and remain mothers, if they feel or fear that society through its legal system is ready to punish them by depriving them of their children any time they stray from the traditional, constraining path of "true mother-and-wife," then it makes a certain practical and logical sense for them to hold on to one thing they can affirm with certainty: that they have a natural, biological bond, and right, as mothers, to their children.

I read Chesler's book as a terrified reaction to what she perceives as a terrifying reality. To reaffirm, as she does, the biological bonding between mother and child and to claim that the mother is the child's "natural" guardian may be an ideologically and psychologically regressive move (one that overlooks, furthermore, the rights of adoptive mothers), but it is also a self-protective move, as regression often is.[6] Until and unless American women feel that society offers them a trustworthy surrounding in which they can safely pursue both their desire for self-creation and their desire to mother, they will be unwilling to share their child with "other mothers" and will cling to the fantasy of ultimate responsibility. It will appear to them as their best, perhaps their only, hope.

The popularity of Chesler's book underscores the connections between the fantasy of maternal splitting that I have analyzed in *Men and Angels* and women's real-life situations. Although it is theoretically hazardous to draw neat parallels between fiction and life, in practice we often do read fiction as an illumination of, and commentary on, real-life predicaments. That being the case, I would suggest that changes in the representation of maternal conflicts and fantasies in fiction by American women writers will have to be accompanied (perhaps even preceded) by efforts to create a trustworthy surrounding for women in American social life. As a first step, such efforts might be directed at the creation of a system of excellent, universally available day care that would allow biological mothers to rely on "other mothers" instead of feeling threatened by them, and would encourage all of us to think of motherhood and self-creation as complementary rather than as mutually exclusive categories in women's lives. In concert with other social policy reforms, this action would contribute to and reflect the broader thinking that is necessary about the family, the social roles of women and men (both those who are parents and those who are not), and how these will be linked to the needs, values, and ultimate goals of American society at the turn of a new century.

Notes

This essay, which appears in my volume *Risking Who One Is: Encounters with Contemporary Art and Literature* (Cambridge, Mass.: Harvard UP, 1994), was first published in a slightly different version in *Signs*. I am grateful to the "other mothers" in the Cambridge mothers group—Mieke Bal, Teresa Bernardez, Carol Gilligan, Marianne Hirsch, Evelyn Keller, Amy Lang, Ruth Perry, and Gail Reimer—for our ongoing discussions, in 1985 and 1986, of the issues treated here.

1. Freud's 1912 essay can be found in Sigmund Freud, *Sexuality and the Psychology of Love* (New York: Collier, 1963, 58–69). See also J. Swan, "*Mater* and Nannie: Freud's Two Mothers and the Discovery of the Oedipus Complex," *American Imago* 32 (1974): 50 and passim.

2. Interestingly, the question of the mother's sexuality is once again foregrounded in Sue Miller's best-selling novel, *The Good Mother*—in which, perhaps most significantly, the mother's sexuality becomes a determining factor in a legal conflict over what is beneficial or destructive to the child. The cultural-ideological implications of this novel and of its extraordinary popular success are yet to be fully explored.

3. See Erik H. Erikson, *Childhood and Society*; Nancy Chodorow, *The Reproduction of Mothering: Psychoanalysis and the Sociology of Gender*; Dorothy Dinnerstein, *The Mermaid and the Minotaur: Sexual Arrangements and the Human Malaise*; Jessica Benjamin, *The Bonds of Love: Psychoanalysis, Feminism and the Problem of Domination*.

4. Among the works that Chodorow and Contratto critique are Adrienne Rich, *Of Woman Born: Motherhood as Experience and Institution*; Jane Lazarre,

The Mother Knot; *Feminist Studies* 4, no. 2 (Summer 1978), a special issue entitled "Toward a Feminist Theory of Motherhood."

5. I call my reading of *Men and Angels* both detailed and partial because,
although it explores at some length the phenomenon of maternal splitting and
uses it to make sense of the novel as a whole, that is all it does. In other words,
it makes *one* sense of a work that invites many other readings and constructions
of sense. Such a partial reading is inevitable, given my theoretical frame; in any
case, no reading of a novel can claim completeness, although some readings may
be more complete than others.

6. This is even clearer in Chesler's more recent book, based on her involvement on behalf of Mary Beth Whitehead in the "Baby M" case, *Sacred Bond*.
Here, too, although Chesler's claims may be sweeping, the cases she documents
are sobering. See also Daniel Golden's "What Makes Mommy Run?" *Boston
Globe Magazine* 24 April 1988.

Works Cited

Balint, Alice. "Love for the Mother and Mother Love." Michael Balint, *Primary
Love and Psychoanalytic Technique*. New York: Liveright, 1965.

Benjamin, Jessica. *The Bonds of Love: Psychoanalysis, Feminism, and the Problem of Domination*. New York: Pantheon, 1989.

Bettelheim, Bruno. *The Uses of Enchantment: The Meaning and Importance of
Fairy Tales*. New York: Vintage, 1987.

Chesler, Phyllis. *Mothers on Trial: The Battle for Children and Custody*. New
York: McGraw-Hill, 1986.

————. *Sacred Bond: The Legacy of Baby M*. New York: Times Books, 1988.

Chodorow, Nancy. *The Reproduction of Mothering: Psychoanalysis and the Sociology of Gender*. Berkeley: U of California P, 1978.

Chodorow, Nancy and Susan Contratto. "The Fantasy of the Perfect Mother."
In *Rethinking the Family*. Ed. Barrie Thorne and Marilyn Yalom. New York:
Longman, 1982.

Dinnerstein, Dorothy. *The Mermaid and the Minotaur: Sexual Arrangements and
the Human Malaise*. New York: Harper and Row, 1976.

Drabble, Margaret. "The Limits of Mother Love." *New York Times Book Review* 31 Mar. 1985: 30.

Erikson, Erik H. *Childhood and Society*. 2nd ed. New York: Norton, 1963.

————. "Human Strength and the Cycle of Generations." *Insight and Responsibility*. New York: Norton, 1964.

Feminist Studies 4.2 (1978). Special Issue: "Toward a Feminist Theory of Motherhood."

Freud, Sigmund. "The Most Prevalent Form of Degradation in Erotic Life." *Sexuality and the Psychology of Love*. New York: Collier, 1963. 58–69.

Friday, Nancy. *Jealousy*. New York: Morrow, 1985.

Gilligan, Carol. *In a Different Voice: Psychological Theory and Women's Development*. Cambridge: Harvard UP, 1982.

Golden, Daniel. "What Makes Mommy Run?" *Boston Globe Magazine*. 24 April 1988.

Gordon, Mary. "A Cabin of One's Own." *New York Times Book Review* 31 March 1985: 30. (Interview with Herbert Mitgang.)

———. *Men and Angels*. New York: Random House, 1985.

———. "On Mothership and Authorhood." *New York Times Book Review* 31 Mar. 1985: 1.

Kaplan, E. Ann. "Mothering, Feminism and Representation: The Maternal in Melodrama and Women's Film, 1910–1940." *Home Is Where the Heart Is*. Ed. Christine Gledhill. London: British Film Institute, 1987. 113–37.

Klein, Melanie. "Weaning." *"Love, Guilt and Reparation" and Other Works, 1921–1945*. New York: Doubleday, 1977.

Lazarre, Jane. *The Mother Knot*. New York: McGraw-Hill, 1976.

Mahler, Margaret, Fred Pine, and Anni Bergman. *The Psychological Birth of the Human Infant*. New York: Basic Books, 1975.

Miller, Sue. *The Good Mother*. New York: Harper and Row, 1986.

Rich, Adrienne. *Of Woman Born: Motherhood as Experience and Institution*. New York: Norton, 1976.

Suleiman, Susan Rubin. "Writing and Motherhood." *Risking Who One Is: Encounters with Contemporary Art and Literature*. Cambridge: Harvard UP, 1994.

Swan, James. "*Mater* and Nannie: Freud's Two Mothers and the Discovery of the Oedipus Complex." *American Imago* 31 (1974): 50 and passim.

Weitzman, Lenore J. *The Divorce Revolution: The Unexpected Social and Economic Consequences for Women and Children in America*. New York: Free Press, 1985.

12

Be True: Moral Dilemma in *The Scarlet Letter*

Donna D. Simms

"Shall we not meet again?" whispered she, bending her face down close to his. "Shall we not spend our immortal life together? Surely we have ransomed one another, with all this woe! Thou lookest far into eternity, with those bright dying eyes! Then tell me what thou seest?"

"Hush, Hester, hush!" said he, with tremulous solemnity. "The law was broke!—the sin here so awfully revealed!—let these alone be in thy thoughts! I fear! I fear! It may be that, when we forgot our God—when we violated our reverence each for the other's soul—it was thenceforth vain to hope that we could meet hereafter, in an everlasting and pure reunion. . . ." (233)

The appeal of Nathaniel Hawthorne's *The Scarlet Letter* rests to a large degree on his psychological portraits of the adulterous lovers, Hester Prynne and Arthur Dimmesdale. In the passage above, which occurs after Arthur has confessed his sin on the scaffold and is about to die, we see his and Hester's radically different interpretations of a shared experience. They have loved one another unlawfully and suffered as a result; but Hawthorne makes it clear that they each understand their love differently and that, moreover, there is no way to resolve their conflict. Hester's " 'surely we have ransomed one another' " shows that she clings to the possibility of a relationship, if only in the afterlife; Arthur, on the other hand, having finally confessed, holds fast to principles that forbid a relationship with Hester.

Feminist psychologists, by exploring gender differences and providing a more complex understanding of moral decision making, offer insights that help us to better understand this irreconcilable difference between Hawthorne's protagonists. Carol Gilligan's distinction of two moral perspectives, which she has labeled "justice" and "care" (63), is particularly useful in this analysis. To Lawrence Kohlberg's description of a morality that values rules and principles, separation and autonomy—a description based on an all-male sample—Gilligan added the missing voice of care and responsibility that she first heard by listening to women (18–19). She defines the difference as follows: "One voice speaks of connection, not hurting, care, and response; and one speaks of equality, reciprocity, justice, and rights. . . . The pattern of predominance, although not gender specific, [is] gender related" (Gilligan, Ward, and Taylor 8).

Nona Lyons, analyzing interview responses that elaborate Gilligan's two perspectives, notes a difference between the *justice* of "an individual alone deciding what ought to be done," for whom "morality becomes a discrete moment of rational 'choosing'" and the *care* of "an individual aware, connected, and attending to others" for whom "morality becomes a 'type of consciousness,' which, although rooted in time, is not bound by the single moment" ("Two Perspectives" 21–2). According to Lyons, in a moral dilemma, a person motivated by the ethic of justice wants to be fair, meet obligations, and obey rules, while a person motivated by the ethic of care behaves in terms not of what is right but of what is responsible, and is concerned with taking care of others and not hurting them ("Listening to Voices" 34, 42–3). A gender difference related to these two moral perspectives appeared in a study of images of violence conducted by Gilligan and Pollack: i.e., that "each sex perceives a danger which the other does not see—men in connection, women in separation" (Gilligan 42).

Gilligan's theory of two moral orientations, and its elaboration by Lyons, is clearly applicable to Hawthorne's protagonists. In the scaffold speeches quoted above, Hester's expectation that they will " 'meet again'" and her fear of abandonment are pitted against Arthur's obsession with the " 'law [that] was broke'" and his fear of this threatening relationship. It is Hawthorne's master-stroke in *The Scarlet Letter* not only to have based his case study in moral decision making on adultery, an act which puts relationship in conflict with law, but to have localized this conflict in the relationship between the lovers themselves. The fact that Arthur sees only the broken law and Hester sees only the broken relationship illustrates just how "judgment depends on the way in which the problem is framed" (Gilligan 167). Clearly, the one character most fears what the other most desires. As one would expect, given the patriarchal Puritan setting, Arthur's voice is dominant in this dialogue, and his " 'hush'" carries into eternity his negation of their connection. Hester is left with only the discouraging crumb of his " 'may be'" to give her hope.

Be True: Honesty and Justice

Arthur Dimmesdale is notable for his commitment to transcendent and inflexible religious principles. He is "a true priest, a true religionist. . . . It would always be essential to his peace to feel the pressure of a faith about him, supporting, while it confined him within its iron framework" (113). This faith dictates that he not love a married woman and, having done so, that he confess his sin. Although Hawthorne describes Arthur, in contrast to Hester, as one who "had never gone through an experience calculated to lead him beyond the scope of generally received laws" (183), it is clear, too, that Arthur's legalistic personality needs what his religion dictates.

Unable to live by his religious credo, Arthur chooses to substitute " 'penance' " for " 'penitence' " (176), flagellating himself and wasting away throughout the novel. Furthermore, when Hester encourages Arthur to leave his torture behind and begin his life anew, the idea only *seems* to be liberating. His agreeing to renew their unlawful relationship confirms Arthur's notion that he is evil, and he undergoes "a revolution in the sphere of thought and feeling . . . nothing short of a total change of dynasty and moral code" that causes him to do "strange, wild, wicked [things]" (198). Through Arthur's deviant behavior, Hawthorne tells us that he cannot escape his moral code: for the moment, he has merely changed sides within it and is still unable to interpret his love for Hester as anything but sinful.

If devotion to a system of rules keeps Arthur from affirming his relationship with Hester, so too does his status in the Boston religious hierarchy. Arthur's separation from Hester is reinforced in the novel by his priestly vows, his spotless reputation, and his elevated position in the community. Thus, his very success as a man of God provides another hindrance to his full conformity with, or his growth beyond, Puritan morality. The outward symbols of his dominant status are too precious to Arthur to be sacrificed, until his imminent death makes their retention in any case impossible. Unfortunately, Arthur too easily moves from actual superiority to egocentric delusions. During the second scaffold scene, in a "highly disordered mental state," he interprets the meteor as a scarlet "A," extending "his egotism over the whole expanse of nature, until the firmament itself should appear no more than a fitting page for his soul's history and fate!" (142).

Arthur's rigid moral framework prevents the fulfillment of his need for a more liberal perspective that would sanction his relationship with Hester. On the scaffold, he demonstrates his lack of sympathy with her when he says: " 'Is not this [i.e., my confession] better . . . than what we dreamed of in the forest [i.e., a life together]?' " Facing death, Arthur can think only of himself: " 'For thee and Pearl, be it as God shall order . . . Let *me* now do the will which He hath made plain before *my* sight. For, Hester, *I* am a dying man. So let *me* haste to take *my* shame upon *me*!' " (231, italics added). At this moment Arthur's self-absorption is understandable, and any change in his perspective unlikely, but nonetheless, he represents "the blind willingness to sacrifice people to truth," which Gilligan has identified as a "danger of an ethics abstracted from life" (104).

Just as Arthur resists affiliation, so he neither recognizes nor accepts responsibility. When, early in the novel, Governor Bellingham reminds him of his responsibility for Hester's soul (62), Arthur acts only upon the most literal denotation of the warning. Bellingham's remark is obviously ironic, since Arthur ought to own his responsibility to his lover by confessing, but Arthur is also clearly responsible for Hester in a much broader sense: he owes both financial and psychological support to the woman he has disgraced and the child he has fathered. Far from acknowledging this responsibility and finding a way to contribute to Pearl's upbringing, however, he admits to Hester his fear of Pearl and of having his crime discovered because of her resemblance to him (189). Jean Baker Miller, in her analysis of men and women living in dominant-subordinant relationships, asserts that "members of the dominant group . . . do not have to feel the necessity to develop, as a *primary part of their personhood*, the conviction that they are, in a profound and real sense, responsible for each other ("Construction" 187). In this insight, we can see the connection between Arthur's social and gender dominance and his difficulty recognizing his responsibilities. Arthur's self-protective fear for his reputation outweighs any concern for his personal obligations.

Hawthorne creates a powerful irony when he places this man, who resists a love relationship, in public, long-term intimacy with his direst enemy. Roger Chillingworth lives with Arthur in order to discover his secret, torture him, and ensure his final damnation. Although Arthur finds Roger's proximity disquieting, he cannot extricate himself from this socially acceptable connection. On learning at last from Hester that she has allowed him to live for years with her husband, Arthur explodes in embarrassment and wrath: " 'Thou little, little knowest all the horror of this thing! And the shame!—the indelicacy!—the horrible ugliness of this exposure of a sick and guilty heart to the very eye that would gloat over it! Woman, woman, thou art accountable for this! I cannot forgive thee!' " (178). In this response, Arthur again betrays his egoism, here so powerful as to overwhelm his religious principles; and his anger shows that he is unable to imagine how Hester had acted on her best reckoning of his interests when she agreed to protect Roger's identity in order to protect his own. We are also struck by the fact that the relationships in

Arthur's life seem to become either a threat to his moral sanctity or an example of his poor judgment or both.

Arthur's interaction with his world is predictable from his moral perspective. He influences people from a distance with his moving sermons, but, in spite of his sympathy with the sinners in his congregation (131), does not seem to actually interact with his parishioners. He tells Hester in the forest that children do not trust him and that " 'even little babes, when I take them in my arms, weep bitterly' " (190). His penance is worked out alone, in closet self-flagellation; his stirring sermons, although they transform his listeners, tend to isolate him further, both because they elevate him ever higher in the public esteem and because in them he consciously transforms "the very truth"—confessions of his unworthiness and guilt—into "the veriest falsehood"—the appearance of humility and sanctity (133).

Arthur Dimmesdale is clearly a man constricted by his ethical orientation, and Hawthorne criticizes that perspective when he suggests that a change might be beneficial for Arthur. For example, he has Arthur identify Hester as his appropriate role model, his " 'better angel' " (185), when they meet in the forest; and his decision to resume the relationship has positive as well as negative effects: Arthur suddenly feels healthy and energetic, has a ravenous appetite, and writes an extraordinary sermon. His new energy comes from having been involved with Hester in " 'an empowering interactive process' " of a type which, according to Jean Baker Miller, quoted in Surrey, results in " 'increased zest, empowerment, knowledge, self-worth, and desire for more connection' " ("Relationship" 167–8). Ultimately, however, in spite of his brief experience of human affection and sympathy, described as "a new life, and a true one" (184), Arthur cannot change; he is constrained by the "regulations . . . principles, and even . . . prejudices" (183) of his theocratic community. By placing Arthur in a situation in which his moral conflict paradoxically makes him a more effective religious spokesman even as it sickens and kills him, Hawthorne underscores his criticism of both the moral perspective and the religion that shackle Arthur.

Be True: Loyalty and Care

In Hawthorne's contrast of the "iron framework" (113) of Arthur's inescapable faith with the "iron link" (146) of Hester's relationship with him, the words "framework" and "link" prefigure Gilligan's categories of justice and care, and the repetition of the adjective "iron" suggests that these perspectives are equally binding. As Arthur exemplifies a morality based on justice, so Hester exemplifies one based on care; her actions and choices are as consistent and predictable as his. The governing element in Hester's life is the connection she feels to others and, in particular, to Arthur. Although Hawthorne insists that "she hid [this] secret from herself," Hester stays in Boston because "there dwelt, there trode the feet of one with whom she deemed herself connected in a union that, unrecognized on earth, would bring them together before the bar of final judgment, and make that their marriage-altar for a joint futurity of endless retribution" (74). Hester defines herself as connected: her commitment is illustrated both at the moment when she chooses to stay in Boston to be near Arthur and seven years later when she finally stands with him on the scaffold. She bears out Janet Surrey's suggestion that "for women at all life stages, relational needs are primary and that healthy, dynamic relationships are the motivating force that propels psychological growth" ("Relational" 37). Just, however, as Arthur's relationship with Hester exists in direct conflict with his morality, so Hester's love for Arthur is in conflict with the realities of her life situation. Hester is legally married to Roger Prynne when she meets Arthur, and there is no behavior or condition that will allow her to legitimately associate with Arthur in any meaningful way. The important relationship in her life cannot be dynamic; therefore, Hester's growth, like Arthur's, is stunted.

From her initial choice to protect Arthur and his position in the community to their meeting in the forest, Hester's devotion is never in doubt. Her relationship with Arthur Dimmesdale takes precedence over received social and religious considerations: her belief that their affair " 'had a consecration of its own' " (179) and her vision of their marriage, even one consisting only of eternal retribution, are evidence of her priorities. When Arthur asks for her support to begin a new life, Hester is willing to throw away seven years of penance and good works in accompanying him to England (183): in fact, she has clearly been hoping for this opportunity to reestablish their relationship. Her ethic of care is based not on choosing between right and wrong at discrete moments, but rather on maintaining her commitment and responsiveness whatever the consequences.

As Gilligan's model would predict, Hester's morality is concerned not with adultery or hypocrisy, but with betrayal. For her, to be true is to be loyal. Early in the novel, when Roger extracts from her a promise not to reveal his identity (perhaps perceived by both as an echo of her marriage vow), she anticipates its moral significance: " 'Hast thou enticed me into a bond that will prove the *ruin of my soul?* ' " (72, italics added). This phrase, which in Arthur's mouth would signify the commission of certain concrete, well-defined sins, is evidently used by Hester to denote the possible betrayal of her " 'responsibility . . . in reference to the clergyman, which she owed to no other' " (146). When her fear is borne out, she laments to Roger that " 'having cast off all duty toward other human beings, there remained a duty toward him; and something whispered me that I was betraying it, in pledging myself to keep your counsel. In permitting this [Roger's torture of Arthur], I have surely acted a false part by the only man to whom the power was left me to be true!' " (156). Hester realizes that keeping her promise to Roger has been wrong because she has betrayed her deeper emotional loyalty; but she takes steps, in finally revealing Roger's identity to Arthur, to rectify this mistake, realizing that her protection of Arthur, under Roger's malignant tending, is causing greater harm than if his crime were to be exposed. Furthermore, Hester's identification of mortal sin with a betrayal of responsibility is consistent with her moral orientation.

Hester's relationship with her husband Roger Prynne/Chillingworth, is also fraught with issues of justice and responsibility. Hawthorne, however, reduces Hester's accountability for this relationship by describing her marriage as inappropriate (69). Although Hester acknowledges her responsibility to Roger, she also "deemed it her *crime* most to be repented" (161, italics added) that she had married Roger without loving him.

In Hester, Hawthorne creates a character who, as exemplified by the badge that proclaims her adultery, literally defines herself in relationship. While she has no choice but to accept the punishment exacted by the community and outwardly behaves in conformity with their expectations, there is no moment when she repents her love. In fact, she comes to wear its symbol, the scarlet letter, proudly and resists all bribes and offers to remove it, saying to the Reverend Wilson, " 'It is too deeply branded. Ye cannot take it off. And would that I might endure his agony, as well as mine!' " (64). This heroic expression of commitment to the person she loves and her willingness to bear the entire weight of their shared responsibility illustrate the strength of Hester's self-definition in relationship.

Because, in her patriarchal Puritan context, Hester cannot expect to experience validation or acquire status, she must live her life on two levels, symbolized by her "burning blush and yet . . . haughty smile" (50) as she endures her punishment on the scaffold. Hawthorne states specifically that the scarlet letter, which was intended to reform as well as humiliate Hester, had failed (152). Although Hester appears to conform, the scarlet letter actually serves to "set her free" (183), and thus, "the world's law was no law for her mind" (150–1). She is morally untroubled by her and Arthur's putative sin, whatever consequences she allows it in the afterlife. Moreover, she is visited by revolutionary thoughts "which our forefathers . . . would have held to be a deadlier crime than that stigmatized by the scarlet letter" (151). Hester's independence is characteristic of the creative, effective women discussed by Carolyn Heilbrun in *Writing a Woman's Life*. Heilbrun posits that women become able to think and act independently when they break society's rules and escape the conventional woman's role (48–51), as Hester has certainly done. This freedom of thought and tolerance of moral ambiguity are also strengths associated by Gilligan with the ethic of care (ch. 3, *passim*).

Hester's need for connection, however, has its negative side. For example, when she is caught between competing loyalties to Roger and Arthur, she is slow to realize that in promising to keep Roger's secret she has betrayed Arthur. In addition, Hester can be blind to Arthur's real needs: Her belief that leaving Boston to assume a new identity and begin a new life, which is a real possibility for her, and which Arthur gives her some slight reason to imagine will be revitalizing and liberating for both of them, is actually deadly for him. In this case, her nurturant impulse is effectively insensitive and destructive. Also, Hester is vulnerable because she depends on others to give her life meaning. Hawthorne shows us that, while Arthur counted as unforgivable the fact that Hester had allowed his isolation to be breached by Chillingworth's malice, she, in turn, "could scarcely forgive him . . . for being able so completely to withdraw himself from their mutual world" (218) when he gave her no sign of recognition during the Election Day procession. Lastly, in her original decision to stay in Boston to be near Arthur, Hester is also choosing isolation and unhappiness. Her willingness to live with so little of what she wants and needs, and to suffer humiliation and ostracism unnecessarily, exemplifies a potential weakness of one whose life is defined in relationship; i.e., "the identification of goodness with self-sacrifice" (Gilligan 80).

It is ironic that Hester's commitment to a relationship forces her to live such a lonely life. Limited not only by the ostracism she suffers but also by the confinement of single parenthood, she does, however, adamantly resist total isolation. When the authorities threaten to take Pearl from her, Hester even risks alienating Arthur in demanding that he intercede for her: " 'Speak for me! Thou knowest,—for thou hast sympathies which these men lack!—thou knowest what is in my heart, and what are a mother's rights, and how much stronger they are, when that mother has but her child and the scarlet letter! Look thou to it! I will not lose the child! Look to it!' " (104). Her veiled threats in this speech succeed on this one occasion in provoking Arthur to responsible action on her behalf. Hester's ultimate commitment to her relationship with Pearl also inhibits her in the long term from overt acts of rebellion and even greater consequent isolation from the community (107–8, 151).

Despite her lonely life, Hester, in contrast with Arthur, interacts closely with others; and just as Arthur's isolation is predictable from his moral orientation, so is Hester's affiliation predictable from hers. She works out her penance by taking responsibility in personal and intimate ways for those who are suffering. She makes clothes, delivers food, tends the sick, and later in life, becomes a counselor to troubled women. She provides "a well-spring of human tenderness, unfailing to every real demand, and inexhaustible by the largest"; and, as people come to appreciate her extraordinary sympathy, they reinterpret the scarlet letter as meaning "Able; so strong was Hester Prynne, with a woman's strength" (148). Even though her relationships with others do not seem to afford Hester any meaningful intimacy, Hawthorne still chooses to show her defining herself through caring interactions.

While Arthur's life is lived upon the rack of solitary moralizing, Hester's is shaped by her need to maintain relationships. These two ways of defining the self correspond to the extreme positions these characters take on the moral spectrum, and, as stated above, both Hester and Arthur pay a heavy price for their limited points of view.

Blended Perspectives

When we examine the ways in which the two secondary characters, Pearl and Roger Chillingworth, relate to the primary characters and their relationship, we find that each personifies important aspects of both care and justice. The secret and unlawful love relationship between Hester and Arthur constitutes a betrayal of both Pearl and Roger. Roger has been robbed of the marriage that he believed would provide him comfort in his old age, and Pearl has been deprived of a father and an accepted place in the community.

Pearl embodies considerations that motivate both her parents. She is described as having the dual purpose of "justice and retribution" and "mercy and beneficence" (165). She is a child who, in spite of her unpredictable behavior, "[possesses] affections" and also "steadfast principles" (165). She can be loving, tender, and supportive; and she recognizes connections, such as the one between her mother and the minister, and presses to understand them. She wants to experience love, but nonetheless, holds this love to certain standards; for example, she makes clear that the relationship that exists in secret is not adequate. On the occasions when her father acknowledges her—at midnight on the scaffold and later in the forest—she asks him to make the acknowledgment public and hence real, desiring both a link with her father and her right of acknowledgment as his daughter. Since Pearl embodies the true relationship between Hester and Arthur, it is appropriate that she insist on truth and openness.

Because she senses falsity surrounding her mother and the minister and because she has been deprived of an accepted place in the community, Pearl, in exacting a kind of revenge against both parents, functions as an instrument of justice. Scornful of falsehood and knowing instinctively where significant truths lie, Pearl makes both Hester and Arthur uncomfortable with her pointed questions. In addition to asking about and decorating Hester's "A," Pearl chastises her father in the midnight scaffold scene, and later in the forest, for his lack of courage.

While Pearl tortures her parents with her intimations of the truth, at the same time she symbolizes their ideal union, something beautiful and unconventional. She is "the living hieroglyphic, in which was revealed the secret they so darkly sought to hide . . . Pearl was the oneness of their being" (189). As a symbol of the relationship between Hester and Arthur, Pearl demonstrates that, when their attributes are combined and freed from the polarities of the Puritan setting, their love can be healthy and happy. In Pearl's ability to survive and flourish, and in her final acceptance of both her mother and her father, Hawthorne suggests the importance of integrating the perspectives of justice and care. Gilligan's analysis yields a similar insight: "Development for both sexes would therefore seem to entail an integration of rights and responsibilities through the discovery of the complementarity of these disparate views" (100).

In addition to embodying attributes of both her parents and providing Hester with a meaningful relationship, Pearl also suggests the possibility of a more humane order to come. When she adorns herself with a green "A" made from eel-grass, she demonstrates her transformative power. The connotations of the "A" shift from fiery, passionate, and even hellish to natural, life-giving, and healthy. Its association with the eel, i.e., serpent, evokes the pre-Christian "good snake" linked with life-giving female power, and suggests that the tempting knowledge of passionate love and sexual union is a step toward life and growth, as embodied by Pearl herself.

Hawthorne's striking image of Pearl in the graveyard scene reinforces her potentially revolutionary role in the novel:

> So she drew her mother away . . . among the hillocks of the dead people, like a creature that had nothing in common with a bygone and buried generation, nor owned herself akin to it. It was as if she had been made afresh, out of new elements, and must perforce be permitted to live her own life, and be a law unto herself, without her eccentricities being reckoned to her for a crime. (124)

In this image of a liberated Pearl, the use of the word "eccentricities" suggests a revision of context in which Hester's "crime" might also be reduced to the status of an eccentricity. The primary lesson in this description, however, is that Pearl's individual assertiveness has empowered her to transcend the dead Puritan law. She survives in this rule-bound society without either conforming or being destroyed. In fact, she outlives her identity as the bastard child, becoming an envied heiress and leaving home to live a happy life in some unidentified location in Europe. Although Hawthorne gives us no more than a suggestion that Pearl becomes the prophetess that Hester dreamt of being (239), he does create in Pearl a figure who never compromises either her insistence on truth and justice or her demand for meaningful relationship.

Because she grows up alone with her mother at the margin of the Puritan community, Pearl lives in a peculiarly female environment. When asked by the Reverend Wilson if she is a Christian child, she responds, " 'I am mother's child' " (101), thus rejecting his attempt to define her in patriarchal terms and, in a larger sense, illustrating a girl's natural psycho-social development free from exposure to society's female stereotypes. Pearl has, however, noticed some aspects of the external world: for example, she knows from experience that it is hostile, and she may intuit from her mother's pain and isolation that it is particularly difficult for women; but this knowledge has freed, not crushed, her. From the beginning Pearl seems to be what Brown and Gilligan call a female "resister" (87 and *passim*); her reaction to threats is not to submit but to fight, to stand up for herself and speak what she knows. Not only does she frighten off a group of self-righteous, mud-throwing Puritan children (94), but she forces her mother back to her familiar identity when Hester tries to throw off her scarlet letter (i.e., displace Pearl) in the forest (192–3). Pearl's isolation from patriarchal society and her unmitigated exposure to the difficulties in a woman's life have trained her in both interdependence and autonomy. Having given Pearl the strength to survive society's hostility to women, Hawthorne also provides her an experience—public recognition by her father as he dies—that "[develops] all her sympathies" so that she can "be a woman in [the world]" (233). Although there is little evidence in the novel that being a woman offers any advantages, nonetheless Hawthorne gives Pearl a unique frame of reference to illustrate the sources of human completeness.

If Pearl is the character who points us toward the future and new possibilities for women, Roger Chillingworth reminds us of the past that Pearl is leaving behind and the dark side of a morality based on justice. An unregenerate patriarch who has succeeded in limiting Hester's possibilities, Roger is, according to Pearl, the " 'old Black Man' " who " 'hath got hold of the minister already . . . But he cannot catch little Pearl' " (123). Roger, like Pearl, combines qualities of the justice and care perspectives. He seeks justice, believing in an eye for an eye or a betrayal for a betrayal, and dedicates his life to seeking Arthur's damnation. To succeed in this, however, he must develop a close relationship with his patient-victim. It is significant also that the woman with whom he intended to spend his life loses her appeal when Roger can see in her "nothing but the contagion of her dishonor" (108); and he instantly takes up his rights as an aggrieved husband to spurn his marriage, resolving "not to be pilloried beside [Hester] on her pedestal of shame" (108).

Roger is like Arthur Dimmesdale in his willingness to allow Hester to suffer her punishment alone and in his solitary, scholarly approach to life. He has been disappointed in his half-hearted attempt to center his life on a love relationship with Hester, so he shifts his focus to justice and revenge. Roger's relationship with Arthur is illuminated by Jessica Benjamin's observation that male domination is "rooted in a struggle for recognition between men in which women are mere objects or tokens: the prize" ("Bonds" 55). Roger, whose malevolent attentions to Arthur appear motivated by rage at having been worsted in the competition for Hester, engages in a contest for power, albeit a contest in which Arthur does not realize he is involved: a struggle for hierarchical dominance aiming at his rival's destruction.

Ironically, Roger pursues his goal by means of "a more *intimate* revenge than any mortal had ever wreaked upon an enemy" (128, italics added). In describing Roger, Hawthorne illustrates how care can be perverted in the service of justice, in this case a version of justice reduced to simple revenge. Hawthorne shows Roger consciously arranging his life in a new pattern of relationships, and his hatred of Arthur inspires a more passionate involvement than his love for Hester ever did. Roger anticipates his new sense of connection when he is tending Hester in the jail: " '. . . elsewhere a wanderer, and isolated from human interests, I find here a woman, a man, a child, amongst whom and myself there exist the closest ligaments. No matter whether of love or hate; no matter whether of right or wrong! Thou and thine, Hester Prynne, belong to me. My home is where thou art, and where he is' " (71). Roger demonstrates not only the twisted force of a passionate relationship aiming only at justice but also, as he works *on* rather than *with* the subject of his attentions, an egoism equal to Arthur's. Using intimacy to harm, Roger ultimately destroys himself rather than the object of his hatred.

Roger and Pearl, complex amalgams of the perspectives of justice and care, function similarly as agents of retribution to those with whom they are most closely connected. They also represent, however, opposing directions in the novel. Roger is cold, calculating, demonic, and false. A figure from the dying past, he perverts the goals of intimacy from nurturance and support to competition and control. His role as physician appears to be curative when it is actually vindictive. Pearl, on the other hand, is passionate, unpredictable, redemptive, and true, and functions as the harbinger of a more humane, compassionate future. In ultimately choosing Pearl as his heir, Roger expresses a degree of care and commitment missing from his life and, by acknowledging his kinship with Pearl, frees her for new possibilities.

The Ambiguity of Truth

Separating "truth" from its opposites, falsehood and betrayal—finding a way to "be true"—is the challenge for characters in *The Scarlet Letter*. Arthur's and Hester's different definitions of truth become a shorthand for their opposing moral orientations. When writing of Arthur that, "by the constitution of his nature, he loved the truth, and loathed the lie, as few men ever did" (133), Hawthorne refers to abstract truth and honesty in the service of abstract justice. Hester's " 'I have surely acted a false part by the only man to whom the power was left me to be true' " (156), on the other hand, defines being true as being loyal, faithful, and empathic to another person. Pearl is the one character whose words and point of view seem to combine the two meanings of being true. When, on the scaffold at midnight, she says to her father: " 'Thou wast not bold!—thou wast not true! . . . Thou wouldst not promise to take my hand, and mother's hand, to-morrow [sic] noontide!' " (144), the standard to which she is holding him can be interpreted as including both honesty and loyalty—the confession and the acknowledged relationship.

At the close of the novel, Hawthorne explicitly addresses the issue of truth: "Among many morals which press upon us from the poor minister's experience, we put only this into a sentence: 'Be true! Be true! Be true! Show freely to the world, if not your worst, yet some trait whereby the worst may be inferred!' " (236). Telling us here that his novel has been Arthur's story all along, Hawthorne also suggests, as throughout the novel, that Arthur has needed to act or change; but, despite the repeated imperative of these lines, it is still not perfectly clear what Arthur should have done. One possibility is that he should have made a public confession akin to Hester's; clearly, if he had been capable of confessing his sin and leaving it behind, he would have been relieved of his hypocrisy, even though no closer to a satisfactory relationship. Hawthorne's characterization of Hester and Arthur's relationship, on the other hand, as not just a " 'wreck and ruin' " (181) but also "a flood of sunshine" (182), suggests another possibility; namely, that Arthur should have been true to his lover in spite of his principles. Perhaps, as Pearl suggested, Arthur should have combined these possibilities, not merely confessing, as he himself wished, nor merely running off with Hester, as she wished, but publicly acknowledging his relationship. Hawthorne does not apply his moral to Hester, who, having of necessity confessed her sin and by choice remained loyal to Arthur, appears to have been true by both standards. Although her unwavering commitment to Arthur makes her whole life, in religious terms, an adulterous act and, although her saintly behavior, like Arthur's, is suspect throughout the novel, Hester, at least technically, is able to integrate Hawthorne's two definitions of truth.

While Hawthorne's repetition of "Be true!" may operate not to reinforce but to proliferate meaning, we are still brought back to the fact that Hester Prynne and Arthur Dimmesdale do not live by the same truth. On the simplest level, when he is true to his principles, he cannot make room for an attachment to Hester; defining himself in terms of legalistic religious doctrine, he cannot recognize that love and responsibility for another human being might take precedence over his Christian commandments. And, characteristically true to the significant relationships in her life, Hester cannot understand the guilt Arthur suffers for breaking a commandment. For Hester, dogmatic Puritanism, which condemns her emotional attachment and attempts to crush her spirit, provides no incentive to appreciate and share in Arthur's point of view.

The only solution Hawthorne can imagine to the dilemma in the lives of his characters is relegated to some future time. It is consistent with the novel as a whole that Hester's message, when she returns to Boston as a counselor to other women, is an assurance "that, at some brighter period, when the world should have grown ripe for it . . . a new truth would be revealed, in order to establish the whole relation between man and woman on a surer ground of mutual happiness" (239). But Hawthorne circumscribes this future hope when he makes Hester connect it, not to a change in law or religion, but to a sanctification of the prophetess who will establish the sexes in a new relation. In describing "the angel and apostle of the coming revelation" as "a woman . . . lofty, *pure*, and beautiful; and wise, moreover, not through dusky grief, but the ethereal medium of joy; and showing how *sacred* love should make us happy" (239, italics added), he shows the Puritan-induced blindness that prevents Hester from appreciating her own strength and freedom. Hester realizes that the world needs to change, but does not realize that, in fact, she is precisely the woman with the knowledge to change it.

In the story of Hester Prynne and Arthur Dimmesdale, Hawthorne has dramatized two conflicting definitions of the self and the moralities that correspond to these definitions. Hawthorne's nineteenth-century novel, like many other works both before and after, demonstrates that these perspectives are neither new nor unexploited in literature. Hawthorne's innovation, however, is, like Gilligan's, to argue for the validity of both perspectives: Arthur ultimately triumphs in his own terms when he confesses and thereby saves his soul; but Hester triumphs, too, by preserving her love over a long period and refusing to be crushed by the social and religious conventions that condemn her. Nevertheless, in his dismal historical setting and intentionally frustrating plot, Hawthorne allows no room for either of his protagonists to grow and develop—to reach the "integration of rights and responsibilities" (100) that Gilligan defines as most fully human. Instead, his characters live their lives in tragic conflict; and, although individually they may triumph—Hester over vilification and Arthur over hypocrisy—their relationship is the victim in this tragedy. Hawthorne's ambivalence in the face of the conflict he created is borne out in the novel's final image of the graves of Hester and Arthur placed side by side, "yet with a space between, as if the dust of the two sleepers had no right to mingle. Yet one tombstone served for both" (239). And one symbol serves for both: a scarlet letter, representing the law that divides these troubled personalities and the love that unites them.

Works Cited

Benjamin, Jessica. "The Bonds of Love: Rational Violence and Erotic Domination." *The Future of Difference*. Ed. Hester Eisenstein and Alice Jardine. New Brunswick: Rutgers UP, 1980.

Brown, Lyn Mikel and Carol Gilligan. *Meeting at the Crossroads: Women's Psychology and Girls' Development*. Cambridge: Harvard UP, 1992.

Gilligan, Carol. *In a Different Voice: Psychological Theory and Women's Development*. Cambridge: Harvard UP, 1982.

Gilligan, Carol, Nona Lyons, and Trudy Hanmer, ed. *Making Connections: The Relational Worlds of Adolescent Girls at Emma Willard School*. Cambridge: Harvard UP, 1990.

Gilligan, Carol, Janie Ward, and Jill Taylor, ed. *Mapping the Moral Domain*. Cambridge: Harvard UP, 1988.

Hawthorne, Nathaniel. *The Scarlet Letter*. New York: Bantam Books, 1981.

Heilbrun, Carolyn G. *Writing a Woman's Life*. New York: W.W. Norton & Company, 1988.

Jordan, Judith V., Alexandra G. Kaplan, Jean Baker Miller, Irene P. Stiver, and Janet L. Surrey. *Women's Growth in Connection. Writings from the Stone Center*. New York: The Guilford Press, 1991.

Lyons, Nona P. "Listening to Voices We Have Not Heard." Ed. C. Gilligan, N. Lyons, and T. Hanmer 30–72.

———. "Two Perspectives: On Self, Relationships, and Morality." Ed. C. Gilligan, J. Ward, and J. Taylor 21–48.

Miller, Jean Baker. "The Construction of Anger in Women and Men." Jordan, et al. 181–96.

Surrey, Janet L. "Relational Self in Women" (Individual section of the collaborative chapter, "Women and Empathy: Implications for Psychological Development and Psychotherapy). Jordan, et al. 35–43.

Surrey, Janet L. "Relationship and Empowerment." Jordan, et al. 162–80.

Index

adolescence, 1, 2, 83; experiences of girls in, vi, 1–6, 28–42, 46–64, 70, 71–72, 81, 83, 85; friendship among girls in, 4, 28, 30–39, 81; girls' resistance in, 2, 3, 4, 5, 28, 30, 39, 40, 41–2, 46, 47, 48, 54; girls' transformation in, 28, 46, 87–88

African-American women writers, 101, 144, 162, 163, 217

Apter, Terri, 2, 6n1, 72, 83, 88

art (artists), v, 6, 29, 40, 170, 177–8, 182–3, 184–5

Asian-Americans, 117–118, 131, 136n4, 136n5. *See also* Japanese culture

attachment. *See* connection

Atwood, Margaret (*Cat's Eye*), 4, 27–42

authority (epistemological), 103, 104, 108, 109, 110; as authors, 158, 201, 202

autobiographical fiction. *See* autobiography

autobiography, viii, 62, 200; autobiographical fiction, 49, 51–52, 126, 135

Belenky, Mary, v, 91n12; Belenky et al. (*Women's Ways of Knowing*), 2, 99, 103, 105, 106, 108, 111, 113, 114, 120, 125, 130, 133, 137n10

Benjamin, Jessica (*Bonds of Love*), 72, 74, 78–9, 88, 89n1, 157, 170, 175–76, 180, 187, 189, 207, 208, 209, 212, 215, 218, 226, 250

Bernikow, Louise (*Among Women*), 86–87

Bettelheim, Bruno, 68–69, 70, 89n4, 89–90n5, 224, 225

Brown, Lyn Mikel, vi, 2, 3, 4, 63n4, 63n11, 76–77, 78, 79, 87–88, 249

Cat's Eye (Atwood), 4, 27–42

Chodorow, Nancy, 2, 3, 9, 15, 16, 23n4, 71, 88, 89n1, 13712, 142, 144, 148, 149, 155, 171, 192, 226, 234; "The Fantasy of the Perfect Mother," 89n1, 226, 227, 228, 233, 236–37n4; *Feminism and Psychoanalytic Theory,* 10; *The Reproduction of Mothering,* 2, 23n1, 2; 83, 136n9, 168

Christie, Agatha, 99, 103, 105, 106, 113, 115; *The Body in the Library,* 99, 103, 106, 107, 110, 113–115; *The Mousetrap,* 105

Clinchy, Blythe, v

Collins, Patricia Hill, 69, 91n15, 163n1

connection (connectedness), viii, 10, 28, 50, 51, 92n18, 126, 128, 130, 132, 135, 141, 142, 148, 155, 161, 170, 178, 180–81, 240, 246, 247, 250; failure of (among women; between women and girls), 36, 38, 39–40, 88, 126, 180, 193–5, 196, 198; girls' with their mothers, 2, 40–42, 83–4, 129, 168–69, 192, 193, 193–95, 205; loss of: *see* separation

Contributors

Lyn Mikel Brown is assistant professor and co-chair of the Education and Human Development Program at Colby College. She is co-author (with Carol Gilligan) of *Meeting at the Crossroads: Women's Psychology and Girls' Development* and has written numerous articles on girls' and women's psychological development, girls' education, and feminist research methods. Her new book is entitled *Stones in the Road: Anger, Class, and White Adolescent Girls*, to be published by Harvard University Press.

Susan Currier is associate dean and professor of English at California Polytechnic State University. She is a recent American Council on Education Fellow and she has written on a variety of British and American twentieth-century women writers.

Jerilyn Fisher is assistant professor of English at Hostos Community College, City University of New York, where she teaches Literature and Psychology; Women and Literature; and basic writing classes. Just before immersing herself in the making of this book, she published several articles about feminist pedagogy, as well as studies of writer Kim Chernin and her work.

Sally L. Kitch is professor and chair of the Department of Women's Studies at Ohio State University. Her research focuses on feminist theory and epistemology. Among her recent publications are *This Strange Society of Women: Reading the Letters and Lives of the Woman's Commonwealth* and *Chaste Liberation: Celibacy and Female Cultural Status*.

Kathleen Gregory Klein is the author of many articles on women writers and the award-winning book *The Woman Detective: Gender and Genre*.

She is the editor of *Great Women Mystery Writers: Classic to Contemporary*, which was nominated for the Edgar Allen Poe and Agatha Christie awards, and *Women Times Three: Writers, Detectives, Readers*. She is currently editing a collection of essays on cultural diversity and detective fiction.

Gail L. Mortimer teaches American literature at the University of Texas at El Paso. The author of *Faulkner's Rhetoric of Loss: A Study in Perception and Meaning* and of *Daughter of the Swan: Love and Knowledge in Eudora Welty's Fiction*, Mortimer has also published in such journals as *The Psychoanalytic Review, Novel: A Forum on Fiction, The Faulkner Journal, The Southern Literary Journal*, and *American Literature*.

Annie G. Rogers, a developmental and clinical psychologist, is assistant professor in Human Development and Psychology at the Harvard Graduate School of Education. A founding member of the Harvard Project on Women's Psychology and Girls' Development, she directed the study "Strengthening Healthy Resistance and Courage in Girls." She has co-edited a book with Carol Gilligan and Deborah Tolman, *Women, Girls & Psychotherapy: Reframing Resistance* and recently published *A Shining Affliction: A Story of Harm and Healing in Psychotherapy*.

Betty Sasaki is assistant professor of Spanish at Colby College. She is the author of articles on Spanish poetry and prose of the early modern period, multiculturalism, and identity politics.

Barbara Schapiro is professor of English at Rhode Island College. She is author of *Literature and the Relational Self* and *The Romantic Mother: Narcissistic Patterns in Romantic Poetry*. She is also co-editor with Lynne Layton of *Narcissism and the Text: Studies in Literature and the Psychology of Self*.

Mirella Servodidio is professor of Spanish at Barnard College. She is the author of *Azorin, escritor de cuentos* and *The Quest for Harmony: The Dialectics of Communication in the Poetry of Eugenio Florit* and the editor/contributor of *From Fiction to Metafiction: Essays in Honor of Carmen Martin Gaite* and *Reading for Difference: Feminist Perspectives on Women Novelists of Contemporary Spain*.

Ellen S. Silber is professor of French at Marymount College Tarrytown, where she also teaches women's studies. She is the director of the Marymount Institute for the Education of Women and Girls and the publisher of *Equity* for the Education of Women and Girls, a national newsletter. She is the editor of *Critical Issues in Foreign Language Instruction.*

Donna D. Simms has taught English at Emma Willard School since 1978, where she currently offers an elective in which Gilligan's categories inform the analysis of literary works. Between 1981 and 1985, she was a participant in the Dodge Study of adolescent female development conducted at Emma Willard by Carol Gilligan and Nona Lyons. Simms currently teaches an American literature elective in which Gilligan's categories inform the analysis of works by authors such as Hawthorne, Chopin, Hurston, Glaspell, and Baldwin. She devotes her spare time to subsistence farming, flowers, and the fruitless study of modern Greek.

Susan Rubin Suleiman is the Chair of Romance Languages and Literatures at Harvard University. She is the author of numerous books and articles on modern literature and culture and has also published poetry and autobiographical sketches. Her most recent book of criticism is *Risking Who One Is: Encounters with Contemporary Art and Literature.* Her newest memoir is *Budapest Diary: In Search of the Motherbook.*